T0265810

DONALD AUTEN

BLACK LION ONE

TOPGUN
Trailblazer

Capt. John Monroe "Hawk" Smith
IN COMMAND OF VF-213

SCHIFFER MILITARY

4880 Lower Valley Road ■ Atglen, PA 19310

Designed by Justin Wakinson
Cover design by Brenda McCallum
Type set in Helvetica Neue LT Pro/Minion Pro/Univers LT Std
ISBN: 978-0-7643-6344-3
Printed in Serbia

Published by Schiffer Publishing, Ltd.
4880 Lower Valley Road
Atglen, PA 19310
Phone: (610) 593-1777; Fax: (610) 593-2002
Email: Info@schifferbooks.com
Web: www.schifferbooks.com

For our complete selection of fine books on this and related
subjects, please visit our website at www.schifferbooks.com.
You may also write for a free catalog.

Schiffer Publishing's titles are available at special discounts
for bulk purchases for sales promotions or premiums. Special
editions, including personalized covers, corporate imprints, and
excerpts, can be created in large quantities for special needs.
For more information, contact the publisher.

We are always looking for people to write books on new and
related subjects. If you have an idea for a book, please contact
us at proposals@schifferbooks.com.

Dedication
To Torpedo Squadron 8, Battle of Midway

Lt. John Monroe Hawk Smith's commissioning ceremony into the regular Navy. *J. Monroe Smith*

Early in the morning of June 4, 1942, the aircrews of Torpedo Squadron 8 (VT-8) assembled in their ready room. Waiting for them was a memo from Lt. Cmdr. John C. Waldron, commanding officer of VT-8. It read, "My greatest hope is that we encounter a favorable tactical situation, but if we don't, and the worst comes to the worst, I want each of us to do his utmost to destroy our enemies. If there is only one plane left to make a final run-in, I want that man to go in and get a hit. May God be with us all. Good luck, happy landings and give 'em hell."

It was a sobering message. All aircrew knew their responsibilities. They had accepted them. And all, to a man, were prepared for the consequences.

They received their briefs and donned their flight gear, and then "Pilots, man your planes" blared over the 1-MC. Pilots and crew assigned to that first strike rushed to the flight deck, strapped in, and cranked up.

They flew with the throttle full forward, straight and level at almost 180 knots, without fighter cover into the roaring guns of the Imperial Japanese Navy. Fifteen obsolete Douglas TBD Devastators were destroyed; all aircrew, save one, were slain; a squadron was obliterated; and for their gallantry and sacrifices, a battle was won.

Black Lion One is dedicated to these brave Americans.

We will strike, regardless of the consequences.

—Lt. Cmdr. John C. Waldron, VT-8 commanding officer
June 4, 1942

Epigraph

The primordial elegance and immense splendor brought Hawk solitude, clarity of purpose, and thankfulness. Cocooned snuggly in his Tomcat, thousands of feet above the worries and stresses of mortal man, he felt alive, free, and energized with a realization that he was doing what he was supposed to be doing. He was in perfect harmony with his destiny. Embraced by the sheer beauty surrounding him he had found complete tranquility. When he returned to earth, when the landing gear hit the steel deck of the *Enterprise*, he would be just a man again, but for a little while, a moment frozen in time, he felt immortal.

—Don Auten, from *Roger Ball!*

Contents

Dedication 3
Epigraph 4
Foreword 8
Preface 9
Prologue 12

Chapter 1: Behind the Wing Line **16**
The "Gunfighters" 16
The Man 16
The Machine: The First "Third-Generation" Fighter 28
The Reunion 28
The Butcher, the Baker, and Everything Else 31

Chapter 2: The Black Lions **32**
Lineage of the Black Lions 32
The Fly-In 33
Assault on a Windmill 38
Gator Takes the Conn 39
Leadership 101 40
Friday the Thirteenth: Nightmare on *Enterprise* 42
The Supply Totem Pole 44
Call Sign "Thunder" 45
Weapons Detachment in the High Desert 48
USS *America*: First Impressions 50
Workups 51

Chapter 3: *America* Sails **53**
Casting Lines 53
Between a Badger and the Deep Blue Sea 54
Bad Karma 57
Entropy in the Supply Department 58
Ship's Habitability Improvement Team 59
Port Visits 61
Bombing under the Flares 62
Land of Camel Herders and Fighter Pilots 62
Independence Day in the Med 66

Chapter 4: I Relieve You, Sir! **68**
Command 68
Harpoon Shoot 71
MAYDAY from Bad Bob 74
The Far Turn 75
Convertible Tomcat 77
America Turnover with *Nimitz* 79

Chapter 5: Homeward Bound **80**
Animal House 80
Chaos at Cannon 82
Budley to the Rescue 84
Home Is the Sailor 85

Chapter 6: "On the Beach" **87**
Forging Alliances 87
Stand-Down 89
ADMAT Inspection 89
Hitting the Wall 91
Miss Jenny's Fire 92
Epiphany 93
TARPS Mission 93
Call to Action 94
Gator's Big Push 96
Hawk's Junkyard Dream 97
Renaissance 99

Chapter 7: Hardening of the "Lions" **101**
The Young "Lions" 101
The Science of Maneuvering Flaps 102
Scopes for the Fleet 104
Have Drill 105
Mugs McKeown: To Kill a MiG 106
Constant Peg 109
Pride Runs Deep 110
Fastest Gun in the West 112
The Training Carousel 113

Chapter 8: A Clattering of Sabers **114**
Fighter Super Bowl 114
Hawk vs. Toado: Gunfight at the OK Corral 114
Lessons Learned . . . Again 121

Chapter 9: Counting Coup **122**
The Debrief 122
All Things in Competition 122
Happy-Hour Banter 123
Pipper's On! 124
On the Podium 126

Chapter 10: Here There Are Lions **128**
Ascent to Mount Olympus 128
Change of Command 129

Chapter 11: Blue Skies, White Water **131**
Last Romp in the Big Blue 131
Follow-On Orders 131
Full Circle 133
Fly Navy! 134

Epilogue 135
Endnotes 139
Bibliography 147
Glossary 151
Index 164

In *Black Lion One*, author Donald Auten masterfully incorporates the challenges of the era following the Vietnam War with the fighter community's reevaluation and discovery of the lessons coming out of Vietnam. From this chaos of war, a new apogee in the fighter war arts was born through deities of the air warfare tribe—warriors such as Mugs McKeown, Randy "Duke" Cunningham, Dave "Frosty" Frost, Bad Fred Lewis, and many more.

Capt. John Monroe "Hawk" Smith was in this congregation of savant fighter pilots and tacticians in the midst of the tempest who pushed forth naval TACAIR forces to its rightful place of superiority. Hawk's vision, tenacity, and unsinkable enthusiasm were known and admired throughout the fighter community. Successful tours at VX-4 as the F-14 Tomcat project officer and commander Air Group 14 senior landing signal officer for the first-ever F-14 deployment equipped him for assignment as the executive officer, then commanding officer, of the famous Naval Fighter Weapons School—TOPGUN. Hawk's tour there, a grueling but highly successful assignment, caught the attention of decision-makers in the highest tiers of Navy leadership. He was rewarded with a second command tour as skipper of VF-213—the Black Lions.

Black Lion One captures the true spirit of a Navy fighter pilot's career, especially the two defining command tours as commanding officer of TOPGUN and the Black Lions. Hawk's story is one of persistence in the face of adversity, success and achievement when confronted with stagnation, and extraordinary leadership when embroiled in havoc. As Auten weaves the history of world events and incorporates the many real-world challenges within the fighter squadrons and community, the key and most potent ingredient of true leadership highlighted is that of taking care of your people. In fact, this book should be required reading by every potential commanding officer, regardless of community. The other vital element captured by Auten is the importance of support from senior leadership, as demonstrated by RAdm. Paul Gillcrist.

Hawk was a warrior in the realm of great fighter pilots, and a visionary leader totally dedicated to resurrecting naval TACAIR as the finest, most lethal force in the world.

Black Lion One is the conclusion of the odyssey of a great Navy fighter pilot—Capt. John Monroe "Hawk" Smith.

Michael Bucchi
VAdm., USN (ret.)

Preface

Capt. John Monroe "Hawk" Smith, USN, is just a man, but his story, his life adventure, is a rich tapestry of achievements for naval tactical aviation, devotion to a cause, and service to his nation.

It was a time during and shortly after the Vietnam conflict that America became ideologically divided. The military was disillusioned with the intrusion of nonwarriors in the White House over the conduct of the war, and tactical aviation of all the services was struggling to catch up to the realities of the war's hard lessons. It was a time when the Navy needed leaders and strong-willed thinkers to set things right again.

John Monroe Smith, call sign "Hawk," was a legend in the fighter community. He joined the Navy in 1963 and retired in October 1993. During his thirty-year career, he forged a reputation as a skilled and lethal aviator in the air-to-air combat arena, a natural tactician, and consummate leader. All who knew Hawk or knew of him believed he was one of the most essential pathfinders in the modernization of the naval air warfare arts.

As significant as Hawk's contributions were to the fighter community, there was another important dimension to Hawk. Built on the bedrock of his core beliefs, he was a magnificent and charismatic leader. Throughout his career he was known for his steel resolve, unwavering loyalty, and a willingness to stand tall for those things and people he believed in—regardless of the consequences.

Vexing as it was, Hawk would admit that it was those same personal qualities that elevated him to the CO position at TOPGUN, which were responsible for his own near demise. In pursuit of an objective, Hawk was innovative and often unencumbered by established Navy procedures, especially those that delayed or denied logical and swift solutions. Occasionally, Hawk's solutions weren't received well by the temple acolytes. He was an idea factory connected to a dynamo, and, to be truthful, to the commander who was concerned with his cannon being securely fastened to the deck before the coming storm, Hawk could be problematic.

Any way one studied Hawk, they would conclude that he was in the eye of a tempest during the fighter modernization era and became a standout in a small but courageous phalanx of dedicated warriors, innovators, and tacticians. His story was a piece of history that needed to be told.

As early as 1999, I asked Hawk if I could write his story. He replied then as he would for the next several years: "I didn't do anything special. Hell, I wasn't even in direct combat. Write about a hero. Write about a warrior!" For the next three years I remained determined to write Hawk's story, and he remained humbly reluctant. In late June 2002, my persistence paid off. Hawk agreed to allow me to begin the project. I started the manuscript of *Roger Ball!* on July 1, 2002.

Roger Ball! was released in 2006. It is a historical biography of a Navy fighter pilot during the crucial, transformational years throughout and after the Vietnam War. At first blush this work may appear to be yet another biography of a combat pilot caught up in the hell of an overseas military fiasco—but it is far more than that. It is an odyssey of a Navy fighter pilot—Capt. John Monroe "Hawk" Smith—a detailed history of the evolution of modern Navy fighter tactics. And it is a very personal account of the forging of a fighter pilot and naval leader.

Since its release, it has received enormous praise and many inspiring comments. *Roger Ball!* concludes with the end of Hawk's tour as commanding officer of TOPGUN, but not his saga. Many readers urged me to complete the telling of Hawk's story. *Black Lion One*, the sequel to *Roger Ball!*, does just that.

In 1978, following Hawk's tour as CO of TOPGUN, he began his assignment as executive officer and commanding officer of VF 213—the Black Lions.

As the reader courses through Hawk's saga, I would hope that they can divine the underlying essence of the substory that, in addition to being a tactical genius and, when the occasion required, a hardheaded bomb thrower (when he realized the apoplexy of Navy fighter doctrine and tactics at the behest of the shrine sycophants), he is also a magnificent and devoted leader.

Hawk stands tall among many of those who were willing to risk their reputation, their career, and, all too often, their very lives in pursuit of a calling. On occasion, Hawk complained about the tremendous strain placed upon his shoulders in caring for his troops and all the frustrations of command. Whether by DNA coding or the fortuitous alignment of the constellations, he was a leader we needed so badly to right the ship in TACAIR during that time.

When guts and gallantry are part of the composition of heroes, the pilots and crewmen of Torpedo Squadron 8 (VT-8) immediately spring to mind. On June 4, 1942, during the Battle of Midway, USS *Yorktown* (CV-5), USS *Enterprise* (CV-6), and USS *Hornet* (CV-8) launched strike aircraft against the Imperial Japanese Navy warships. VT-8 made a series of heroic torpedo attacks on the Japanese ships. These remarkable American aviators, who flew with steady hands and full awareness of the consequences of their action, charged into lead-filled skies and into the history books in one of the most stunning and consequential naval engagements in world history. In that single attack, a squadron was destroyed and all but one of the crewmen were slain. It is to these valiant few that this work is dedicated.

When America and the world were imperiled, courageous Americans responded to the call to arms, knowing full well that they put their very lives on the line for something far more important than themselves.

Through the aperture of life in America today, it is hard to imagine this same sense of purpose, that same intrepidness and selflessness in American generations. I often wonder if we, as a nation, could muster warriors with such determination, dauntless commitment, and patriotic devotion to make a similar stand. I hope we will never have to find out.

When I began this endeavor, I had grand hopes to provoke action from a few of the young-adult readers. There is a great big world out there, and for a chosen few, those with aspirations to be a part of something magnificent, those who would help shape our future heritage, I hope this work sparks a passion to take up such a challenge.

Black Lion One is the compilation of the efforts of several subject matter experts who, by their individual (and remarkable) competences and energetic efforts, greatly improved this work, maintained the historical fidelity, and helped make it an enlightening read.

Many thanks to Sgt. Alan J. Weiss, USAF (ret.), for his quick eye and remarkable grasp of worthy and appropriate prose.

If you happened to visit the aircraft carrier exhibition at the Smithsonian's National Air and Space Museum, quite likely you remember the museum's impressive 1:100 scale model of USS *Enterprise* (CVN-65). This was the stunning artwork of Steve Henninger, who invested a thousand hours per year for twelve years in its creation. I am in his debt for bringing that same level of detail, focus, and persistence in improving the story flow of this work.

Cmdr. Jan Jacobs, USN (ret.), was an F-14 RIO and later an editor and writer for *US Naval Institute Proceedings* and the managing editor for the *Tailhook* magazine. Who would have guessed that a fighter guy would have such an incredible grip on naval aviation history and such a vivid recollection of the evolutionary events in Navy tactical aviation. And no wonder—Jan completed a stint with VF-21 on Yankee Station during the end of the Vietnam War, logged more than 1,440 hours in the F-4 Phantom and another 350 hours in the F-14 Tomcat, and held the record for being the only ensign to complete the demanding TOPGUN syllabus. For his dazzling assistance in setting me straight in so many areas I seem to have forgotten since my carrier days—thank you greatly!

Long ago I met a TOPGUN instructor during one of my visits to the Navy Fighter Weapons School, Lt. Michael Bucchi (now vice admiral, USN [ret.]). He was a junior officer under Hawk during his assignment at TOPGUN and one of the most talented instructor pilots at the school. I have fond memories of times we flew together. Those were the days. I am humbled and in debt for the very gracious foreword. Thank you, sir!

My wife and my own Navy nurse took the responsibility of reviewing my many versions of this work during its evolution. I am always amazed at her patience and perseverance. Thank you, Katie, for your suggestions, guidance, and all the time you invested in *Black Lion One*. I owe you big! (as usual).

And then there's the man who lived the story, Capt. John Monroe "Hawk" Smith, without whom there would be no story, and naval tactical aviation might not be held in such high reverence as it is today.

Prologue

Once you have tasted flight, you will forever walk the earth with your eyes turned skyward, for there you have been, and there you will always long to return.

—Leonardo da Vinci

It was a funny thing; a few moments ago Hawk was besieged by a hundred issues—personnel matters, administrative dilemmas, command projects, operational concerns, logistic obstacles, and a complete set of additional knee-knockers associated with his pending change of command. All these issues begged for his undivided attention.

Cmdr. John Monroe "Hawk" Smith was commanding officer of the Black Lions, VF-213, and as such these concerns were as much a part of his job as taking care of 250 officers and enlisted personnel and flying fast jets from aircraft carriers. He pondered these things as he strode though the passageway clad in 30 pounds of flight gear.

He mounted the short steps from the O-3 level and then stepped onto the grimy flight deck of USS *America* (CV-66).[1] As soon as his boots hit the scarred, nonskid surface, it happened: all those issues, problems, and dilemmas vanished like smoke rings in the breeze. He couldn't remember half of them. Those he could remember were now distant and of no importance. Hawk's total focus was now on the mission, his F-14, and the return flight to Naval Air Station (NAS) Miramar, California. As he strode toward his assigned Tomcat, all his senses went on high alert. Here, death came noisily and swiftly—sucked into a jet intake, squashed by 30 tons of aircraft, blown over the side of the ship, or sliced into large bloody chunks by a spinning prop. It was the flight deck of a carrier and probably the most lethal piece of real estate on earth, but to Hawk it was always exciting, enthralling, seductive . . . and home.

It was almost impossible now to think of anything but manning up and flying. If there was something more important at this point, Hawk didn't know what it could be.

It was still a few minutes before the prelaunch symphony began. A few deep breaths away from the loud barks of the air boss over the 5-MC,[2] the ear-shattering whines of the start carts firing up, the annoying scraping of chains across the flight deck, the dull thud of chocks slamming to the deck, and the unmistakable rumble of the steam-driven catapults tossing 72,000 pounds of men and machinery into the air as if they were Frisbees. Now, and for a few minutes more, Hawk was treated to the familiar waving of the "remove before flight" flags; the unforgettable bouquet of cable grease, steam, JP-5, and sweat; and the invigorating vista of the sea—quiet now and deep electric, luminous blue.

It was the same scene he'd enjoyed a thousand times before as a fighter radar intercept officer (RIO), a landing signal officer (LSO), and a fighter pilot; the same dazzling splendor—a persistent blue tableau—yet, it was all different, since this would be Hawk's last shot from the deck of a carrier. This was his last sojourn into the wild blue, his last romp through the clouds in his Navy jet—his last hurrah.

As Hawk approached his F-14, he realized the paradox—he was fully charged by the thought of flying, yet deeply saddened by the significance of this day—his last carrier sortie.

Hawk scanned the scene around him as he closed the distance to his airplane. He took in the sights, committing everything to memory.

Mighty *America* cut a dazzling white swath across the Caribbean, running downwind before she commenced her turn to bring 85,000 tons of iron and men into the wind to launch airplanes. There were seventeen- and eighteen-year-old kids in charge of moving, arming, fueling, and launching billions of dollars' worth of machinery into the air, and entrusted with the lives of their shipmates. And then there were the airplanes: A-6 Intruders, medium-attack aircraft; A-7 Corsair IIs, light-attack jets; the big antisubmarine S-3 Viking; SH-3 Sea King—the antisubmarine warfare helicopter; and, finally, Hawk's favorite—his Grumman F-14 Tomcat. These were the things that made up Hawk's life. These were the things he was going to miss—every single thing about them.

But, he thought, *would I do it all over again? A career as a Navy fighter pilot has not been easy.*

Hawk strolled up to his Tomcat, scrambled up the ladder for a quick cockpit check, and dumped his rifle scope and helmet bag in the seat. He climbed back down the ladder and was joined by his RIO, Lt. Dan "Chief" Anderson.

Chief was a talented RIO, a solid tactician, and an invincible RIO in a dogfight. He was perhaps best known in the fighter world for his keen sense of situational awareness in every flight, from takeoff to landing. Moreover, Chief had those two critical professional components necessary when operating a fighter around the ship—competence and fearlessness.

Chief and Hawk were scheduled for a morning launch and a three-leg flight from a point just south of Guantanamo Bay, Cuba, to NAS Miramar, California, home base for his VF-213 "Fighting Black Lions."

"Big day, Skipper." Chief gave Hawk a bright smile.

"A big day, a perfect day. I never had a better day, Chief." This was standard fare for Hawk, and the strange thing was, everybody who knew him actually believed him. Hawk was the perennial optimist—unsinkable, positive, smiling, always moving forward.

"Bigger for you than for me, Skipper. This isn't my last flying day," Chief lightheartedly replied.

"Last flight or not, we've got a long day in front of us, and we're burnin' daylight, son. Let's git 'er done!"

"Roger, Skipper. Git 'er done, aye!"

Hawk gave Chief one of his famous "mule eatin' green briars" grins, then went to work on his portion of the preflight. This was by now second nature and a task they'd both done hundreds of times.

Hawk began on the left side of the airplane, his hands touching everything within reach and his eyes carefully scanning that which was out of reach.

How many times have I done this? How many preflights have I completed?

His thoughts ricocheted back to his first flight as a student basic naval aviation officer (BNAO) training some sixteen years previous: *I've come so far, accomplished some good things. I've lost a few battles along the way, and I guess I did most things right, but was it all worth it? Were the few victories I managed to rack up, the chance to serve my country as a frontline fighter pilot, worth all the effort; to work alongside the most professional and dedicated men and women I've ever known, and do a thousand things I never could have done in any other profession? Well, it makes me feel good inside, but was it all worth it? The head-butting with the oligarchy during the F-14 introduction, the humiliation my TOPGUN people suffered at the whims of a rancorous admiral, the near loss of my TOPGUN command, the hardships and months of loneliness I put my wife and son through—was it all worth it?*

Hawk shook himself out of his reverie and finished his preflight. He scrambled up the three steps to the left side of the cockpit and checked his ejection seat carefully. He took a sideways glance at Chief, who was already strapped in the rear cockpit, and received a big smile, a thumbs-up, and a "Good to go, Skipper!"

Click! "On the flight deck, pilots and crews are manning aircraft for the first launch of the day." The flight deck hymn sung by the air boss over the 5-MC snapped every able-bodied seaman and air crewman to full alert.

"Check helmets on, chinstraps buckled, goggles down, sleeves rolled down, and flotation vests securely fastened."

The air boss was Zeus of the flight deck. Nothing happened and nothing moved on the 1,000-foot flight deck without his approval, and when his words blasted from the 5-MC, it seemed everything moved at once in exquisite synchronization. Flight ops had begun.

Ten minutes later, USS *America* came hard to port in a wide turn into the wind. By the time she steadied out on her upwind course, Hawk had the canopy down, both engines online, and, with the help of Chief, most of the takeoff checklist items complete.

A series of hand signals among Hawk, a brown-shirted plane captain, and a yellow-shirted taxi director followed. The chocks were pulled and Hawk gently added power to taxi out of his tie-down area. A quick tap on the top of the rudder pedals in response to the taxi director's signals ensured that the brakes were operating. Once clear, Chief keyed the ICS switch: "Radar's in standby. We've got the checklist complete except for the wing sweep and flaps."

"Wings and flaps to go, Chief," Hawk quickly echoed.

The yellow-shirted taxi director passed control to another director positioned just behind the giant jet blast deflectors (JBDs). He followed up with a starchy salute and a thumbs-up. Hawk returned the salute and the thumbs-up and shifted his attention 20 feet forward to the waving arms of his new taxi director. Hawk followed the hand commands of the director, which were somehow instantly translated without any conscious brain activity into foot and hand muscle movements to the rudder pedals and throttles, which in turn precisely aligned the 63-foot jet with the number 2 catapult. His taxi director then passed control to the catapult director, who, with small movements of his hands and tiny twitches of his head, carefully guided the Tomcat's long nose directly over the catapult shuttle.

Clenched fists signaled Hawk to stop the jet. With his gloved right hand, the director touched his nose, then extended his arm in front of him. Hawk responded by lowering the launch bar, which then engaged the shuttle. At the director's signals, Hawk squatted the nose strut, extended the wings full forward, set the flaps, and, one more time for Miss Jenny and young Jack, rechecked the trim. "Wings and flaps set; trim rechecked, Chief."

After thirteen years of successful carrier operations, it would be a bad show to drill his Tomcat into the water on his last flight, all for the lack of a proper flight control setting.

"Concur—wings, flaps, and trim set," Chief returned.

With that, the director passed control to the cat officer, the *shooter*. For the next several seconds the shooter controlled the lives and determined the future of Hawk and Chief.

The shooter recognized Hawk by his helmet. He smiled and nodded. With a slight tip of his helmet, Hawk returned the gesture.

As two final checkers made a last inspection of doors, panels, and external stores and checked for fluid leaks, the shooter noted the weight scribbled in chalk on the nose gear fairing and scanned the configuration of the Tomcat. He then raised his right hand and gave a two-finger turn-up signal. Hawk responded by moving both throttles forward to the throttle stops. The nose of the beast crouched low, nose down, tail up—a tiger ready for the attack.

The shooter's two-finger turn signal changed into a clenched fist, followed by an open hand. He then repeated the gesture a second time. Hawk brought both throttles around the detent position into afterburner. The Tomcat bucked and quivered and shook side to side. A tremendous howling, a chest-rattling roar that would have deafened anyone on the flight deck without earplugs and sound suppressors, erupted from the twin TF30 infernos.

Hawk made his final scan of the engine instruments, gauges, indicators—those last-chance telltales of the wellness of the jet. He cycled the flight controls through all four corner stops and checked the center mirror to ensure the seat pin was out.

Satisfied their Tomcat was good to go, Hawk yelled above the rumble, "You ready, Chief?"

"Up and up, Hawk.

"And Hawk," Chief declared almost as an afterthought, "it's been a pleasure to serve with you, Skipper!"

"Thanks, Chief. Truly, the pleasure's been mine. But it ain't over yet!"

CHAPTER 1

Behind the Wing Line

I have seen the curvature of the earth. I have seen sights most people will never see. Flying at more than 70,000 feet is really beautiful and peaceful. I enjoy the quiet, hearing myself breathing, and the hum of the engine. I never take it for granted.

—Lt. Col. Merryl Tengesda

The "Gunfighters"

The day looked like any other spring day in Southern California: 75 degrees, a light breeze from the west, and a thin, low scud layer hugging the coast. For Cmdr. John Monroe "Hawk" Smith, it was far from just another day in paradise.

It was mid-April 1978. He had taken a few days leave following his change of command at the Navy Fighter Weapons School, a.k.a. TOPGUN, and today he was checking into VF-124.

He had kissed Miss Jenny goodbye and driven the 12 miles from Escondido to NAS Miramar—Fightertown USA. Miss Jenny, his wife of nearly sixteen years and his first love, was confident and comfortable in knowing she was not in competition with Hawk's second love and the reason for which he was checking into VF-124.

VF-124, the "Gunfighters," was the West Coast F-14 Fleet Replacement Squadron (FRS). Their hangar sat just a few hundred yards from TOPGUN's. Hawk was scheduled to complete an abbreviated flight syllabus at VF-124 and become reacquainted with the mighty Tomcat— the second love of his life.

It seemed like years since he'd last climbed in the cockpit of the F-14, and it seemed like an eternity since his very first thoughts of flying anything at all had sprouted.

The Man[1]

Hawk had just departed the hallowed halls of TOPGUN as the commanding officer. To the untrained eye, he may have appeared to be an average man, but a deep dive into his character, an examination of his physical and cognitive attributes, and an analysis of his moral and ethical codes would prove he was anything but.

There were a number of ground-rattling events in Hawk's life that had shaped, prepared, and guided him into the very unusual occupation as a Navy fighter pilot.

Hawk's clearest memory of being drawn toward the mystery of flight was at the tender age of about twelve. He and his young friends often rode their bikes to Owens Field, in

Columbia, South Carolina, a mere fifteen minutes from his home. There they spent countless hours watching the light, prop-driven airplanes take off and land. Airplanes weren't new, but they were new to Hawk and his friends and captivating stuff in the active imaginations of young boys.

It was in 1952 that Hawk and his friends decided to expand their horizons and ride their bikes to Shaw Air Force Base (AFB). It was a longer ride but promised greater rewards and excitement. It was then, while pressed against the security fence, their eyes lined up with the holes in the chain links, that something magnificent and life-changing took place. Hawk saw an F-86 Sabre take to the air, clean up, and climb out. Suddenly, Hawk's sense of amusement became a pestering obsession—a dream that he too, one day, would be able to fly.

But even at that age, Hawk, always the pragmatist, realized that dreams were just that— dreams—a fleeting flirtation with illusion, and seldom did that cross the line into reality. This awareness, however, never stopped him from, at least, keeping his occasional romps down the rabbit hole alive.

By the age of ten, in 1950, Hawk was developing character elements that further distinguished him from other kids his age. He hosted an energy level, an eternal quest to unravel the mysteries of life, and a competitive spirit that caused him to stand out and, sometimes, away from others.

That competitive spirit and energy level seemed to demand an outlet, and that drove Hawk into team sports, specifically the city league baseball team. This was Hawk's second life-changing experience.

Lean and strong, with exceptional hand-eye coordination, he was noticed by the coaches. They put Hawk on the pitcher's mound. He didn't disappoint, but his exuberance for organized team sports was prematurely doused due to two independent experiences.

During a very important baseball game, the ump made a bad call. Despite all the evidence to the contrary, the ump refused to revisit the ruling. Hawk realized that somebody needed to make the tough calls in a game, but he felt that person should be objective, fair-minded, and, most of all, willing to fess up when he made a bad call.

The second disappointment was a sad realization that not all of Hawk's teammates committed themselves to the same level of enthusiasm, the same measure of determination, and dauntlessness in the heat of competition. In Hawk's words, "Success in team sports comes down to the skill, strength, and commitment of the weakest player. We can be great and do everything exactly right, but if one guy can't hit, or doesn't care, we can lose the game. So much for teamwork!"

It was several years later that a different sport became part of Hawk's life: flat-track, wheel-to-wheel motorcycle racing—another life-changing experience.

This new sport seemed to draw out the best of many of his strengths: independence, a competitive nature, a special skill set for all things mechanical, and a complete indifference for personal safety. It didn't escape Hawk that this new event had nothing to do with "team."

He seemed to be a natural at this sport, and his reputation as a flat-out, go-for-it racer grew accordingly.

This sport was interrupted for a short time, and maybe for the better considering the inherent risks, when his family moved to Norfolk, Virginia, in October 1957.

Hawk graduated the following year from Granby High School and immediately enrolled in the engineering curriculum at the Virginia Tech extension program at Norfolk College of William and Mary, leading the way for two other events that would alter Hawk's life forever—a fraternity dance and a chance encounter with a vivacious and gorgeous young lady.

Gorgeous would not properly describe her—she was a showstopper. Virginia Patricia Hudgins, known to her friends as Miss Jenny. She stood 5 inches shorter than Hawk. She was slender and had lustrous brown hair, luminescent blue eyes, and an infectious smile. Hawk had stolen glimpses of her at the school canteen for some time. It was by chance that he spied her on the other side of the dance hall. She was glorious to look at during school, but on this night she was utterly beguiling.

Hawk finally cowboyed up, walked over to her, and started a conversation. Hawk was fully prepared to be sent on his way, but his crazy notion paid off. They talked and danced away the hours, and by the end of the evening, much to Hawk's surprise, she seemed wholly infatuated with him.

On October 5, 1962, four years later, they were married. The justice of the peace performed the services. It was a quiet affair with no announcement and no reception. While the ceremony may have seemed small, it in no way reflected the enormity of their love or their dedication to one another.

This was a sobering epiphany. Hawk was no longer an independent and carefree student and hair-on-fire motorcycle racer. From this point forward, his responsibility to and love for Miss Jenny would be a seminal factor in all of Hawk's future plans . . . whatever they might be.

A little annoying war, far away in 1963, turned a distant improbability into a horrible possibility. The Vietnam conflict was gaining momentum, and the United States was caught up in the tempest of a war few understood and no one wanted.

Hawk was still in college when the draft board invited him to take the entrance exams and physical. There was no lack of patriotic commitment with Hawk, but rather than put his military commitment and his life in the hands of perfect strangers, Hawk vied for at least some control over his future. At the urging of a frat brother, Hawk took the Navy entrance exam in hopes he might avoid being drafted. He scored so well that the proctors offered him advanced testing oriented toward naval aviation. It was a welcome shock to Hawk that he also passed these with high marks.

Hawk was ecstatic, but at the same time his thoughts were muddled somewhere between his responsibilities to Miss Jenny and in his childhood fantasies of flying.

It was later, during his flight physical, that his dream was rained on. A small anomaly with his vision disqualified him from pilot training. On the basis of his test and physical exam results, Hawk was still qualified for NFO training. He could go through the Naval Flight Officer[2] program, but piloting an aircraft was a nonstarter. This was a frigid dose of reality he did not see coming. Now, he was relegated to the back of the airplane.

Hawk explained everything to Miss Jenny with complete sobriety. Miss Jenny, always the magnanimous Miss Jenny, sensed Hawk's disappointment and agreed to support him in his decision—whatever it might be.

After considerable introspection and deliberation, on August 23, 1963, Hawk signed the papers and began his naval career.

Life in the military was not easy on anyone, least of all the spouses. Hawk and Miss Jenny moved three times in the following seventeen months for various aspects of basic and advanced naval aviation training.

With his usual total commitment and focus, Hawk was selected for radar intercept officer (RIO) training in fighters. This, for naval flight officers, was the brass ring, the objective that almost all NFO students aspired to.

In February 1965, Hawk completed RIO training and reported to his first fighter squadron, VF-102 "Diamondbacks," at NAS Oceana Virginia—right back to Miss Jenny's and Hawk's stomping ground.

The "Diamondbacks" were assigned to the carrier air wing deployed aboard a brand-new ship, USS *America*. Nine months after joining VF-101, Hawk and USS *America* departed on his and her very first deployment.

This first cruise was a whirlwind adventure, cram-packed with exciting exploits but also several unwanted experiences. One in particular was a major disappointment and cause for another major character-shaping event.

Early in the cruise, *America*'s carrier task force (CTF) and the French military were tasked with a NATO exercise. Exercise Fairgame IV"[3] was conducted from February 28 to March 10, 1966. It "simulated conventional warfare against a fictitious country attempting to invade a NATO ally." It was *America*'s mission to provide air strikes, fighter cover, and logistics in support of an amphibious operation.

To the aircrew of *America*, it was a war-at-sea exercise pitting the frontline Navy aircraft and *America*'s newest aircraft carrier against Korean-vintage French fighters and attack aircraft.

From the start, it portended to be a tactical disaster for the Navy crews. Although the French aircraft were of 1950s design, the pilots were aggressive and knew their machinery. They also seemed united in the belief that the rules of engagement (ROE) did not really apply to them, and most of the international flight regulations were pretty much optional.

From the French aspect of instilling confidence, vanquishing the Yankees, and adding to their repertoire of war stories, it was an overwhelming success. Taken from the viewpoint of *America*'s air wing, it was a humiliating and disastrous tactical defeat.

According to Hawk, "We had our collective asses handed to us by a second-rate military club flying a bunch of cheap, little airplanes by pilots who didn't even hold down an honest sixteen-hour-a-day job. We looked like a bunch of buffoons, a bunch of toothless boxers growling at the milkman. All we did was make noise, smoke, and good targets!"

Hawk took the humiliation hard. He believed the victory should go the bold, the stout hearted, the swift of foot . . . not to those who didn't play by the rules. Years later, Hawk explained: "This wasn't fair, but it did reflect the real world, and I learned the true meaning of the dictum *If you ain't cheating, you ain't trying.*"

"Know the rules; they'll set you free, and sometimes," Hawk concluded, "the main rule is—there ain't no rules."

Operation Fairgame IV marked a cathartic moment in Hawk's life—a wake-up call. There was something very wrong with the tactics and training in the Navy fighter community. The reality of the situation was more than an annoyance to Hawk; it was downright vexing. Ultimately, it launched Hawk on a quest, a mission to help improve tactics and training for the Navy fighter community. As a young lieutenant junior grade (Lt. j.g.), he had far more questions than answers—the root problem and the solution were utterly baffling—but his goals were clear: he needed to help fix a very broken system.

Sometime after the exercise and just prior to returning to CONUS,[4] Hawk received a reprieve of sorts, a second shot at Navy pilot training.

With a clean bill of health from the squadron flight surgeon and a strong endorsement from Cmdr. Max Morris, the commanding officer of VF-102, Hawk applied for and was accepted for pilot training. A few months before *America* completed her deployment, he returned to the states, grabbed Miss Jenny, and headed south to Pensacola, Florida, to begin pilot training. This was a dream since childhood, and he was blessed with a second chance in life. He could not have asked for more.

Hawk performed well in the pilot-training syllabus, but he was eye-watering in the air combat maneuvering (ACM) phase. There were several reasons for this: he was spatially adapted to the three-dimensional arena of air combat maneuvering based on his RIO training, he was competitive by nature, and he was highly motivated. But there was a fourth reason more overpowering than the others—the humiliation his air wing suffered at the hands of the French compelled him to be the very best he could. While other guys were at the beach, in the bars, or out on the golf course, Hawk studied diligently to discover solutions to the dynamic and three-dimensional mysteries of air combat.

As his air combat training phase progressed, he advanced so far and so fast that the syllabus instructors, unbeknown to Hawk, pitted the best tactics instructor pilot in the command against him—a Marine fighter pilot.

Hawk flew his final flight in ACM phase flight in the AF-9J, the lead sled, against the Marine instructor. Following the brief, they manned up and took to air. Three gut-busting engagements were flown that day. When they finally headed home, the fights were declared a draw.

Hawk was exhausted but exuberant, and even more so when he was told that his mystery instructor was a ringer—a combat vet and a vaunted fighter pilot.

The lesson attributed to this experience was this: in all things, do your best, strive for perfection in all challenges, and, pertaining to Hawk's last tactics hop in the syllabus ... *never give up!*

Hawk received his naval aviator Wings of Gold on the first of July 1967 and reported to the F-4 Phantom FRS, VF-101, at Key West with one of the highest academic and flight grade averages ever recorded.

It was a cinch he'd receive orders to a fleet squadron when he completed the FRS curriculum—but which one? Most of the carriers ordered into the Vietnam theater were West Coast ships whose fighter squadrons were stationed at NAS Miramar, California. Hawk was one of those who always rode to the sound of gunfire, so it was no surprise to anyone, including Miss Jenny, when he lobbied heavily for orders to a West Coast squadron.

That was not to be, however. Early in 1968, Hawk received orders to VF-103, the Sluggers, aboard USS *Saratoga* (CVA-60), an East Coast ship.

Though mightily disappointed, he was no quitter. He was convinced that as the war heated up (and surely it would), *Sara* would be called to action to save the day.

Sara was scheduled to deploy for a Med cruise on July 9, 1969. For some time before that, Hawk and Miss Jenny felt the stirrings of their parental responsibilities. They loved kids, and both of them were equipped with all the requisite parental instincts and skills to properly raise a child. Miss Jenny, with all her goodness and love, would make an extraordinary mother. When they were informed that they couldn't have children of their own, they decided to adopt. And so it was that Jack Smith was delivered on January 9, 1969, to his new and loving parents, Lt. John Monroe and Miss Jenny Smith.

Fatherhood brought a sense of fulfillment; there was no ignoring it. In sharp contrast with his new role as a father was a responsibility as a Navy pilot whose job it was to man America's first line of defense. Hawk understood, full well, that his duty as a new father would have no effect on *Sara's* sail date: July 9, 1969.

Sara's 1969 cruise was without any significant international crisis, and that was a disappointment to Hawk since he was hoping they'd be ordered into the war. Gravely disappointed, he looked to the future and his next set of orders.

As one of the high-trajectory junior officers of his day, Hawk would have had pretty much his first choice of assignments. Initially, Hawk had designs of returning to VF-101, the Fleet Replacement Squadron, at NAS Oceana.

Cmdr. J. R. Winkowsky, the XO of VF-103, had a different idea. He recognized in Hawk certain traits and skills that made him a natural for a bigger challenge, something that would test his mettle. There was an outfit at Pt. Mugu, California—a fighter squadron that few knew about, VX-4, the "Evaluators."[5] Cmdr. Winkowsky was a straight shooter and spoke of the tremendous matchup between VX-4 and Hawk. Hawk's inquisitive mind, unflappable determination, good people skills, and demonstrated superior airmanship made him a natural for the assignment.

After some contemplation and many hours discussing their choices with Miss Jenny, Hawk took the XO's advice and accepted orders to VX-4. Despite his many initial misgivings, Hawk saw it to be the opportunity of a lifetime and the gateway to greater things.

Hawk reported to VX-4 on April 10, 1970. Eight months later, and a shock to no one, Hawk was assigned as the VX-4 project officer for the most expensive and comprehensive aircraft acquisition program in the history of naval aviation—the Grumman F-14 Tomcat project.

There were a number of different agencies and offices involved in the testing and evaluation of the Tomcat, to include Naval Air Systems Command (NAVAIRSYSCOM), the Pacific Missile Center (PMC), and others, but the big ball carrier was VX-4, and a great deal of that load fell on Hawk's shoulders.

After months of preliminary groundwork and administrative functions, the F-14 airframes began to arrive at VX-4. In October 1973, after months of testing and scores of hours in the airplane, Hawk's evaluation team certified the F-14 as "operationally suitable for service use." This finding paved the way—just in time—for the Tomcat's first scheduled deployment in September 1974.

The honeymoon didn't end with the Tomcat fleet certification at VX-4. Hawk's tour at VX-4 coincidentally concluded just before the Tomcat entered fleet service. Hawk was strongly encouraged (some might say shanghaied) to deploy on the big bird's first cruise.

At the urgings of several very senior Navy officials, Hawk accepted orders to CVW-14[6] as the air wing's landing signal officer (LSO) for a western Pacific (WestPac) deployment. It was a gargantuan responsibility, but no one knew the Tomcat—its quirks, moods, and technical challenges— as well as Hawk. He was the perfect match for the Tomcat's first overseas deployment.

By early fall 1974, CVW-14's two fighter squadrons, VF-1 "Wolfpack" and VF-2 "Bounty Hunters," had received their inventory of F-14s, their crews were trained and certified, and the air wing and ship's company embarked aboard America's first nuclear-powered warship, USS *Enterprise* (CVN-65), for the Tomcat's first deployment. On September 17, 1974, USS *Enterprise* glided under the Golden Gate Bridge, bound for Hawaii and points west.

But barely into the deployment, a high-priority mission was assigned to the "Big E," radically changing the cruise schedule. During the last days of the Vietnam War, in April 1975, *Enterprise* and escorting ships were tasked to provide support and security for US and Allied forces during Operation Frequent Wind, a joint-forces emergency extraction operation.

Though Frequent Wind would be judged a success, there was just no way to flavor the war's outcome to make it palatable. The *Enterprise* crew was part of an epochal event in world history. They had just witnessed the end of America's longest war and her first major military defeat. The greatest military power in the world just had her clock cleaned by a nation smaller than California.

After eight months on deployment, *Enterprise* and her air wing came about and sailed east, returning to where it had all begun. The cruise had come and gone. The months at sea had produced a flood of emotions that can happen only in the military: sadness, excitement, exuberance, anger, reward, loss, fear, anxiety, and the agonizing humiliation of losing the war. It was a barrage of feelings catapulted by events not theirs to control.

The *Enterprise* and Air Wing 14 cruise was a capstone achievement, and despite the technical sophistication and newness of the F-14, it had acceptable availability and performed well beyond expectations.

For Hawk's part, it was a cruise of firsts: the first cruise of the mighty Tomcat, which all predicted would be followed by many more; his first time waving[7] an F-14 into the barricade, which he hoped he would never do again; his first WestPac deployment; and his first combat mission, of which he hoped there would be more. All in all, he was satisfied with the adventure, but he was glad it was behind him.

There were many experiences among the collage of events sprouting from *Enterprise*'s '74 cruise that could have been catastrophic had they not been managed timely and correctly. These were marked by an unusual degree of brilliance and innovation. This gave a booster shot to Hawk's already stellar performance.

Hawk was coming up for orders, and with the hard work behind him he puzzled over the possibilities.

There was a small squadron at NAS Miramar. Its mission area lay in the arena of tactics, training, and weapons system development. It was a pathfinder of sorts and had a significant shaping effect on the entire Navy fighter community, proportionally well beyond the size of its footprint.

The Navy Fighter Weapons School, known throughout the fighter world as TOPGUN, was something more than a school and more than a fighter squadron. It was the single touchpoint for fleet air combat training and the development of fighter tactics. TOPGUN was the higher-learning center, the "grad" school for fighter crews: pilots and RIOs.

This, for any number of reasons, captivated Hawk's attention. The billet he had his eye on was none other than the executive officer (XO) position.

The TOPGUN CO and XO slots were the garlanded prize for all Navy fighter pilots worth their salt. Politics, of course, would play some role in the assignment of such a coveted position, but most of the decision would be based on the performance of the eligible candidates. In that arena, Hawk had a distinct advantage: his tour at VX-4 as the F-14 project manager and, more recently, the remarkably successful first cruise of the F-14. Few of Hawk's running mates could match his credentials.

But there is the old adage "Be careful what you ask for. You just might get it."

Hawk had no idea when he lobbied for the TOPGUN XO slot just how close to home that statement would strike.

Drafting on the monumental successes of TOPGUN's previous COs and XOs, TOPGUN continued to make stellar headway in developing fighter tactics and delivering those to the fleet. This progress continued while Hawk was the XO, and, no doubt, had definitive influence on changing the ground rules for the selection of the follow-on CO.

Since the inception of TOPGUN, the prospective commanding officer had been ordered into the position directly; the executive officer did not fleet up to the CO slot, as was the protocol in fleet squadrons. But in late 1976, the policy had changed, and for good reason.

Leadership within the fighter community believed that the best man for the position was already in the squadron—the executive officer. Advancing Hawk would put a man well known for shepherding over his people and completing the tough missions into a position where he could do what he did best—lead.

On December 13, 1976, at a ceremony on the NAS Miramar parade ground, Cmdr. Cobra Ruliffson passed the scepter of responsibility for seventy enlisted personnel, eleven officers, twelve aircraft, a multimillion-dollar budget, and the most treasured brain trust in the Navy to Lt. Cmdr. John "Hawk" Smith, the sixth commanding officer of the Navy Fighter Weapons School.

Hawk was just one of many TOPGUN commanding officers, but during TOPGUN's most tumultuous and epochal period, he was precisely the right man in the right place at the right time.

From its earliest days, the monumental success of TOPGUN was borne on the backs of those who toiled and sacrificed to improve Navy fighter lethality. The instructor pilots and RIOs worked tirelessly and diligently to devise new air combat tactics and deliver those to the frontline fighter outfits. The commanding officers, steeped in the wisdom of their experiences and empowered by their conviction in the TOPGUN mission, guided their people, fortified their mission, and defended their command.

Hawk's orders to TOPGUN seemed to trigger a culmination point. It was here in Hawk's dream factory where grand ideas and true believers fused. He had become the kinetic force, that spark of inspiration, that harnessed the imagination and determination of a few stout souls who would help change some of those things that badly needed changing in naval fighterdom.

During Hawk's sixteen-month CO reign, TOPGUN racked up a number of lofty and ground-shaking achievements. The TOPGUN staff had incorporated the lessons learned from a number of joint, high-level air combat evaluations (AIMVAL/ACEVAL)[8] into new fighter tactics, techniques, and procedures. They developed innovative antimissile countermeasures and designed defensive air combat tactics for the attack communities. Fleet-services squadrons were being baptized in the TOPGUN teaching techniques and trained to provide adversary services for all TACAIR[9] fleet squadrons to include US Marine fighter commands.

Most simply, TOPGUN pushed a revolutionary change in air-to-air warfare and delivered it to the TACAIR units. TACAIR aircrews, fighter and attack, were, for the first time, trained to engage in the future battlefield.

While little energy was devoted to touting the deeds and accomplishments of TOPGUN, the Navy higher-ups followed these things, and well before the end of Hawk's CO tour, he had been screened and slated for the XO/CO posting to the "Black Lions" of VF-213.

But no good deed should go unpunished. All would have been well, and Hawk would have had a magnificent and productive command tour, but for an event that came to be known as the TOPGUN Christmas Card incident.

It was really a nonevent, or should have been, but what started as a prank from the very imaginative and sometimes overly energetic instructors careened into a nearly career-ending crater.

TOPGUN, in keeping with most of the TACAIR squadrons of the day, sent Christmas cards to other commands, commanders, high officials, and friends.

The TOPGUN JOs were a serious and professional lot. When it came time to play and banter about, however, owing to the adage "Anything worth doing is worth overdoing," they consistently swept all three positions on the podium in the buffoonery competition.

The 1977 TOPGUN Christmas card was right up their alley.

It was a jaw-dropper to be sure, hilariously funny to anyone with a modicum of a sense of humor, but there were those, even in the fighter industry, who had virtually no sense of humor or were so consumed by political correctness that nothing was considered funny.

The TOPGUN JOs connived to design a Christmas card that would capture the spirit and the whimsy, grab-assing that is part of the fighter community. There were several Christmas card prototypes, but Lt. Cmdr. Charles "Heater" Heatley's wife, Kay, a professional graphics artist, designed the Christmas card that won the JO's vote hands down.

On the front cover of the card, she laid out a cartoon of Santa and his reindeer flying through a cloudless night sky. Santa was looking over his shoulder with a bewildered expression. A gunsight was laid over Santa's sleigh with a perfect gun solution. The caption on the front of the card read, "Only an asshole would gun Santa."

On the inside cover was a picture of a perforated, fiery sleigh in a radical descent, with Santa and eight reindeer in parachutes. The greeting, "Merry Christmas and a Happy Ho, Ho from the Assholes at TOPGUN," was printed on the right inside cover. Below the greeting was a photo that had been taken some months earlier and featured the TOPGUN JOs, with their flight suits down to their ankles, mooning the camera. A brand-new F-5E that posed in the background, for the most part, went unnoticed.

Hawk about fell off his chair when the prototype card was presented to him for comment. When he composed himself, he gathered his team together and explained, "It's great guys, but we can't use it. It's too risky. I want a reasonable card we can send to the world. This ain't gonna cut it!"

Instantly, the JOs came up with an option. They suggested that the cards would be sent on a "restricted basis." They would limit distribution to only close friends and selected senior officers who shared a similar sense of humor. Hawk was certain it had all the potential to backfire, but the JOs were relentless.

Against his better judgment, Hawk finally yielded to their wishes.

RAdm. Fenner was not well known for his fondness of many things, but very early during his tour as the chief of staff and, later, as COMFITAEWWINGPAC,[10] it was clear that he had cultivated a strong dislike for TOPGUN. According to those who knew him, "The admiral thought that 'NFWS was staffed by a bunch of rabble-rousing upstarts and out-of-control junior officers led by a cavalier cowboy.'"

Almost immediately after RAdm. Fenner's arrival at Fightertown USA, it was clear that the entire fighter community was in for some draconian changes in management. Many would suffer the consequences of his reign. Hawk, it seemed, was to be the first notch on Fenner's pistol grip; TOPGUN, the second. It took not long for the preverbal pooh to hit the blades.

In pursuit of his tyrannical objective, to dispose of Hawk and corral TOPGUN, RAdm. Fenner had ordered several reports and judge advocate general (JAG) investigations against Hawk and his command. These were seemingly nonevents.

The other skippers and senior officers were initially incredulous that the fighter wing commander would be so petty and waste so much time conducting investigations against a fellow commanding officer for such trivial breaches of rules: section taxiing of aircraft, minor course rules violations, and a confusing charge of misappropriation—none of which gained traction.

These accusations seemed to have two objectives: to nail Hawk and bring to heel the other commanding officers of Fightertown. But there may have been a third objective—to send an unmistakable message that there was a new sheriff in town.

In the words of Lt. Cmdr. Rich "Turtle" Reddit, who recalled the witch hunts, "There were common denominators in each of the JAGs. Each was initiated with the slimmest presumption of wrongdoing. Each JAG commenced without the benefit of solid research. Each seemed to be directed more to denigrate than to discover evidence, and finally, when Hawk and TOPGUN were cleared of all wrongdoing—no apology was offered."

The fact was that Hawk never expected or desired an apology from the wing. More than anything, he simply wanted to be left alone so TOPGUN could continue "God's work." His staff was running full tilt on several important projects—projects critical to all TACAIR squadrons. Time was of the essence. Being ignored by fighter wing was not in Hawk's future, however.

In December 1977, the TOPGUN Christmas card was released. It was, by design, a big hit, and though the address list was restricted, it somehow made its way to the one office that it should not have gone to.

When RAdm. Fenner became aware of the Christmas card, he thought he had Hawk by the short and curlies, and he might have had if it weren't for a well-known senior officer, both objective and forthright.

Cmdr. Leighton Warren Smith, call sign "Snuffy," was selected and assigned by the admiral as the JAG investigating officer. He was a war-hardened, light-attack pilot, accepted in all TACAIR communities. Community origins aside, he was a distinguished and decorated combat pilot, objective, honest, even-tempered—a no-nonsense professional naval officer on a fast track to stardom. But what probably drew the attention of Fenner to Snuffy was his credibility. When Snuffy spoke, people, even the fighter guys, listened. Snuffy was clearly and precisely the right choice for RAdm. Fenner's JAG assignment.

In mid-December, Cmdr. Smith began the infamous TOPGUN Christmas card JAG investigation. The findings of Cmdr. Smith's investigation would have primary bearing on determining Hawk's fate, and Hawk had much to lose: his command at TOPGUN, and his next assignment as XO of the Black Lions. But what bothered Hawk even more was the loss in credibility and respect for TOPGUN and the carnage to the morale and pride of the JOs.

While the JAG investigation was moving ahead under Cmdr. Smith's guidance, there were two behind-the-scene acts playing out.

Cmdr. Smith interviewed each one of the TOPGUN JOs. It became quickly apparent that there was an insurgency brewing within the JO ranks. Each of the pilots and RIOs explained that they would turn in their wings and resign their commission en masse if the admiral took Hawk's command from him.

The second event was an act of valor and loyalty worthy of a combat ribbon, and one that could happen only in the military. Lt. Cmdr. "Heater" Heatley visited, one on one, with RAdm. Fenner. Heater confessed that the entire Christmas card idea was his. It was he who led the drive to convince Hawk to release it. Further, if punishment were to be imposed, Heater should pay the price for the breach of common sense, not the skipper. Hawk, at the time, was unaware of any of this.

On December 30, Cmdr. Snuffy Smith hand-delivered the JAG investigation report to the admiral. It was comprehensive, objective, and fair. He dropped it squarely in the middle of the admiral's fairway with no English.

Sometime earlier, the admiral had requested direction from the CNO. None was forthcoming. So, when the admiral read Snuffy's report, it was obvious he was in a box. Without CNO guidance, the admiral was obliged to follow the recommendations of the JAG report.

Purely from a disciplinary perspective, the admiral would be well within his authority if he stripped Hawk of command and canceled his follow-on orders to VF-213.

The admiral believed it would set a bad precedent if a senior officer, especially a commanding officer, was allowed to continue in command after such a breach of judgment. If, on the other hand, the admiral removed him, it would confirm what many in the fighter community suspected all along—the admiral was out to hang Hawk from the git-go.

There was another outcome to consider, and on the basis of the unvarnished report by Snuffy, a dozen of the Navy's most gifted and experienced fighter crews would resign in protest. That, by all indications, was not an idle threat. The TOPGUN staff was committed to the Navy, but it had become painfully obvious that their loyalty to their skipper was unswerving and absolute. This event could be a coup de grace for the admiral.

In the investigation report, Cmdr. Snuffy Smith recommended a more broad-minded reach, something that would send a signal to the community. His recommendation would avoid a wholesale walkout by the TOPGUN staff and would not destroy a good officer's career. He recommended that Lt. Cmdr. Smith receive a nonpunitive letter of caution, and a fitness report that reflected poor judgment. The punishment was not inconsequential, but neither was it the body blow that would take Hawk out of the game. RAdm. Fenner considered his options, addressed the risks and benefits, and, in the end, agreed with all recommendations.

When Hawk was informed of the admiral's decision, he was quietly jubilant. He fully expected to be out of the Navy in a matter of months, stripped of his command, humiliated by the revocation of his next assignment, and responsible for TOPGUN's fall from grace.

He was disappointed in himself, and yet, there was much to be grateful for. Cmdr. Snuffy Smith could have taken the investigation and the recommendations in any direction. To his credit, he recommended an appropriate punishment commensurate with the crime of poor judgment. It made a statement but did not emasculate an officer who had dedicated his life to the Navy and who, up until now, showed nothing but brilliance, honor, and integrity. Hawk knew he owed the rest of his naval career to Snuffy Smith.

Additionally, Hawk believed that his JOs had taken his advice not to do anything stupid. It wasn't until sometime later that he learned of the JOs' blood oath to resign if the admiral relieved Hawk from command. Although Hawk did not agree with their position, it confirmed a very important lesson: loyalty is a two-way street.

There was an additional twist in the wake of the Christmas card fiasco. From the defiant position the TOPGUN staff had taken in Hawk's defense, and the insight Cmdr. Snuffy Smith had provided, the admiral could not help but realize that there was more to this high-energy country boy than met the eye.

Lt. Mike "Smiles" Bucchi,[11] a well-respected TOPGUN instructor, recounts the incident: "The Christmas card incident gave us all a clear look at the tenacious character of the man who was our skipper. He was always positive, unsinkable, and unstoppable. He exerted tremendous energy and a willingness to protect his people at all costs. It seemed to me, just when things were at their worst, Hawk was at his best!"

"In the end," "Turtle" reflects, "Monroe managed to protect one of the crown jewels of naval aviation—Navy Fighter Weapons School. From my standpoint, that's what he was there to do. To do all this, to fight so many powers from so many directions so valiantly, was incredibly selfless and courageous. And it wasn't without some battle damage to Hawk, but I'm sure he'll tell you today—it was all worth it."

By the end of his tour at TOPGUN, Hawk had become something of a legend in the eyes of the officers and men at TOPGUN and in the fighter community on both coasts. He had weathered the worst of the admiral's assaults, accusations, and investigations and was resolute in his perseverance. His actions, though controversial at times, were always buttressed by the virtue of the results. His decisions were made in the void of the political crucible and always for the ultimate good of his command, the fighter community, the fleet, and the Navy.

Hawk's life experiences were many, and all had profound and lasting impacts that shaped his mien and forged his mettle. Several had negative effects upon his character, festering a degree of hardheadedness, skepticism, and, occasionally, an aversion to compromise.

The incidents while at TOPGUN, for a lesser person, could have completely alienated him to the Navy and all forms of authority, but Hawk was made of stouter stuff. He recognized the error of his ways. He blamed no one but himself.

When he departed TOPGUN, he took with him a Copernican learning experience: loyalty and example are crucial to good leadership. He was as protective of his people as a lioness is of her cubs—this inspired loyalty. He was also exceptionally successful in energizing people to achieve the improbable by conjuring up a vision of the great could-be and urging them forward by personal example. By any measure, Hawk was an extraordinary leader.

At the end of a West Coast formal TACAIR dining out in 1977, during the time set aside for honoring the commander in chief, military heroes, fallen warriors, and POWs, a toast was offered: "To Rear Admiral Fenner, the greatest contributor to the ranks of Naval Reserve aviation in recruiting history."[12]

"Hear! Hear!" was heard throughout the dining area. It was an accurate but highly un-complimentary statement, and it took a moment for it to register. It suggested that Fenner was responsible for driving people out of the active-duty Navy and into the Naval Reserve.

The Machine: The First "Third-Generation" Fighter

The arrival of the Grumman F-14 Tomcat gave the Navy the world's first third-generation fighter.[13] It had completed the most comprehensive gauntlet of tests, assessments, evaluations, phased certifications, and capabilities demonstration ever designed for any aircraft. The Tomcat passed them all in a flurry of triumph and a wall of happy faces.

The Tomcat project tests at all the supporting agencies, for the most part, were nothing short of spectacular, but the truest test of a fighter is how well it could actually fight. For these "real-world" evaluations, Hawk and his senior project RIO, Lt. Bruce "Peeps" Pieper, conducted an operational evaluation against little jets—actual MiG fighters that, at the time, were part of a black program,[14] Have Drill and Have Doughnut.

Hawk and Peeps conducted the evaluation and wrote the report. In summary they stated that "with minor exception, the F-14 Tomcat held a significant tactical advantage over both the MiG-17 and the MiG-21 throughout the operational performance envelope." In less technical jargon, the Tomcat had its way with the little MiGs. It was a win-win.

With all the data and analysis from the Tomcat op eval assembled, the results across the board were very encouraging. The Navy's fighter community had not only the most lethal, long-range interceptor in the world, but the most vicious dogfighter ever built. The Tomcat was the most technologically advanced fighter in the world, and the Navy's backbone fighter-interceptor of the new millennium.

To suggest that Hawk was professionally involved in the development and the fleet introduction of the F-14 would be a wild understatement. Hawk had ties to and a soft spot in his heart for the Tomcat that went well beyond a simple admiration for the airplane and appreciation for its war-fighting capability. There was a visceral connection, a nexus that normally only fellow pilots understood. It was his project, his pride and joy, his baby. Bringing it to the fleet was one of his greatest triumphs.

The Reunion

It had been only three years since his last sortie in the Tomcat, and Hawk was thrilled to get back into the airplane. Despite all its quirks, faults, personality flaws, and limited availability, the F-14 was still *his* jet. He may not have given it birth, but he and his team did deliver it to the fleet, and that alone qualified him as kin to the big bird.

In designing an abbreviated syllabus for Hawk, the operations department at VF-124 made two assumptions. First, since Hawk had just stepped down as commanding officer of TOPGUN, his tactical skills were probably still intact. Second, since he had been the VX-4 project officer for the fleet introduction of the F-14 and taken the jet on its maiden deployment aboard USS *Enterprise*, he probably still remembered a thing or two about the Tomcat.

The ops department was correct on both counts. They scripted a syllabus that would allow Hawk to plow through the ground course, complete the battery of systems tests and NATOPS[15] exams, and climb into the Tomcat for a minimum number of sorties in familiarization, radar intercept, air-to-air gunnery, air combat training, and carrier qualification.

By the end of April 1978, Hawk had completed the ground school courses and was more than ready to begin flying. His first flight was a familiarization sortie. Hawk looked at his FAM sorties not so much as the first stage of the FRS but as a reunion with his second love.

After a standard 1.5-hour brief by a VF-124 instructor pilot, he and Hawk proceeded through maintenance control and then headed across the tarmac to their assigned Tomcat.

San Diego experiences an interesting weather pattern in mid-spring. Normal days begin with a low, thin, overcast layer that reduces visibility to a couple of miles. Usually before noon, that layer burns off to expose a dazzlingly clear day; a mild westerly breeze flows off the ocean, with temperatures seemingly stabilized by climate control. It's the perfect weather and location for work and for play, and on this day, Hawk's first flight in the Tomcat in three years, he was doing both.

As Hawk and his instructor walked up to their assigned Tomcat, Hawk couldn't suppress a small smile. There was no sense trying to ignore it; he was thoroughly revved to get back into *his* beast.

Hawk stood there and for a moment studied the airplane. He gazed upon the gorgeous lines of the Tomcat, and the numbers, specs, and performance parameters all came flooding back to him. He stared at and admired the contours of the airframe and the sleek magnificence of the big beast. At 63 feet from radome[16] to turkey feathers,[17] with a 64-foot wingspan fully extended and 36 feet fully swept, the Tomcat was a behemoth. Empty, it weighed nearly as much as an A-7 Corsair with a full combat load-out, and by the time the Tomcat was full of gas and fitted with its own arsenal, it was shot off the flight deck weighing in at nearly 37 tons. The two massive Pratt & Whitney TF30-P-412A engines belched 20,900 pounds of thrust per side, giving the F-14 nearly a 0.9:1 thrust-to-weight ratio at combat weight. In the world of fighter aircraft, the Tomcat's thrust-to-weight ratio may not have turned many heads: the F-15 Eagle, F-16 Viper, and then-new F/A-18 Hornet boasted in the neighborhood of 1:1 thrust to weight, and the two Ramenskoye Soviet jets, the MiG-29 Fulcrum and the Sukhoi Su-31 Flanker, had well above a 1:1 thrust to weight.

Knowledgeable fighter pilots and tacticians of the fine art of scuffling, however, shared a secret. At least as important as the amount of thrusties out the back end was the amount of lifties off the wing. That's where the Tomcat confounded the competition in the down-and-dirty art of dogfighting.

Operational analysts might argue that only by a system failure or by human error should an F-14 crew find themselves in the midst of a turning engagement in the visual arena with an enemy aircraft. The popular argument is that to arrive in a turning scuffle, the bad guys would have to first negotiate a gauntlet of long-range AIM-54 Phoenix, midrange AIM-7F[18] Sparrow, and shorter-range AIM-9 Sidewinder missiles. With a crew of two operating the most advanced sensor and weapons system in the world, the probability of a close-in fight in which maneuvering capability reigned supreme would be unlikely. Still, in the fog of war, when either the system or the crew hit that tipping point and became overloaded, it could happen; hence the emphasis on designing both a standoff platform and a street brawler.

In a knuckle-buster, close-in dogfight, the airplane with the best energy sustainability and *pointability*—the ability to point the nose of the fighter at the opponent—was generally the victor. Huge, high-aspect-ratio wings, leading- and trailing-edge maneuvering flaps, and the tremendous lift generated by the undersurface of the Tomcat produced a turn rate that was nothing short of eye-watering. True, the Tomcat rolled slower than a crocodile with a water buffalo in its mouth, and the Tomcat pilots had to be weary of burner blowouts during slow-speed maneuvering, but with the 20-millimeter, M61 Vulcan cannon spouting 4,200 rounds a minute, the front part of the Tomcat was a disturbing place. Even when the pilots of other combat aircraft flew their jets perfectly, more often than not that's where they ended up—in front of the Tomcat.

When Hawk and his RIO instructor completed the preflight, they mounted the steps to their cockpits. Hawk laid his gear on the starboard console, completed the inspection on the Martin-Baker ejection seat, hoisted a leg over the canopy rail, and then slid into the seat. The plane captain climbed up the steps on the left side of the aircraft and assisted Hawk with the seat and comm connections. Hawk reached for his signature blue, Protection Incorporated TOPGUN helmet and slid it on.

For the next several moments he simply sat, listened, and felt the stirrings of his airplane. Three years out of the Tomcat, and the smell, the position of the switches, and the entire *feel* of the airplane all came back in a flood of tactile appreciation. He was back in the cockpit of *his* Tomcat—this was where he was supposed to be.

He was a little surprised that the simple act of climbing into the F-14 would produce such a rush of ebullience. He just didn't expect it, but there was no denying the fact that this, above almost all other experiences, was one of the greatest and most rewarding.

But it wasn't just the simple act of cocooning himself in this magnificent testimony to American ingenuity—this leviathan fighter—that pleased him so. Here he realized he was part of something great. He was an integral component of an organization that is bound by duty and by oath of commission. Hawk and all commissioned military officers were charged with leading men and protecting and defending the Constitution of the United States—his nation.

Hawk was part of the greatest military in the history of mankind. Snuggly cradled in this sleek beast, this apex of human accomplishments, he and his RIO were the critical link in the man-machine loop. He controlled the most technologically advanced, formidable, and dangerous fighter ever built.

The contrast, marked by time, from his early days in South Carolina watching that jet take off from Shaw AFB to this moment, was a virtual collision of improbability and a manifestation of the enormous possibilities that could be realized only in America.

Hawk shook off the reverie. He rechanneled his thoughts to the task, made the final connection from his helmet to the oxygen mask, and began the prestart checklist. Once he was satisfied that each of the scores of switches, knobs, rheostats, levers, handles, and buttons was in the proper position, he pressed the intercom switch and said, "ICS check!"

"Loud and clear, Hawk. Ready to go."

"Roger! We're bringing number 1 online."

Now, using hand signals, Hawk and the plane captain worked together to get the monstrous TF30s to light off.

Fifteen minutes later, Hawk taxied onto the centerline of runway 24 Right (24R), pushed the throttles to the stops, felt the reassuring volcano-like eruption out the tailpipes, and released the brakes.

An hour and a half later, Hawk had completed his first and what disappointingly became his only familiarization sortie. According to Hawk's instructor pilot, there was no reason to waste limited assets and tax dollars on any additional FAM flights, flights Hawk obviously didn't need.

Hawk was slightly disappointed but understood the argument. Besides, as the soon-to-be XO of the Black Lions, he hoped to get plenty of flying.

The Butcher, the Baker, and Everything Else

In conjunction with plowing through the FRS syllabus, Hawk had also stepped up to the plate as the Black Lions' Beach Detachment officer in charge (OIC).

The Black Lions were one of two fighter squadrons in CVW-9 aboard USS *Kitty Hawk* (CV-63). *Kitty* was completing an extended WestPac deployment, and the fly-off was scheduled for May 15, just a few days away.

Hawk had but a short time to process, organize, and begin training the new kids reporting for duty, prepping the hangar for the Black Lions, and making all the spaces habitable before the Black Lions arrived home. This additional duty would require a big chunk of Hawk's time, but even with the demands of the FRS syllabus, compared to the grinder Hawk was part of in the previous two years while at TOPGUN, it was a veritable holiday.

The Black Lions were inbound, and Hawk's holiday was about to come to a halt. That was just fine with Hawk; he was very eager to take his place with the Black Lions and get on with business.

CHAPTER 2
The Black Lions

Never fly the "A" model of anything.
—Edward Thompson, World War II pilot

Lineage of the Black Lions

Hawk's next fighter squadron, VF-213 Black Lions, had a long, proud heritage. The "Lions" were established on June, 22, 1955, at NAS Moffett Field, California. They were then equipped with the McDonnell F2H Banshee. The Banshee, a straight-winged, single-seat, carrier-based jet fighter, was one of the mainstay Navy jets used during the Korean War.

Their first deployment as an operational fighter squadron was aboard USS *Bon Homme Richard* (CVA-31), deploying to the western Pacific. Upon their return, and for their next two deployments, the Lions were assigned to USS *Lexington* (CVA-16). In 1957, the Lions transitioned to the Douglas F4D-1 Skyray.

The Skyray was a bat-winged-design, carrier-based, supersonic fighter/interceptor. It was an odd-looking airplane that had all the eye appeal of a banjo shark. It was never combat-tested, but its claim to fame was the fact that it was the first carrier-based aircraft to break the world's speed record, at 752 mph, and became the Navy's and Marine Corps' first fighter to exceed Mach 1 in level flight.[1]

Flying the finicky Skyray was, thankfully, a short-lived experience, a blessing according to many of those who flew the beast, owing to some unusual (and dangerous) flight characteristics. VF-213 transitioned to the F3H-2 Demon in 1959, giving the squadron a long-range punch with the new AIM-7[2] Sparrow, a radar-guided, air-to-air missile.

Their third and final WestPac deployment aboard *Lady Lex* (CV-16) came in the latter part of 1960, returning in June 1961.

The early 1960s was a busy time for the Lions. Shortly after returning from their WestPac deployment, they moved to NAS Miramar—Fightertown USA. The Lions would call Miramar home for the next thirty-six years.

In February 1964, they took delivery of the first of the then-new McDonnell Douglas[3] F-4B Phantom IIs, giving them a tremendous edge in the air-to-air interceptor and fighter missions . . . and just in time.

The United States' official military involvement in the Vietnam War spanned the period from 1955 to the fall of Saigon in April 1975—twenty years. The first American forces to arrive on scene were military advisors, and war was not far behind. A full military conflict erupted in November 1955. Our involvement, right or wrong, grew exponentially in the early 1960s. On November 5, 1965, as one of two fighter squadrons assigned to Carrier Air Wing 11 (CVW-11) aboard USS *Kitty Hawk* (CVA-63), the Black Lions began the first of nine[4] consecutive combat cruises to the western Pacific and Southeast Asia. These first combat cruises also heralded the debut of the Phantom as a conventional bomber.

The Phantom, a true multirole fighter/interceptor/bomber, would bolster the operational capability and combat efficiency and capacity of three of our nation's services: the US Navy, Air Force, and Marine Corps.

During the Vietnam War years, the Black Lions logged more than 11,500 combat missions and delivered over 6,000 tons of ordnance. Their first air-to-air victory came on December 20, 1966, when Lt. D. A. McRae and Ens. D. N. Nichols downed a North Vietnamese AN-2 Colt. True, the Russian-designed Antonov An-2, a single-engine biplane, was not really built to take on the world's most formidable supersonic fighter, but in the parlance of fighter aviation, *a kill is a kill.*

The "Lions," for many years, had set the gold standard in the fighter community. They had built an enviable record as a squadron chock-full of tacticians, professional warriors, leaders, and long-range thinkers.

Interestingly, Newton's claim of "What goes up, must come down" has application, in some context, to professional sport teams, the stock market, and, yes, even fighter squadrons.

By September 1976, one year after the Vietnam War, the Black Lions had transcended their apogee as one of the most formidable fighter squadrons in the Navy and had begun a descent from their glory days. Sometimes these reversals of fortune are attributable to second-order effects: poor leadership, inconvenient timing, bad karma, or other intangibles, but these can always be circumvented or at least mitigated by building a strategic vision, gathering the right people, providing them with the right tools, instilling in them a hunger to reach an objective, empowering them, applying proven leadership techniques, and taking care of the *team.* Not only did Hawk believe this in his core, but he had committed his personal and professional life to its application.

The Lions' fall from grace was not information unknown to Hawk, and while it was an irksome trend, putting the Black Lions back on the podium would surely tax his resources and test his resolve. He embraced the challenge.

In December 1976, a year and a half following the end of the Vietnam struggle, VF-213 and her sister squadron, VF-114, the "Aardvarks," known throughout Fightertown as the "Varks," transitioned to the Navy's—in fact, the world's—premier supersonic fighter: the F-14A Tomcat. This made CVW-11 the third West Coast Tomcat-equipped air wing. One year later, on October, 25, 1977, *Kitty Hawk* pulled out of San Diego to begin her first deployment with their brand-new Tomcat.

The Fly-In

On May 15, 1978, *Kitty Hawk* was on the horizon northwest of San Diego and well within range of the Miramar-based E-2 Hawkeye and fighter squadrons. It had been yet another seven-month, peacetime WestPac cruise, complete with the usual emotional peaks and valleys that are part of each extended deployment: euphoria, excitement, wonder, loneliness, boredom, melancholy. But today, May 15, all that was behind them. They were back home and soon to be rejoined with loved ones and friends. The fly-in for the E-2 Hawkeye aircraft and fighter squadrons promised much excitement and many blissful reunions.

Hawk probably should have been more stoic during fly-ins. He'd been a part of several and watched many more from the ranks of the welcoming crowd, but standing among the hundreds of family members, loved ones, shipmates, senior officials, news people, and well-wishers, Hawk could not help but be caught up in the thrill of the moment.

Hawk was excited for two reasons. First, he enjoyed the joy of the reunion, and second, it was his first opportunity to meet up with most of the aircrew.

Two large flights of F-14s made a wide, sweeping turn over the hills east of Miramar. Light-gray smoke trails were easily seen, and those with fighter-pilot eyes could make out individual aircraft still in loose formation. As they steadied out on the runway heading, the formations closed up nicely. The fly-in announcer gave a running dialogue of the historical high points of the cruise until he was drowned out by the ground-rattling roar of the Tomcats nearing the approach end of runway 24R.

The "Aardvarks" made up the first formation. Hawk counted eight F-14s in two divisions[5] in right echelon. They rumbled in at 350 knots: slow enough to lengthen the time over the crowd, and fast enough to produce an impressive, vapor-maker break turn.

Despite the adrenaline surge sure to be cursing through their systems, the pilots flew tight, smooth, and well-spaced positions. To avoid any possible risk of a midair collision, the leader of the trail division broke first. He rolled into a crisp 60-degree bank just beyond the runway center point. Three seconds later, number 2 matched the leader's roll and pull. When finally the fourth aircraft broke, the RIO of that aircraft keyed the mic and transmitted, "Clear, Skipper!" That was the signal for the leader of the first division to commence his break turn. Thirty seconds later, the last Tomcat rolled out on the downwind heading. It was, even for those who had seen this before, an awe-inspiring sight.

As the last "Vark" turned off the 180 position, the point abeam the intended point of landing, the lead was already clearing the runway.

A deep-throated peal snatched the attention of the crowd, and a hundred heads involuntarily snapped back to the source of the roar. The Black Lions were approaching the numbers.

Hawk counted six F-14s this time, packaged in two three-plane formations. Although there were two fewer aircraft, the discipline shown by the "Varks" had nothing on the Black Lions. The formation flown overhead and into the break was a study in discipline and grace.

Perhaps a bit confusing to the crowd was that the first of the "Vark" Tomcats still had their engines running and canopies closed even after being chocked and chained for several minutes in front of it. Surely, the aircrew wanted nothing more than to shut down the noisy jets, leap from their aircraft, and run like hell to their family and friends. Aircrew of less disciplined air wings would have done just that and made it look like the start of the Boston Marathon rather than an orderly, drilled march to the awaiting throng.

Hawk knew what to expect. He'd seen this show before, and it was always a crowd-pleaser.

The last of the Black Lions' Tomcats taxied into the tie-down area and braked at the plane captain's signal. Other plane captains scurried around the big jets, chocking the wheels and installing safety pins. Although none of the crowd could hear the transmission on ground control frequency, the CO of the "Varks," in a well-cadenced voice, said, "Stand by . . . shut-down." At that precise moment, all throttles were pulled to idle cutoff, and twenty-eight TF30s began winding down.

A second transmission followed, "Canopies . . . now!," and fourteen canopies lifted in unison as if saluting the near-frenzied congregation.

The gathering was excited before—few of the wives, children, and sweethearts slept well the previous night—but in light of the building tension and the precision shutdown show, it was almost too much.

The cheers of the horde soon drowned out the waning banshee cries of the TF30s. Each of the twenty-eight crewmen dismounted and, in lock step, marched toward the crowd. And that *was* too much. They sidestepped the ribbon barrier and ran to the open arms of the Black Lions and "Varks" aircrew. It was a long seven months, and now they were home!

Hawk was caught up in the pageantry and the flood of emotion. He waded through the scores of people, some braving the huge, crocodile tears and all wearing their best ear-to-ear grins, to greet as many of the Black Lion and "Vark" crews as possible.

He caught sight of Cmdr. Jake Jacanon, CO of the "Lions," beaming with an arm around his wife. Hawk made his way toward him. "Welcome home, Skipper!"

Cmdr. Jacanon turned, smiled warmly, and grasped Hawk's outstretched hand. "Hawk, glad to see you," Jake yelled over the clamor of the crowd. "Honey, this is Hawk Smith, our next executive officer. Hawk, my wife!"

"It's a real pleasure to meet you, Ms. Jacanon," Hawk said genuinely.

"So you're 'the' Hawk I've heard so much about," she returned.

"I am, ma'am, but don't hold it against me!"

The skipper, obviously anxious to speed things up, inserted, "Thanks for showing up and thanks for taking the time to take care of our arrival and making all these arrangements. They look great, Hawk."

"It really wasn't much, Skipper. I'm just glad you're back."

"You and me both, Hawk. The XO's around here somewhere. I'll let you two handle the details. We're heading home, but call me if you have any questions."

"I won't bother you, Skipper, unless something comes up the XO and I can't handle," Hawk responded.

"Good enough, Hawk. See you in a few days."

Hawk turned and scanned the crowd, looking for Cmdr. Terry "Gator" Applegate, the Black Lion executive officer. Hawk found him almost at once and waded through the gathering toward him. Gator must have felt Hawk's eyes on him, since he turned, spotted Hawk, and waved and flashed a large smile."

"Hawk, it's great to see you," Gator said, shaking Hawk's hand vigorously. "We've been following your exploits, and I think I can speak for the entire fighter clan; we're damned glad you survived."

"No more glad than I am, Gator. I've got a lot of people to thank, and that's fer sure."

"Or maybe," the XO said thoughtfully, "the system actually worked like it was supposed to. Anyway, let me take care of a few things here and catch up with you at the squadron."

"Roger, Terry. As soon as we've bedded down the airplanes, I'll track you down."

"See you then, Hawk!"

Hawk took his eyes off the XO for only a moment, and he was instantly swallowed up in the horde.

The throng of people thinned, and Hawk checked with his chief petty officers to quickly review the tow-back plan and ensure that their ground crew had all the required vehicles. Satisfied the plan was proceeding smoothly, he headed to the Black Lion hangar. He scrambled up the stairs to the second deck and found the XO in his office, with his feet propped on top of a gray-steel, government-issue desk, skimming the overflowing in-basket. "Hawk, come on in and sit yourself down," the XO said.

"Thanks, Gator!" Hawk replied as he slid into a chair opposite the desk. "So, how was it?"

"It was like they all are, Hawk—long, hard, and full of challenges. Standard stuff. The troops did great. They worked their asses off and hardly complained, and thankfully we brought them all back in one piece. But this cruise was especially tough because of the jets. They're tired, and we beat the crap out of them. We were lucky to get six up for the fly-off. I'll bet not a one of them is up now."

Hawk could relate to this. His tour at VX-4 and his follow-on orders to *Enterprise* taught him quite a bit about the finicky nature of the F-14. He was quick to realize that once some of the dazzle and new airplane smell wore off, the mighty Tomcat had all the potential of becoming a maintenance nightmare. Its sophistication required daily preening by highly trained technical experts and gobbled up airplane parts at a frightening pace. The historical maintenance data told the story. With a full five years of statistical data available, the Tomcat had proven to have the highest maintenance-man-hour-per-flight-hour ratio and, consequently, had the lowest availability rate of any aircraft in the fleet.

Two additional factors would further complicate their current situation. Since they had just returned from cruise, the Black Lions and the "Varks" were at the bottom of the parts-and-supply-priority stack. To top it off, in the next several months both squadrons would be experiencing a massive exodus of their most experienced technicians, supervisors, and aircrew.

"Gator, I ain't telling you anything you don't know; the Tomcat is the toughest, bad-ass fighter in the world, but because of their technical sophistication they're also the hardest tactical aircraft in the inventory to maintain. At VX-4, even with the best technicians in the Navy, Grumman engineers on hand, and great parts support, the jets sometimes were absolutely cantankerous about flying. Looking back on the experience, during the first cruise with CVW-14, I'm kinda surprised we flew as much as we did. Aside from the fact that we lost three Tomcats in the first few months of the cruise, we ended up doing pretty well."

"Hawk, I followed that first deployment on *Enterprise* very closely. That was a groundbreaking experience for us all. You guys did well, but we haven't ironed out the wrinkles in this jet yet. I'm not sure we can. When they're up, they're great airplanes, but getting them up and keeping them up . . ." His thoughts were left unsaid. Hawk mentally filled in the missing words . . . *that was the problem.*

"We've got other problems too."

Hawk leaned closer, elbows resting on his knees.

"When we and the 'Varks' first took delivery of our F-14s, they were still so new that the F-14 maintenance courses weren't even online yet. Grumman set up the technical training for squadron maintenance personnel before we deployed. This was expensive training, and we had limited seating. To minimize costs and maximize the benefits, NAVPERS required many of our maintenance troops and most of our aircrew to extend in the command until the end of the deployment. Now the problem is, within the next six months, we're not going to lose the usual 30 percent of our personnel; we're going to actually lose about half of our people. And of course these are our core people, our most-experienced, cruise-hardened, veteran technicians and supervisors.

"And one more thing . . ." The XO wasn't done reporting the bad news. "I'm sure you're up on all the rumors running around, and it's now official: CVW-11 is switching decks from *Kitty Hawk* to *America* for our next deployment. They've got the sail date penciled in for March 1979. That's not quite a year from now, and our first refresher training comes in January.

"Now I hate to do this, but I don't think we can give everybody a thirty-day postcruise stand-down period. We may have to cut that short by weeks."

"I'd heard the rumors. I'd hoped they were just that. A short turnaround is bad enough, but everything is going to be far harder when we have to deploy on an East Coast ship. We'll do what we always do, though: bust our butts to make it happen."

"It's not going to be easy, but you're right . . . it's the way we always do it!"

"Hawk, I'm going to head home. I'll be there for the next couple of days. We'll start our official postcruise stand-down next week. That means we'll be down to a skeleton crew. Don't expect any more people than what you have on the beach det right now. As usual, there'll be plenty of unpacking to do, a lot of administrative work, and no flying until we complete the postcruise maintenance inspections. That could take weeks. I know you're still working through the FRS syllabus, and aircraft availability at VF-124 is tight, but fly as much as you can with them. We'll probably have to use our own aircraft for part of your syllabus, but that may be a ways down the road.

The XO stood, glanced at the fresh mess on his desk, and then looked at Hawk. "All right, Hawk, you've got the conn. Call me if anything pops loose, but don't expect me to be checking in any time soon."

"Got it. Don't sweat a thing. And . . . welcome home, Gator!"

Cmdr. Applegate headed out of the hangar to his awaiting family, and Hawk walked out to the flight line to monitor the progress of the ground crew. For a moment he watched quietly as his team carefully moved aircraft into their assigned spots, chocked and chained the big jets, and proceeded to download the external stores.

There was a lot of activity and much to do, but for a time Hawk, lost in thought, walked among the Tomcats. Each was an eyesore that only an aviation enthusiast could enjoy. These were tired airplanes. VF-213 had taken delivery of brand-new Block 90 jets right out of the Grumman assembly line less than a year before *Kitty Hawk* sailed. They weren't even two years old. The high-gloss-gray factory paint jobs were now pockmarked with flat-gray paint splotches, and no two shades seemed to be the same. Brick-red hydraulic fluid dripped from many points on the underside of the wings and fuselage and had streaked aft. Engine oil stained the area underneath the engine bay, and even the telltale purple smudges of JP-5 fuel left their mark on the belly and around the single-point refueling receptacles. Boot marks scuffed the top of the fuselage and wing, and cable grease, the viscosity of peanut butter, splattered the areas around the tailhook and tail assembly. A long, dark carbon smudge began just in front of the 20 mm Vulcan gun port and streaked back as far as the port intake.

Well, Hawk thought to himself: *I've been in the squadron less than a day, and already I can see we've got airplane problems out the gump-stump and, unless I'm reading this wrong, some big personnel problems brewing. And those two conditions always have a way of causing safety and operational problems. The fact that our next cruise is going to be on* America, *an East Coast ship, ain't gonna do anything but make everything harder. Anyway I slice it, we're going to have our hands full.*

Hawk turned and headed toward the hangar, head down, deep in thought. He paused and pivoted back toward the flight line. *Yep, they're exhausted, beat-up, abused airplanes, and these are the ones that were in good enough shape to make it off the ship. They'd never win a beauty contest,* Hawk mused. *They're warhorses and they're our warhorses. We need to make them well again!*

No one familiar with the trials and challenges of a deployment would argue that the CVW-11's most recent cruise was not a successful one, but the breakneck pace of the preparation followed by seven months at sea heavily fatigued both man and machine. In Hawk's words, "The 'Lions' flew the hell out of their airplanes, and consequently they came home with high-time, beat-up, worn-out jets." If they had been a sled-dog team, to conjure up a metaphor, they would have collapsed in their traces with their tongues dangling in the snow.

Assault on a Windmill

In 1978, the Navy introduced PERSMAR[6] to save money and improve personnel assignment efficiencies. Under PERSMAR, assignments were based on squadron manpower requirements and indexed to the unit's priority in the deployment cycle: those commands nearest their deployment dates were given the highest assignment priorities. While this appeared to be a sound concept, the actual execution left much to be desired.

Under PERSMAR, assignment expediency trumped proper personnel-to-billet match. In many cases it appeared that little consideration was given to training, experience, or community association. "It was a new personnel assignment system, and it was broken," according to Hawk.

"Turnover, manning, and training were key problems, and BUPERS[7] was not very approachable. There was no closed-loop detailing for F-14s, so they sent us a first class from the helo side that had never even seen an F-14 till he went through FRAMP.[8] And this is the guy that BUPERS sent to relieve our E-7 power-plants supervisor, who happened to be a walking encyclopedia on TF30 engines? We actually had nonrated guys in the power-plants shop that knew more about changing an engine than this new first class! We literally had to send him to the ship's mess deck master-of-arms to get him out of the way until we could properly train him. It was crazy!"

Hawk worked with his personnel officer, Lt. Cmdr. Charlie "Cajun" Degruy, to convey to the bureau the many frailties of the PERSMAR process. Hawk, never afflicted by political elegance, sent a plain-language message to BUPERS: "We can't live with this shit anymore." In it, he explained that "the program (PERSMAR) is ineffective and greatly constrains the ability of this command to meet mission requirements and tasking schedules."

The message was a minor assault on one of the many windmills inaugurated and vigorously guarded by the Navy. Hawk's mugging of the system likely had no impact on the personnel assignment process, but it was one of those blaring clarions to which, for the good of the order, Hawk was compelled to respond.

The turnaround cycle for the first Tomcat cruise was difficult, owing to the complications associated with transitioning to the new but persnickety Tomcat. And as bad as it was, the turnaround cycle for the follow-on cruise had all the elements of being even tougher. The Black Lions' jets were beat, the turnaround cycle was only ten months long, and, though replacement personnel were slowly arriving, in many cases they were untrained, untested, and unaccustomed to the high tempo of a fleet fighter outfit.

The turd in the punch bowl, however, was that CVW-11's next deployment was scheduled as a MED cruise aboard USS *America* (CV-66), an East Coast ship. The planning, organization, and logistics entailed in a transcoastal deployment would boggle the mind and cause lesser men to head to the showers.

Hawk was deeply involved in reviewing the myriad of issues and obstacles for the next cruise, but in June 1978, all focus of effort shifted to the change of command.

Gator Takes the Conn

Hawk split his days between the FRS syllabus, taking care of a seemingly endless list of tasks at VF-213, and preparing for the change of command for Cmdrs. Jake Jacanon and Terry "Gator" Applegate.

Hawk had met with Gator, the soon-to-be "Black Lion One," almost on a daily basis since their return. At the heart of many of those meetings was the project of organizing the change-of-command ceremony.

Hawk, as the company commander, was responsible for coordinating the band, honor guard, PA system, placement of podium, chairs, and refreshments; notifying base security; and a host of other items that accompany the change-of-command ceremony.

This ceremony is uniquely naval. The Army and Air Force do not have an equivalent event. And while a great deal of time and energy are devoted to this tradition, it is performed for a reason—it sends a clear, unambiguous message to command personnel of the importance of the command structure and attests to two centuries of naval tradition. It emphasizes the authority of command and acknowledges the tremendous accountability and responsibility intrinsic to that authority. Usually the change of command is accompanied by an awards ceremony, which lends the outgoing CO an opportunity to recognize the extraordinary efforts of several of the standout team members. Finally, it allows the incoming commanding officer to address the way ahead, the challenges *their* command will face in the near term, his personal goals, and his expectations.

Parochial, certainly . . . it's a naval institution.

Necessary . . . absolutely!

On June 23, 1978, Cmdr. Terry "Gator" Applegate took the reins of command, and Hawk, though still enrolled in the F-14 FRS syllabus, ratcheted up to the executive officer position. Shortly following the change of command, Gator and Hawk conferred on the several challenges facing the "Lions" in the coming months—the issues seemed daunting.

Hawk, a strategic thinker and global planner in the Clausewitzian model, sketched a midrange plan that identified turnaround milestones, inspections, and certification schedules. He calculated the massive maintenance certification process, factored in those personnel leaving and checking in, and attempted to capture the primary activities in a master schedule. The keystone events were the air wing carrier qualification phase; weapons detachment at NAS Fallon, Nevada; *America*'s workup and refresher training schedule; and, finally, the departure, on March 13, 1978. Everything had to fall into place, and "fall" meant carefully planned, scheduled, and executed. Key and critical to the entire plan was the manpower piece.

Cmdr. Applegate, like Hawk, was a "people person." Both recognized that their squadron personnel were in a deep morale abyss. By the end of June 1978, newly assigned personnel were trickling into the command. Most of the old guard, those who had completed the previous deployment, were short on vivacity and motivation, and it was contagious. The skipper and Hawk agreed that one of the first orders of business was to improve morale and rekindle "Black Lion spirit."

With the help of their department heads and chief petty officers, the CO mounted a campaign to improve the well-being and morale of their troops. It would not be an overnight success. It might take months to rebuild the "can-do" attitude that both the skipper and Hawk were accustomed to in a frontline fighter outfit. They recognized the work in front of them, but they agreed that it was something that needed doing.

Leadership 101

At the time of the change of command, Hawk was thirty-eight years old. He'd spent nearly fifteen of those years in the Navy, something less than 40 percent of his life, yet most things he knew about people and virtually everything he had learned about leadership had been in those formidable years in the service of his country. His leadership lessons were certainly not unique, but, by his thinking, the lack of consistent use of the fundamentals of leadership, at many levels in the service, seemed sadly too often either ignored or viewed as an inconvenience.

"One of the things I did all the time was carry a *wheel book*." Hawk explained. "I wrote down anything and everything about any topic, thought, idea, or issue. It included everything—the names of my branch personnel, phone numbers, schedules, airframe changes, occasional flashes of brilliance, attaboys when I saw one of the boys do something good, and all things in between. I also used it to jog my memory, like a to-do list that I would expand into a loose-leaf notebook every so often.

"I had a 'Leadership' section in the notebook, and I wrote down every single thing I liked that someone was doing, as well as the negative stuff—and there was no shortage of that. I somehow managed to keep all of those little pocket-sized books together.

"On my first fighter squadron tour, as a junior officer in VF-102, I was truly stunned by all the personnel problems we had. I just didn't understand why we couldn't simply fire some guys. Nope, we had to keep 'em. We had to handle letters of indebtedness, sleeping on watch, Executive Officers Inquiry (XOI), captain's mast, and tons of paperwork when we shoulda been focused on flying, tactics, intelligence, assessments, and professional development. But over time, I came to appreciate that every single one of these guys had superb potential and ability to get some job done . . . if we gave them a chance and could keep them focused.

"I found that the average age in the squadron and aboard the ship, about twenty-two, was exactly the same year after year. Yep! Go figure! In a blinding flash of the obvious, I realized that we—the Navy—had a helluva continuing-training problem. We rotated our newest super-junior enlisted personnel through ninety-day TAD assignments, both ashore and afloat, to such attractive jobs as mess cooking, compartment cleaning, master-at-arms, first lieutenant, and the aircraft line division. Those kids had no idea who they were assigned to or who they really worked for, and, many of them didn't realize what squadron they were in for those first ninety days. Unreal! No officer ever checked them in, reviewed their service records, explained what was expected and their part in the big picture, or kept tabs on these folks. That is, all except one old Mustang in VF-102 who worked in Maintenance Control, Mr. Digiovani, a.k.a. 'Mister Dee'! I learned volumes from this guy about how to be a good officer, and it wasn't an easy schoolhouse either. But the outcome—my leadership takeaways—would accompany me through the rest of my time in the Navy, and all through my life—even today.

"All the same problems seem to be with us still. We are constantly relearning the same lessons the hardest way possible, and it all has to do with knowing and taking care of your people first!

"The people approach is really simple. If you have a 'team,' ya need to know your players, their strengths and weaknesses, what their specialties are, their interests, and you need to figure out how to best bring 'em into play. Are they married? What's their wife's name, their kids' names? Where were they born? Where did they grow up? What are their interests? What Navy and civilian schools did they attend? What kind of a car do they drive? Do they have any debts or financial problems? What about their parents? Where do they live? And on and on."

Hawk admitted, "I had a wild side. I know I could be stubborn and, under the right set of circumstances, even belligerent at times, but this was not like Little League baseball. There you could walk off the field if you don't like the rules, the call, or the team. In this league, you were playing the most important game in America. On this team, you had to work with what you had, make your teammates as good as they could be, and play to win.

"Every supervisor, whether a senior petty officer, a CPO, or officer, needs to make time to meet with every single one of their people for an interview, beginning with the most senior enlisted on down to the greenest recruit. And the sooner they do this, the better. They need to pick every subordinate's brain for everything—get an understanding of their thoughts on what's good in the command and what could be improved—anything and everything! And take notes. Everyone will notice that you care, that you ain't just fakin' it!

"And fix every single thing within your power just as soon as you find out something's broke, or are advised of something that could be improved. Then, provide feedback to any and every individual involved with the issue.

"When someone is leaving the outfit, be certain to interview them on their way out. This is your chance to get some of the most important feedback. These are the guys who have been in the command the longest; they have something to say. You've got to listen to them. And, yes, you'll occasionally come across a disgruntled sailor that has nothing good to say about anything. He may just be a complainer. Every squadron has at least one. But maybe not. He could just dump a treasure trove of information, ideas, and thoughts on how to make things better and how to improve the spirit of the command. You need to listen to them too!

"One of the great military paradoxes is that the people who lay their life on the line for America's freedoms and rights have far less of them. They have been called on for hundreds of years to make sacrifices, and all too often to make the ultimate sacrifice, but when it comes to the right of privacy or free speech or not going to work if they don't feel like it, they have no protection under the law. Further, a service member must comply with both civil law and the Uniform Code of Military Justice (UCMJ), a set of laws far more restrictive and harsh than civil law.

"For many of my sailors the Navy was the best thing that could have happened to them. We took in unskilled kids right off the street; we trained them, disciplined them, promoted self-confidence, instilled responsibility, and returned them to America as capable, productive men and women and patriots. We gave America back a more mature individual able to contribute something to his community and his country.

"I truly believe that success for any organization lies with its people, and all ya gotta do is to tap into their inherent skills and fire up their desire to accomplish great things! These kids ain't stupid, and they catch on very quickly when they are properly trained and inspired.

If handled correctly, they'll realize quickly that they are part of something far bigger and far greater than the sum of the individual parts!

"And I love and admire our chiefs. The CPOs, as always, shouldered the responsibility of breaking in the new kids. Complaining, bellyaching, whining was ordinarily met by CPOs, who took that standard chin-out, hands-on-hips pose, leaning into the complainant and recounting their favorite, belittling sea story, which ordinarily began, 'Why, when I was your age, we only had two meals a day. The first one was bread; the second meal was water. We carried cannon balls in our pockets just in case, only slept on Sundays, and we *never* bitched!'

"Certainly, these were sea stories, the ingenious teetering on the ridiculous, but to the new kids, the young seventeen- and eighteen-year-old kids fresh out of high school from big cities, small farm towns, many from broken homes and without the experience of ever having come nose to nose with hard work and absolute authority. This was an epiphany—an awakening to the hard ways of the real world. This, for many, was the first course in becoming a responsible seaman and a team member."

One of the first policies set by the new skipper and executive officer was a liberal leave initiative. "Well, we knew we couldn't give them bonuses, all-expense-paid vacations, or a new car," Hawk recounted, "but we did have the authority to grant liberty on a case-by-case basis, and that's what we did. In fact, by allowing the supervisors, the first-level managers, authority to determine workload and schedule and grant liberty at their level, not only were the sailors ecstatic, but the supervisors received a serious dose of accountability—and that is the requisite for authority.

"If the troops, no matter what department they worked in, didn't have an immediate task or project at hand, we authorized their bosses to let them secure early. That decision was authorized at the lowest decision level, the work center supervisors and division chief petty officers. Of course, they knew they would still be held accountable for production, completing training, and meeting the flight schedule each day, but we gave the first-class petty officers and several second-class POs a taste of authority and a sense of responsibility.

"Several interesting things happened—morale improved. That we expected, but so did aircraft availability, supervisory judgment, and leadership—and that was something of a surprise!

"Our senior petty officers got a whole lot more serious about the responsibilities of their positions and began to understand that with authority comes the heavy burden of accountability.

"It was amazing to me just how many good things can come from such a simple thing as letting supervisors act like supervisors," Hawk recalls.

Friday the Thirteenth: Nightmare on *Enterprise*

All things were proceeding fairly well in the FRS syllabus, but there were the occasional hiccups along the way. Hawk was scheduled for his carrier qualification (CQ) in September 1978—both day and night traps were on the slate aboard the USS *Enterprise*.

There wasn't a carrier pilot alive who didn't enjoy the daytime work, but when it came to the night stuff, well, at least one F-4 pilot, Don Coker, equated it this way: "Night flying is the grown-up equivalent of the bogeyman (whose name shall not be spoken) under the bed. At night, all sensory receptors are on high gain. Night noises are louder, warning lights are brighter, an unanticipated thump or bump in the night causes hands to involuntarily move toward one of the ejection handles, and a simple question like 'What was that?' can take on frantic speculation with the wellness of the airplane."

Hawk took his turn in the night CQ circus, and though he'd much rather be on day air combat maneuvering (ACM) sorties, he kinda liked the solitude and beauty of most nights.

Hawk reflects, "I never really fretted about the cat shot. That was pretty much in God's hands, but getting back aboard the ship, well, there were a whole lot of things to be concerned with. This is when you funnel all your energy into controlling three things: angle of attack, lineup, and glide slope. All that said, there really were some things that could go 'bump in the night.'"

And one of those things went "bump" during a night CQ sortie on USS *Enterprise* on Friday, September 13, 1978.

Day traps went without issue, but as Hawk sat strapped into his VF-124 F-14, awaiting the signal to move up to the jet blast deflector (JBD), he witnessed a horrific mishap involving another VF-124 F-14 flown by friends.

Mark "Tag" Ostertag and Tim "Spike" Prendergast completed their prelaunch checks and were directed to the number 2 catapult. Up to that point, everything went well, but when the shuttle was engaged with the launch bar, it did not properly couple. With final checks complete, the catapult officer waited for the formation lights to come on, signaling that the aircrew was ready for the launch. As soon as that happened, the shooter visually cleared the area in front of the big jet, knelt down, touched the deck, and then pointed forward. The F-14 started to accelerate. Halfway down the stroke, the shuttle separated from the launch bar. Tag pushed the throttles into afterburner zone 5, but it was immediately obvious that even with all that thrust, their Tomcat was not going to reach end speed.

Tag and Spike stayed with the airplane for a few seconds, but, seeing nothing good in trying to ride it out, they opted for ejections. They both received good separation from the Tomcat and full chutes.

Hawk, spotted just in front of the island, had a front-row seat to an unfolding nightmare. Hawk remembers, "The Tomcat dribbled off the bow as they ejected. One hellacious water vapor cloud blossomed up from the F-14, and at first I thought the F-14 went in the water, but there was a strange glow in front of the ship. All of a sudden, the Tomcat reappeared nose up and climbed out as if by its own will . . . sans aircrew. In full burner, the nose continued to arc up, nearly perfectly wings level. It went through a thin scud layer at about 1,000 feet and continued its climb. Once above the layer, the giant TF30 burners made an eerie glow above the clouds like a twin sun, and the F-14 kept climbing."

Hawk, at first mesmerized by the show, suddenly became aware of the chilling fact that the big jet wasn't going to climb indefinitely, and if the F-14 chose the same route coming down as it chose going up, things could get quite sporty.

"Based on the only visual contact of the F-14 I had, the afterburners, the plums gradually went from round to elongated and then finally disappeared altogether, but the glow from the afterburners lit up the sky. That's when I realized things were not good.

"The F-14 broke through the layer nose down. It was going pretty darn fast. It was backlit by its own afterburner against the white overcast. The airplane was completely visible and, for a short time, looked like it was boresighting the ship. Fortunately, the nose of the F-14 continued to arc to the port side of the ship and finally slammed into the water well abeam.

"While all that was happening, Spike was picked up by the plane guard helo, but, for a while, there was no sign of Tag.

"Tag had a successful ejection, but, as the story goes, he got entangled in his chute shrouds when he hit the water. As the chute sank, Tag was being towed under. As if things could not get worse, only one side of his LPA-1[9] lobes inflated, and he couldn't get to the manual inflation tube to blow it up. Because of the sea state and the wake generated from the ship, Tag's breathing time was being reduced in a hurry. Tag was kicking like crazy to keep above the surface and extended his neck and pursed his lips to try to make them reach above the surface of the water in a desperate attempt to suck in air.

"Just as Tag thought there was no hope, a rescue swimmer showed up. The swimmer checked things out and realized that only one side of Tag's LPA had inflated. The swimmer quickly manually inflated the other lobe. The second problem was that Tag was still having trouble floating; he was tangled in the chute shrouds. The swimmer reached for his shroud cutter, realized his had been lost, then searched for Tag's. He couldn't find it!

"The swimmer made a mad dash in choppy cold water back to the hovering helo to get another shroud cutter, a knife, a box cutter, anything to cut through the shrouds. As I came to find out, he was handed a bolt cutter.

"Even weighted down with the heavy bolt cutter, he dashed back to Tag and somehow cut all the shroud lines tangled up with Tag. He towed Tag back to the helo, and they hoisted him aboard.

"It was a horrible predicament," Hawk recounts, "but it had a happy ending considering all the Murphy events that took place.

"When the word of the mishap got out, one of the aircrew recommended that not only should shroud cutters be mandatory survival gear,[10] but that aircrew should also be issued *lip extenders* in the survival vest." Hawk comments, "That was kinda funny, but the whole event could have been deadly. I thought about that mishap for a long time."

The Supply Totem Pole

In late August, the "Lions" were still on the low end of the supply priority list, short on any number of aircraft parts, undermanned, and, consequently, well behind training and readiness milestones. The two-week air wing weapons-training detachment at Naval Air Station (NAS) Fallon was scheduled for November 1978. From that point on, the training schedule was chockablock, with one event after another, and left little time to celebrate the approaching holidays.

By late autumn, there was perceptible improvement on several fronts. The "Lions" had received nearly their full complement of personnel, and their parts support priority had improved somewhat. The backbone of the command, the chief petty officers, concentrated their activities on training and certifying new maintenance personnel. More maintenance personnel were trained, more parts became available, and, voilà, more aircraft made it on the flight schedule.

The operations and training departments were thrilled. It was a major undertaking, but long hours of hard work and deep commitment by the officers, chief petty officers, and enlisted personnel helped turn the corner. It's impossible to accurately gauge the value of high morale in this alchemy, but the effect of motivated sailors and teamwork played a critical role in preparing the squadron for the trip to the high desert—NAS Fallon, Nevada.

Just in time, the Black Lions had cobbled together enough aircraft, aircrew, and maintenance personnel to meet the CVW-11 weapons-training schedule. They now could start the uphill climb to meet air wing aircrew certification and training requirements.

Call Sign "Thunder"

Air Wing 11, tactical call sign "Thunder," has a rich and vibrant history dating back to the early years of World War II. They were established on Navy Day, October 10, 1942,[11] and in the course of the next six decades flew from the decks of seven different carriers.

CVW-11 assumed critical combat roles in World War II, Korea, and Vietnam and took part in at least four other major combat actions.

The Pacific campaign against the Japanese during World War II entailed some of the most brutal fighting imaginable, and under some of the most horrible conditions in our nation's history. It goes without saying that without strong, committed, and strategically adroit leadership, and a nation behind their military, neither the war in Europe nor in the Pacific would have been won by the Allies.

The Pacific campaign against the Japanese was initially a two-service show: the Navy and the Marine Corps.

The US strategy during World War II committed forces primarily to Europe in the "Germany First" operations plans. The Army and the Army Air Corps[12] were deeply committed to the European front. The war in the Pacific, which began December 7, 1941, following the Japanese sneak attack on Pearl Harbor, was largely a come-as-you-are conflict for the Navy and the Marine Corps.

At the opening scenes of the Pacific campaign, the entire inventory of Navy carriers totaled seven. When the Japanese attacked Pearl Harbor, only three were on the West Coast; USS *Lexington* (CV-2), USS *Saratoga* (CV-3), and USS *Enterprise*—the "Big E" (CV-6). Within several months, three East Coast carriers made transits to the Pacific theater, but within the year, three of the entire Pacific carrier fleet had been sunk: USS *Lexington* (CV-2), Battle of Coral Sea, May 8, 1942; USS *Yorktown* (CV-3), Battle of Midway, June 6, 1942; and USS *Wasp* (CV-7), near San Cristobal Island, September 15, 1942.

Owing to the strategic innovation of military leadership in the Pacific theater, the dauntless courage of our forces in the face of horrific odds, and a whole lot of luck, the inertia of the Pacific campaign began to slowly shift in favor of US naval forces following the Battle of Midway. The next four-year period was a tough slog against a well-equipped, well-trained, and determined enemy—quarter was neither asked for nor given.

In testimony to America's industrial might, by war's end twenty-seven frontline carriers had deployed. Not only did the carriers change the face of the Pacific campaign and make victory possible; the carrier battle groups (CVBG) greatly changed US military doctrine, strategy, and operational concepts of major regional conflicts for the future.

Carrier Air Group 11 was just a part of a military juggernaut pieced together to first stop Japan's aggression in the Pacific, build forces, and then hopscotch across the Pacific to take the battle to the doorstep of Japan's highest spiritual authority and the country's commander in chief—Emperor Hirohito.

In February 1943, embarked aboard USS *Altamaha* (ACV-18) and then USS *Long Island* (ACV-1),[13] the air group steamed toward the Fijian Islands. While in transit, they continued to train and fly simulated combat missions. By the time they arrived in the Pacific theater, only one aircraft carrier was operational. This forced the entire air group to be transferred to Guadalcanal at Henderson Field. They arrived on April 15, 1943, and though this was an unplanned change in assignment, it did not take them out of the action.

The bomber and torpedo squadrons conducted patrol, search, and reconnaissance missions; strike operations; and night minelaying operations, while the VF-11 fighters flew escort missions and provided cover for the strikers.

During the bloody fighting in the Solomon and New Georgia areas of the operation in June 1943, Air Group 11 aircrews engaged in the first daylight combat missions upon those islands.[14]

On June 16, 1943, at the peak of combat operations in the Pacific, greatly outnumbered but not outclassed, twenty-eight pilots from VF-11 engaged a reported 120 Japanese planes. The Navy fighter pilots counted thirty-one kills that day.

Finally, on September 29, 1944, Air Group 11 came aboard USS *Hornet*, replacing Air Group Two. *Hornet* promptly steamed west into battle, engaging the enemy at Okinawa, Formosa, the Philippines, French Indochina, and Hong Kong.

Challenged almost daily, the air group defended the strike group against Japanese kamikaze attacks and were constantly hampered by foul weather, poor communications, and thick antiaircraft fire.

During the deployment aboard *Hornet* from September 1944 to January 1945, Air Group 11 aircrews shot down an estimated 105 aircraft in air engagements and destroyed another 272 aircraft on the ground. In excess of a hundred Japanese ships were damaged or sunk, which amounted to over 100,000 tons of enemy shipping.

These achievements came at great cost to Air Group 11: more than sixty men were killed, missing in action, or wounded, and over fifty aircraft were destroyed.

Air Group 11 returned to Alameda, California, on February 24, 1945—six and a half months before VJ-day.[15] For these and other operations, CVG-11 was awarded the Presidential Unit Citation.[16]

A short five years of world peace separated the end of World War II from the beginning of the Korean War. Carrier Group 11 was again called to action.

The Korean War,[17] often called "the Forgotten War," began when Communist North Korea invaded South Korea on June 25, 1950. When the war ended in July 1953, Korea was still divided and remains so to this day. Thousands died or were wounded, and nothing was settled.

In this conflict, Carrier Air Group 11 was the first air group to engage and down MiG jet fighters. During the early phases of the war, they played major roles in defending the Pusan Perimeter and assisted in the breakout when US and UN troops were pushed into a small toehold in the southeast tip of South Korea. Air Group 11 and other units were tasked with protecting US-led American and UN forces during the amphibious landing at Inchon. This action was a major milestone because it halted North Korea expansion into the south, saved South Korea, and provided a strategic reversal of the war for a time.[18]

During the Chosin Reservoir Battle from November 27 to December 13. 1950, CVW-11[19] and other air combat units flew around the clock, providing strikes, reconnaissance, and attack missions against the North Koreans engaged in a strategic attempt to destroy the 1st Marine Division, US X Corps, and 30,000 United Nations troops. Although US and UN forces were cut off and attacked by over 100,000 Chinese troops, our forces mounted a fighting withdrawal against the Chinese and inflicted heavy casualties.

So crucial and well executed was the battle at Chosin Reservoir by the 1st Marine Division that it stands today as one of the most legendary and gallant engagements in Marine Corps history[20]—its survivors are called the "Chosin Few."

CVW-11 deployed aboard USS *Kitty Hawk* (CVA-63) for a WestPac cruise in October 1963 and flew the first offensive missions against North Vietnam in the spring of 1964. Unfortunately, they were also the first to experience the losses of US Navy aircraft.

Shortly after returning home, in 1965, CVW-11 received new aircraft: the RA-5C Vigilante, A-6 Intruder, and E-2 Hawkeye. This represented the most modern, complex strike group ever assembled under wartime conditions. The upgraded aircraft enhanced combat capability, as was demonstrated by improved strike results between December 1965 and May 1966.

When the wartime data were analyzed, the results proved to be astounding. In their nine back-to-back combat deployments during the Vietnam War, CVW-11 established a number of operational records, including a sixty-one-day line period—the longest of the war. Prior to the limited bombing announcement in March 1968, CVW-11 bombed operational targets well into North Vietnam, striking enemy power plants, rail yards, and lines of transportation and communications. CVW-11 broke all records for combat sorties flown and ordnance dropped during its sixth WestPac deployment, from November 1970 to July 1971, and then busted their own record during their following cruise. During this period, CVW-11 deployed with 107 aircraft, thereby making the command the largest air wing ever to go to sea with tactical aircraft and antisubmarine aircraft on the same carrier.

Air Wing 11 earned two Navy Unit Commendations for their actions in the Vietnam War. But the cherry on top was the awarding of the Presidential Unit Citation delivered to *Kitty Hawk* and CVW-11 for their role in the Vietnam conflict—the first battle group to earn that award.[21]

In 1975, CVW-11 and *Kitty Hawk* deployed for their first noncombat cruise in nine years. It was a long time coming.

In 1978, CVW-11 was one of fifteen Navy air wings. It represented a significant chunk of naval war-fighting capability, and when integrated with its assigned carrier, CVW-11 projected a fearful conventional and strategic military force for the United States and was a first-line provider of two of the Navy's strategic missions—Forward Presence and the long-range reach with a big stick, Power Projection.

Three thousand personnel supporting eleven squadrons, flying nine different aircraft—fifty power-projection shooters and over twenty combat support and logistics aircraft—were assigned to CVW-11.

VF-213 Black Lions and the Aardvarks of VF-114, the two fighter squadrons, were complemented with two A-7E light-attack squadrons: VA-192 "Golden Dragons" and VA-195 "Dambusters" from NAS Lemoore. The VA-95 "Green Lizards," flying A-6E and KA-6D (tankers), were stationed at NAS Whidbey Island, Washington. The long-range radar surveillance and air intercept missions were flown by E-2Cs from VAW-122[22] "Steel Jaws," home-based at NAS Norfolk, Virginia. VFP-63 (Det 4) flew the aging RF-8G photoreconnaissance aircraft, often described as an airplane with fire at one end and a fool at the other. They were stationed at NAS Miramar. VAQ-131 "Lancers," stationed at NAS Whidbey Island, were assigned the EA-6B prowler and provided the electronic-warfare assets. VS-33 "Screwbirds," out of NAS North Island, California, flew the submarine-killer S-3A and the latest carrier onboard delivery aircraft, the US-3A.[23] The HS-12 "Wyverns," flying SH-3H helicopters, had three primary missions: antisubmarine warfare, vertical replenishment, and search and rescue. Finally, the "World Watchers" of VQ-1,[24] stationed at NAS Agana, Guam, flew the electronic-reconnaissance EA-3B Whale, the largest and one of the oldest aircraft in the air wing.

Weapons Detachment in the High Desert

High in the desert in western Nevada lies a remote naval air station—NAS Fallon.[25] It is situated 72 miles east of Reno. Other than Reno, Fallon is very distant to anything resembling civilization, and therein lies Fallon's great attribute—its remoteness. It's an ideal site for the highly advanced weapons and tactics training required by the air wings and many other specialized forces.

From its beginnings during World War II as an Army Air Corps airstrip, Fallon had been assigned a number of missions for all the services. Originally envisioned as an auxiliary airstrip to oppose Japanese forces in the event of an attack on the West Coast (should they reach the West Coast), Fallon has evolved into a versatile, full-service training facility that provides unique training opportunities. It is considered the pinnacle for all air warfare training.

What the station lacked in number of physical structures was more than made up for in land mass of the adjoining training ranges.[26] Surrounded by over 240,000 acres of not-so-prime desert real estate, the Fallon ranges allow aircrews to deliver live ordinance at designated impact areas and provide electronic bomb scoring and electronic-countermeasures training, with thousands of cubic miles of restricted airspace for air-to-air training.

Prior to 1972, the base was known as Naval Auxiliary Air Station and was heavily used during the Vietnam War by air wing squadrons prior to deploying to carriers headed for Vietnam. Even now, because of the extreme variance of temperatures—an average low in January of 21 degrees to an average high of 91 degrees in August—ground units are temporarily assigned to NAS Fallon for hot- and cold-weather training.

In the late 1970s, the station footprint was relatively small, but the facilities were quite adequate, with three runways ranging in length from 7,000 to 14,000 feet.

Impact areas and bombing ranges dot the surrounding valleys and hillsides, including Lahontan and Dixie Valley. Dixie Valley also contains a network of simulated air defense systems that include twenty operational radar installations. In the impact areas, scores of surveyed military vehicles, some captured equipment, are scattered throughout the area.[27]

The immense real estate spread at NAS Fallon allows the entire amalgamated carrier air wing to conduct comprehensive training and complete certifications in realistic battle scenarios for nearly all missions and tasks: power projection, strike warfare, operations, joint battlefield operations, close air support (CAS), and combat search and rescue (CSAR). The air wing comes here to test their mettle and consecrate their warfare skills as a unified and integrated carrier air force.

The air-to-air mission tasks include basic fighter maneuvering (BFM), air combat maneuvering (ACM), and threat tactics, and strike scenarios are flown against top-tier, highly trained adversary pilots and instructors credentialed by the Navy Fighter Weapons School—TOPGUN. One of the most effective projects launched by TOPGUN leadership was an expansion of specialized adversary squadrons whose pilots and instructors were indoctrinated in the fine art of threat simulation. The *bogies* or *bandits* provided realistic threat tactics in the guise of A-4 Skyhawks simulating MiG-15s and MiG-17s—first-generation aircraft.[28]

Second-generation simulators, the F-5 Tigers, with performance capabilities very similar to the MiG-21 Fishbed and the MiG-23 Flogger, performed as the second-generation threats.[29]

These platforms brought substantial realism to the training environment. That they were not actual threat platforms was more than compensated for by the fact that the bogey drivers were far more skilled in the dark art of air combat than almost all of the actual enemy pilots the air wing aircrews might face in the real world.

To add to the fidelity and realism, occasionally the air wing staff would arrange to have USAF fighters added to the mix of Navy strikers in order to improve good-guy force level and exercise joint operations, and to enhance the success of the strike. Unfortunately, not always do these forays turn out as planned.

Case in point: On October 3, 1979, during an air wing strike, the strike package ran south down the Dixie Valley.[30] The F-14 fighter sweep was deployed and accelerated out in front of the strike group. They were successful in simulated kills against many of the dozen adversary aircraft protecting the target complex.

At about the time the A-6 and A-7 strike package arrived on target, several F-15 Eagles entered the fray from the east. Unbeknown to the bogies, these were late entries to assist the air wing in taking out the adversaries.

Two of the Eagles converged in a very high "g" turn on an A-4 that was prosecuting an A-6. In the ensuing maneuvering, the F-15 wingman lost sight of his lead but continued to work for a weapons solution on the A-4. Unfortunately, the lead F-15 was in the heart of the envelope on the A-4—the same position in which the F-15 wingman maneuvered for. The wingman of the defensively engaged A-4, at this point struggling to get a gun solution on the lead F-15, did something that the F-15 wingman did not do—he eased off the turn to reestablish situation awareness (SA), to search for other airplanes in the immediate vicinity. What he saw brought a shot of ice-cold blood down his spine.

The F-15 wingman, still in a hard port turn, was belly up to the lead F-15. The wingman never saw the lead F-15 and unknowingly continued to close on the big jet.

A violent explosion upon impact between the two Eagles resulted in massive damage to the wingman's airplane and the loss of the port horizontal stabilizer and the port vertical stabilizer, and the separation of about 8 feet of the left wingtip. The wingman immediately ejected. The pilot of the lead Eagle stayed with his jet and regained control.[31]

A "knock it off" call immediately was broadcast on strike frequency and transmitted again on Guard[32] frequency, terminating all activity associated with the strike.

In testimony to the superb training of the Air Force fighter pilots and to the structural sturdiness of the McDonnell Douglas F-15, it continued to fly. But anyone who had seen the airplane missing so much of its flight control and stabilization surfaces would ask the same question—How?

There was a happy ending to this near catastrophe. The wingman was quickly recovered by a Navy search-and-rescue helicopter from Fallon and was unharmed after his ejection. The pilot of the damaged Eagle landed safely at Fallon despite the fact that his jet could make only left turns—an impressive demonstration of skill, coolheadedness, and composure under very dire circumstances.

From a "lessons learned" perspective, all the players—once again—were reminded of the very real perils involved in combat training and of the fallacy of the big-sky theory. The *big sky* isn't!

And so it was that in November 1978, CVW-11 spent two action-packed weeks at NAS Fallon completing one of the primary training events prior to their deployment—the Air Wing 11 Weapons Deployment. This det was not without its daily challenges and occasional traumas, but it was ultimately a complete success. The achievement sparked an unmistakable surge in squadron identity, camaraderie, and esprit de corps. The Black Lions were slowly but unmistakably forming up as a team, as was the entire air wing.

CVW-11 completed the Fallon detachment and returned to their home bases just prior to Thanksgiving. With just a few days to celebrate Turkey Day, CVW-11 squadrons embarked aboard *Enterprise* out of Alameda (December 1978) for three weeks to complete additional training.

In late December 1978, the "Lions" returned to Miramar. Christmas and New Years flew by in a blur. On January 2, 1979, CVW-11 was shuttled to Norfolk for their first deployment aboard *America*.

Happy New Year!

USS *America*: First Impressions

CVW-11 was a West Coast air wing, but for the upcoming deployment, several East Coast squadrons had been reassigned to CVW-11 to take advantage of their proximity to *America*'s berthing location—Norfolk, Virginia.

CVW-11's first trip to their new ship, USS *America* (CV-66), came in early January 1979 and extended through the month. On the second of January, Hawk was scheduled to lead a flight of ten of Black Lions' Tomcats on a nonstop flight from NAS Miramar to NAS Oceana in Virginia Beach—over 2,300 miles as the crow flies. Ens. Brock McClung, fresh out of the F-14 FRS and assigned as Hawk's RIO, received the weather brief and filed the flight plan at NAS Miramar Base Operations. The ensign dutifully reported to Hawk that a cold front had settled in near Tinker AFB, Oklahoma City, and extended east. It was a monstrous front and brought poor flying conditions throughout much of the East Coast, including their destination.

On the basis of the forecast weather at their time of arrival, all the primary and divert airfields on the Eastern Seaboard were clobbered. The weather at Oceana was forecast to be overcast, with low visibility, and cold and blustery winds—generally dismal weather at their estimated time of arrival. The new ensign briefed Hawk on computed fuel levels and forecast weather along the route. He was clearly perplexed when he completed his report to Hawk. Hawk, sensing something was amiss, asked, "Something's bothering you, Brock. What's up?"

In response, Ens. McClung asked a perfectly logical question, "XO, why do they stuff our heads with sayings like 'Safety First' and teach us about all the problems of flying into areas of awful forecast weather, make us memorize all the rules associated with minimum weather at our destination and alternate airfields, and then we go out into the real world and file for a place we know is going to have dog-doo weather with no suitable alternate airfields?"

"Well Brock . . . because we have to," Hawk replied. "We have a schedule to keep and a job to do. Welcome to the fleet, son!"

When the Black Lions landed that night, the weather was true to the forecast—cold, blustery, and dog doo in all quadrants.

CVW-11 squadron maintenance, operations, and administrative personnel moved aboard USS *America* on the third and fourth day of January 1979. Many of the air wing, those designated as permanent ship's detachment personnel, remained on board the ship from that time until *America* departed for cruise.

It is a mystery to no one that Norfolk is cold in January, but through some oversight by ship's company, the boilers had not been lit. No boilers, no heat. That was a big habitability problem, but not the only problem. According to the ship's supply department, there were enough blankets for only 50 percent of the crew, and only one sheet per man. Sadly, this portended to the condition of the ship and the responsiveness of the ship's leadership through much of the deployment.

Workups

Under a gun-metal winter sky, *America* pulled away from her berth on the morning of January 5. Capt. Meyer commanded the ship, and Cmdr. A. W. Fredrickson was his executive officer. RAdm. Dunn, commander of Carrier Group 8, and his staff were embarked and responsible for certification inspections in preparation for the deployment. On the basis of the reputation of the certification team, no one expected this to be a pleasure cruise.

From January 5 through February 13, *America*'s crew and air wing were subjected to a vigorous training and exercise schedules. General quarters drills, damage control training, and daily air operations continued until January 24, when the ship pulled into St. Thomas for five days of rest and recuperation (R&R). But for the air wing personnel, R&R was an elusive thing. There were airplanes to fix, certifications to prepare for, equipment and material to bring aboard and store, and spaces to take care of.

On January 29, *America* cranked up her power plants and made way into the operating areas in the Caribbean. No sooner had she hit blue water than the training began again. For three days commencing on February 6, the CARGRU staff set a grueling Operational Readiness Evaluation[33] (ORE) tempo that all too faithfully simulated wartime conditions.

Ultimately, the CARGRU[34] staff assigned a grade of "excellent" for the ship's ORE performance. With some fidelity, the grade correctly addressed the operational capabilities and readiness of the ship and air wing team, but habitability, cleanliness, and morale issues were clearly not considered in the grading calculus. Although blankets and sheets had finally been distributed to the crew, and heat flowed through the ship's spaces, that was about the extent of the success story.

Hawk was thoroughly unimpressed with that first at-sea period and recalls, "I wasn't an ensign on my first cruise, and our troops weren't indentured servants. They were grown men, doing an incredible job under tough conditions. I knew what was right and what wasn't, and conditions on *America* were completely unsatisfactory. The ship was dirty, run down, poorly maintained, and a 'give-a-shit' attitude prevailed amongst the ship's crew. The condition of the ship and the discipline problems, by my thinkin', were a direct reflection of command leadership—they needed some.

"There were complaints about the quality and quantity of food in the mess decks, reports on broken heads, poorly maintained berthing compartments, malfunctioning heat and air-conditioning systems, filthy conditions throughout the ship, and . . . on and on it went.

"Although this at-sea period was designed to bring the ship's company and air wing together as a team, it did the opposite. Several fights broke out between the ship's company and our air wing crews. To top it off, there seemed to be little incentive to make things right.

"*America* was a dirty, run-down ship. Even the all-hands activities to clean her up for her fourteenth birthday on January 23 were an utter failure. In my mind the filth and grime on her deck plates was symptomatic of a much-deeper problem. Scrubbing her down was the equivalent of putting earrings on a pig.

"We pulled into Norfolk on February 13. By that time, every department and each squadron on board was suffering from problems with the ship's supply department. They didn't seem to have a current inventory of parts or supplies, and what they had on board often couldn't be found. Unfortunately, this was a situation which did not improve prior to the sail date on March 13."

When *America* returned to Norfolk, Black Lions set up a small maintenance and administrative detachment at NAS Oceana to coordinate with the ship's offices while the remainder of the squadron returned to Miramar. During this time, Black Lion squadron equipment, support gear, airplanes, and personnel were split between Miramar and Oceana. And although an earnest attempt was made to rotate people back to Miramar to see their families and take care of last-minute details before *America* cast off, it was difficult. Many of the troops took off what time they could, and many others relocated their families with their parents and close friends.

Hawk remembers, "Maintaining morale, keeping our people happy, and instilling faith in the Navy was a full-time job and our highest priority. Skipper Applegate, the department heads, and our chiefs made a major effort to assist families separated by thousands of miles, but we had a lot to do, and contending with the distances from home and all the issues that came up prior to the cruise . . . well, it just really complicated an already unacceptable situation."

The sad fact was that as precarious and poor as the ship's condition and cruise preparation had been, the actual deployment would get much worse before things improved. Hawk and many of the cruise veterans could sense this.

After months of preparation, fixing aircraft, training maintenance personnel, qualifying aircrew, and a bold attempt to assist families, the Black Lions loaded their equipment, tools, aircraft, and personnel gear aboard the ship.

On March 13, 1979, *America* pulled out of Norfolk for her seventh Mediterranean deployment and her tenth major deployment.

CHAPTER 3

America Sails

I was always afraid of dying. It was my fear that made me learn everything I cared about my airplane and my emergency equipment. I was always respectful of my machine and always alert in the cockpit.

—Gen. Chuck Yeager

Casting Lines

Scores of Navy and Marine Corps personnel, all in their winter dress-blue uniforms, lined the entire circumference of *America*'s 3.5-acre flight deck. They felt rather than heard the deep, chest-thumping rumble reverberating from deep within the bowels of the ship. A tiny fraction of *America*'s 280,000 shaft horsepower was unleashed to the driveshafts, and four 25-foot propellers (66,000 lbs.) began to turn. *America* was under her own steam now and slowly making way into the James River. Like faithful dogs watching their master leave for work, three tugs drifted away from *America* but hovered close enough to come to aid the mighty warship should she need assistance.

Capt. Meyer, commanding officer of *America*, ordered a heading that would take the ship into the main channel of the Chesapeake Bay, then into the frigid March waters of the western Atlantic.

Her 84,000 tons slid rock-steady through the water at 5 knots until she entered the main channel. When *America* passed between Hampton to the north and Willoughby Bay to the south, the captain ordered 8 knots. That order was answered deep in the engineering spaces as *America* made her way into the western Atlantic.

Although March 13, 1979, was only a week away from the first day of spring, Mother Nature was showing no signs of releasing her icy grasp on winter. It was cold. A tenacious northwest blow common to this latitude churned up white caps in all quadrants, completed the frigid seascape, and caused even the stoutest seaman to shiver under his peacoat.

The cruise had begun. This was Hawk's fourth deployment, his third to the Med. This time Miss Jenny and young Jack were not on the pier waving goodbye, and this time the trip across the Atlantic held no excitement and little mystery.

If all went well, *America*, in less than seven months, would be steaming these same waters but heading in the opposite direction. And if all went well, she'd have her entire complement of air wing and ship's personnel with her. If all went well.

The deployment had commenced and, after the donkey show that the ship's company tried to pass off as "predeployment training," it was almost a blessing. At least now the ship's crew and the air wing had a starting point by which they could gauge the days until their return. And at least now, most of the unknowns and chaos was behind them, they hoped.

America rendezvoused with her battle group on the Eastern Seaboard. The *America* carrier battle group (CVBG) was composed of *R. K. Turner* (CG-20), *Lawrence* (DDG-4), *Sampson* (DDG-10), *King* (DDG-41), *Barry* (DD-993), *A. W. Radford* (DD-963), and *Joseph Hewes* (FF-1078).

High sea states and brisk winds were the order of the day, and while *America*'s crew steamed in relative stability, the small boys, the guided-missile destroyers and destroyers, rolled and pitched like barrels in a fast river.

It was on the second day of the deployment that *America* set the Bear watch. This was standard fare for an alert condition in response to anticipated overflights by Soviet Long Range Aviation (LRA).[1]

The LRA of the Russian navy, primarily the Tu-95 Bear, M-4 Bison, and Tu-16 Badger, never missed an opportunity to try to detect, intercept, track, photograph, gather intelligence on, and generally annoy every CVBG.[2] The battle group's TACAIR assets, in turn, attempted to detect the inbound aircraft far enough from the CVBG to intercept, escort, and otherwise dissuade them from performing their mission.

To give the battle group practice in intercepting LRA aircraft, a P-3 Orion from NAS Bermuda conducted a scheduled BEAREX[3] against *America*. The P-3 simulated the profile that LRA aircraft would fly during their missions to gather imagery and signal intelligence against a US ship. In this exercise, CVW-11 F-14s and A-7s scrambled into action and successfully intercepted the P-3 miles away from the *America* battle group.

There are generally four outcomes that can result from these types of missions: (1) no contact; the fighters miss the intercept of the reconnaissance aircraft but there is no overflight; the good guys are happy; (2) the fighters complete a successful intercept on the reconnaissance aircraft and convince them that a run on the CVBG is not in their best interest; the bad guys go home and the good guys are happy; (3) the reconnaissance aircraft make a successful run on the CVBG, shoot lots of photos, gather intel, and depart; the bad guys go home happy, and the good guys are not happy; and (4) the fighters join on the reconnaissance aircraft, they press the issue, a horrible calamity takes place, and nobody goes home happy.

During another deployment aboard another carrier, Hawk and his RIO, Lt. Buck Rogers, came within a few feet of having this fourth kind of encounter, an experience that would live in Hawk's memory forever.

Between a Badger and the Deep Blue Sea

It was in late October 1969, and "Super Sara," USS *Saratoga* (CVA-61), was "showing the flag" in the eastern Mediterranean. Hawk and his RIO, Lt. Buck Rogers, were on a real-world, night combat air patrol flying a VF-103 F-4J Phantom and armed to the gills with a full combat load-out: two Sidewinders and two Sparrows.

An hour into their hour and a half mission, Combat Information Center[4] (CIC) transmitted, "Club Leaf two-one-one, vector 1-zero-5 degrees. Two unknowns at 64 miles from you at angels twenty-five, tracking 2-8-5."

Up until that time, *Sara* had conducted several BEAREXs and drills, but none of them had been anything to get excited about. It wasn't until CIC modified their transmission with "Suspect a Badger section" that Hawk and Buck perked up.

"Roger, 2-1-1 coming right to 1-oh-5 degrees and looking," Buck responded. He had hardly completed the transmission when, more excitedly, he said into the ICS, "Hawk, I got two on the nose at fifty-eight. Come further right to 1-2-5 and check out your screen."

There, on the radar, were two of the largest targets Hawk had ever seen. They looked like crushed cotton balls under glass and marched rapidly down the scope as the distance closed.

"Contact your call," Buck confirmed. "I show two large targets at angles 25 and 55 miles, tracking 2-8-zero degrees at 270 knots."

"Roger, Club Leaf. Those are your targets. They currently appear to be on the international airway."

"Roger, Judy!"[5] Buck transmitted.

The fact that they *might* be on an international airway and they *might* be on a legitimate flight plan did not alter the fact they were about to be intercepted, identified, and escorted if they came too close to *Sara*. By Hawk's reckoning, there'd been quite a bit of activity in the region, and this was no time to get complacent.

Without appearing too provocative, but to ensure the Badger crew knew they were being intercepted, Hawk put his nose on them and pressed in while Buck lit them up on the radar. As they closed on the Badgers, Hawk switched off all external lights. There was no question that the Badger crew knew they were under surveillance by an air-to-air radar, but he saw no reason to help them gather any additional information—not yet.

The Badgers maintained track on the international airway. Their westerly course would take them near but not directly over *Sara*. Just as Hawk was thinking that they might actually be on a legitimate flight plan with no intention of an overflight of his ship, Buck cracked the silence, "Hawk, they're descending. I show 17 miles now and passing through 23,000 feet. They haven't altered course, though, and right now they should clear well to the north of the ship."

Hawk quickly built a mental target plot. There was nothing on their current course that would cause them to descend, and therefore there was only one reason they might.

"Buck," Hawk barked, "they're going to make a run on the ship; I know it."

"That's what I'm thinking," Buck agreed.

Buck gave Hawk a new heading for a stern conversion on the lead Badger. Hawk picked up a single set of lights at 9 miles. The wingman, he guessed, was running midnight.[6] It was a dark night, and what little light came from the stars didn't illuminate the wingman.

The Badgers continued their descent through 15,000 feet. They were still 20 miles away from the ship and nearly abeam, but strangely they still did not alter course to the ship.

Hawk and Buck closed on the leader. He was sure the Badger crew knew they were being intercepted, but it was time to let them know by whom. And just so there was no mistaking the seriousness of their intentions, Hawk wanted them to take a gander at what was strapped to the underside of their wings.

As Hawk closed the distance, he decelerated, carefully flew between the two aircraft, and slid alongside the lead Badger. The flash on the tail of the enormous silver airplane identified it as an Egyptian Badger. No surprise, considering the tensions in the area in 1969.

A bright Aldus lamp suddenly flickered on from a window inside the lead Badger and illuminated the Phantom. The spotlight traveled from the Phantom's radar dome, down the fuselage, on to the wing, and then paused. Hawk's Phantom was loaded for bear—or Badgers as the case might be. The light continued to the Phantom's tail, paused, then returned to the ordinance under the wing, as if to come to the realization that this was no drill. The Badger crew now knew they had an *armed* escort.

Hawk squeaked off power, slid to the rear of the lead aircraft, and took up station at dead six o'clock. It gave Hawk some solace in the fact that the Egyptian crew knew the ante was up.

As the Badgers descended through 5,000 feet, they still hadn't made a course change toward *Sara*, but then it got interesting. The Badgers made a turn, over 180 degrees. When they rolled out they were headed directly toward *Sara* and still descending.

Hawk responded immediately: "Well, Buck, no big surprise here. Missiles are selected, tuned, and ready. I'm holding master arm."

"Okay, Hawk. I'm lighting up the lead Badger now."

Buck locked the radar on the lead Badger. The electronic sensor systems on both Badgers were good enough to have been able to instantly warn them that their escort fighter had locked the lead Badger with air-to-air radar.

With Hawk and Buck in trail, the Badgers descended below 500 feet and flew two passes around the ship in a right turn. Hawk turned on external lights again and took position on the left side of the leader, close enough to be seen but distant enough to maintain maneuvering room.

Badger and Bear pilots were well known for erratic flying and conducting maneuvers designed to incite. This was not news to Hawk, and he was not surprised with what happened next.

The lead Badger suddenly reversed his turn and banked left into Hawk and Buck and descended even lower. Hawk anticipated the turn reversal but was caught off guard by the rapid descent. As he took evasive action, he wondered if it was intentional or if the Egyptian pilots just had trouble maintaining altitude. Whatever the case, he had to avoid getting pickled between the water and the Badger. He had very little altitude to play with.

Hawk pushed the stick forward, then heaved it back to bring the nose of the big Phantom back to the horizon. Instantly, Buck cautioned, "Check altitude, Hawk."

"I got it!" Hawk rolled his head back and saw a set of lights cross over his canopy. *That was close!* He stole a glance at the radar altimeter—he was climbing now, and the instrument showed a little over 200 feet, but there was no telling how low they had descended before he pulled back on the stick.

"That son of a bitch just tried to scrape us off in the water," Hawk swore to Buck.

"Yeah, I know. He got my attention; I was slightly concerned," Buck shot back.

"Well, now I'm pissed!" Hawk returned.

Hawk floated his Phantom to the outside of the turn and fell in trail as the Badgers commenced a climb and set their course away from the ship.

Hawk took a couple of large breaths to steady himself. A few seconds later he was fully composed and focused, but all he needed was a small sign of hostile intent and clearance from the controller to turn the two Badgers into an aluminum reef.

To Hawk's and Buck's dismay, that didn't happen.

Well to the east of the ship, CIC called Club Leaf 2-1-1 back home for recovery.

"Okay, I agree; it's open airspace," Hawk commented later, "but if you're coming out to look at my ship, you can stand by to get joined by my fighter. The fighters are part of the power projection package, and power projection is what my ship is all about. Fool with us and we'll power project your ass into the water."

The intercept and escort took no more than thirty minutes, but it was one of those poignant and promising times that spiked the excitement level in an otherwise mind-numbing night combat air patrol sortie in the Med.

Bad Karma

Less than a week after pulling away from Norfolk, two tragic events took place aboard *America*. AMHC Frederick D. Coleman, a VAW-124 chief, died in his sleep on Sunday, March 18. The following day, an F-14 suffered a stuck throttle while taxiing and struck an S-3A. There were no injuries, but to many aboard *America*, these incidents, so close to the beginning of an overseas deployment, were an omen that bode ill for the rest of the cruise.

America's official in-chop to the 6th Fleet[7] took place on March 24, 1979, when the carrier group commander, RAdm. Nagler, received the official turnover brief and mission assignment aboard USS *Saratoga*, the relieved ship. From this time until she out-chopped in September, *America* was commander, 6th Fleet's strategic asset, and the biggest gorilla in the neighborhood.

Her mission was to patrol the Mediterranean, maintain forward presence, perform such humanitarian relief efforts as assigned, deter possible hostile action, and, if deterrence failed, engage in military operations.

An 84,000-ton man-of-war carrying more raw kinetic power than the military capability of most of the world's nations is often looked on as destructive in nature, but, in truth, battle groups such as this are also keepers of the peace. The savings in lives and resources their mere presence often brings to a theater is incalculable. The sheer sight of a carrier battle group on the horizon never fails to have a certain calming effect on would-be usurpers of peace the world over. It exudes a genuine feeling of order, and for many despots and terrorists, it forces a golden opportunity to practice a bit of rational thinking.

Hawk was well aware of *America*'s mission and very familiar with the role his fighter squadron played in the big scheme of things during wartime and peacetime. Owing to the relative global stability in 1979, this cruise had all the earmarks of a standard peacetime deployment chock-full of joint, combined, and NATO exercises; port visits; diplomatic showboat missions; and any humanitarian relief effort that might pop up. These were the bell-ringer events, the things that sailors looked forward to, but between port calls, disasters, and scheduled exercises, *America*'s crew were usually cemented together by long periods of boredom and loneliness.

After just a few days at sea, the daily routine—the meals, training sessions, general quarters drills, evening movies, and even flying—seemed to fall into a familiar pattern for Hawk. It was the standard routine of cruise, and it had lost much of its luster. With several deployments under his belt, Hawk had come to accept that the cruise was the price of admission, an indivisible predicate to fly fast jets from steel ships and be a part of possibly the greatest tribe of warriors on earth.

Flying was still the love of his life, next to Miss Jenny and Jack, but his focal point had expanded. He continued to perfect and instruct his JOs in the fighter warcraft, but his XO duties—taking care of the troops and interfacing with the ship's staff—commanded a large chunk of his time. Simply put, his priorities hadn't changed; he simply and suddenly had more of them.

Capt. Meyer brought his ship through the Strait of Gibraltar early on the morning of March 29, 1979. No sooner had they broken into the Med than they took station for their first exercise: Tap Dance—an antisubmarine warfare exercise. That was followed on April 4 by a port visit to Naples, Italy, Hawk's least favorite port of call in all the Mediterranean, maybe in all the world.[8] About this time, three ceremonies were held: a change of command for VA-95, the A-6 squadron; a promotion for Cmdr. A. W. Fredrickson to captain, the XO of the ship; and the presentation of the Silver Anchor award for "Excellence in Retention" to *America*'s skipper.

Entropy in the Supply Department

Hawk didn't know the XO of *America* well, but he obviously impressed someone at some time because the captain promotion boards didn't just randomly hand out eagle collar devices. But awarding the Silver Anchor was truly a puzzlement, and not just to Hawk. He didn't know what *America*'s leadership did for her crew to receive such an honor, but nothing he had seen thus far would convince him of re-upping, in fact . . . after just a few weeks aboard the ship, Hawk came to the conclusion that "we were on the worst cruise in history and on the dirtiest ship in the Navy, and it will probably never get better until America was under new management."

"There was an attitude of lethargy and irresponsibility that ran the length of the keel. Like so many of the crew's attitudes toward their assigned tasks, the supply system was an absolute disaster," Hawk recalls. "The supply department hadn't conducted a wall-to-wall inventory prior to sailing, and no one in the department seemed to have an accurate account of what parts were on board or where they were located. No matter what we needed or how bad we needed it, the ship didn't have it.

"On one occasion we ordered a dozen rifle scopes. We were trying to mount those on the glare shield in the front cockpit, similar to what the Air Force did during ACEVAL/AIMVAL.[9] Their visual-identification range jumped from about 5 miles head on to almost 15. What we got instead of scopes was a gross; that's right, 144 black, horned-rimmed reading glasses commonly referred to as 'birth control specs.' It was amazing what that ship just couldn't seem to find or deliver.

"Lucky for us, we were blessed with an energetic and resourceful Grumman logistics support representative. His name was Nat Craig, and I'm convinced there are days we wouldn't have had a single airplane up had it not been for him.

"Nat worked at night—all night—to find stuff we needed. He knew the ship, the supply department, and where the parts were stored better than anybody on board.

"When supply personnel returned our parts requisitions, explaining that the requested parts were not on board, we'd sic Nat Craig on the problem. Our maintenance chief, a magnificent manager in his own right, Senior Chief 'Bernie Mo' Mostoller, would pass the same parts list to Nat that he'd given to the supply department. Of course the chops[10] would come up empty handed. Not so surprisingly, the next morning we miraculously had all the parts on the list. Nat wouldn't stop searching until he had found everything we needed."

At times it seemed as though the ship and the air wing were pitted against each other. Parts support was poor for all the squadrons, but what complicated the problem was the unwillingness of the ship's handler[11] to move aircraft between the hangar bay and the flight deck. "They couldn't or wouldn't move airplanes on the ship, because they were concerned that the elevators would get stuck and the deck would be fouled forever. Only the air boss seemed to know if, in fact, there was a real concern, but there was definite resistance to test the system. We could have 'up' aircraft in the hangar deck and 'down' aircraft on the flight deck, and we couldn't get authorization for an elevator move to swap them out. And the deck multiple[12] was so high you couldn't sneeze without hitting your head on a wing.

"In addition to being the most unresponsive, dirtiest ship in the Navy, with the worst supply system ever, it also had the worst-run officer's mess of any carrier I'd ever been on. We paid a ridiculously high mess bill, and the food was terribly lacking. On top of that, a few weeks after in-chopping to 6th Fleet, we heard that the mess officer was under investigation for weaseling money from the steward's subsistence pay. The problems just went on and on."

Hawk had never experienced such frustration in his life. As the squadron's chief morale officer, he worked tirelessly to instill that same level of professionalism, eagerness, and standard of excellence in the Black Lions he had achieved in TOPGUN. In Hawk's mind he'd spent two years with the most professional organization in the Navy, and he wanted to implant that same constitution, that same commitment and dedication, into his "Lions." He wanted to shape the best maintenance department, groom the best middle managers and technicians, develop the best presentations, fly the best-maintained aircraft, and nurture the best future leaders. In the past he'd been successful in generating enthusiasm to an epidemic level, and he worked doubly hard to achieve that in VF-213: "It wasn't easy, but TOPGUN was a blazing example of what could be done when everyone pulled together, when they were inspired and empowered and realized they were a part of something much bigger than themselves. Aboard *America* the air wing personnel seemed to be surrounded by supine indifference and lack of visible leadership and saddled with one impossible situation after another.

"It was very upsetting to me as a naval officer to realize that even as the XO of one of the most advanced fighter squadrons in the world, I wasn't actually in charge of anything, and therefore I was unable to fix many of the things even a blind man could see was wrong!

"There was a serious lesson for me on that ship—no matter how good you are at shepherding your people and trying to make things fun, exciting, and safe, there's always some needle dick with more authority than you to spoil all the fun and make it simply impossible. But despite all the adversity, all the roadblocks thrown in our path, we still managed to hold interesting training lectures, fix airplanes, remain night and all-mission qualified, and achieve all the other stuff required on deployment. It wasn't easy, but our boys never let up."

Ship's Habitability Improvement Team

There was one condition in particular on the ship that commanded Hawk's full attention. The Black Lions were assigned cleanliness responsibility for their ninety-two-man berthing compartment and the head adjoining the compartment. Both VF-213 and VF-114, a total of 180 men, used the head. In January, during the first workup period, VF-213 reported the unsatisfactory condition of the head to the ship's first lieutenant and cited that two of the four mirrors were broken or missing, three of the six urinals were plugged up, four of the six toilets were missing or inoperative, and the air-conditioning in their berthing area was ineffective. In March, when *America* deployed, nothing had changed; nothing had been repaired. Things were as screwed up as they had been.

Hawk was incredulous: "The air conditioners didn't work. Our sailors didn't have enough mirrors to use for shaving, and the urinals were inoperative. The Navy is the only organization in the world that can have a backed-up head 50 feet above the waterline. Are you telling me the Navy couldn't make piss run downhill? It defied gravity!

"I was plenty unhappy with the missing shitters too. The ship just pulled them up, plugged them with big wooden damage-control plugs, and went about their business as if we didn't really need them in the first place. You go into this head, the urinals are backed up, mirrors are broken, and shitters are missing; there's absolutely no shower curtains, no privacy, and the stench was awful. And that's where my guys had to live. Convicts receive better treatment! Not only would they not fix them or give us the equipment to fix them, they dinged us on the condition of the head in every zone inspection. And that was the final straw!

"I took this on as our rallying point, as that all-important tipping point that would solidify the troops and turn the tide of the campaign. I made this 'the' issue.

"We formed the Black Lion 'Ship's Habitability Improvement Team,' 'SHIT Team' for short. We ordered blue jumpsuits so they had a little identity and wouldn't ruin their dungarees, and I found a second-class petty officer smart enough to figure things out and aggressive enough to get things done. I gave him First Lieutenant Division and put him in charge of the 'SHIT Team.' I just pointed him in the right direction, told him what we needed fixed, turned him loose, and made sure nobody messed with him. The boy was incredible!

"When the ship's maintenance people couldn't fix something—which seemed to be everything associated with habitability—the SHIT team fixed it. For example—the air-conditioning system in our berthing compartment was broken and had been since who knows when. We'd write up a discrepancy report and send it to the 3M[13] office, where it was assigned a work order number. Sometime later the work order was routed to the planning and estimating office. Finally, weeks later, some guy would come to the space, walk around the area, and then say, 'Oh, this . . . we can't do nuthin' about this. We'll have to fix it when we put into port.' It was ridiculous—but consistent!"

Despite the many casualty reports, zone inspection discrepancy reports, and several conversations Hawk had visited upon the ship's XO, it was clear that neither the head nor the air-conditioning system was going to be repaired if left up to ship's company.

When that was clear, Hawk decided that the squadron would pay for the material and fix it themselves. "Well guess what. The squadron didn't hold the correct type of funding to purchase parts to repair the head. As far as I was concerned, that was a moot point and a distant second behind providing our crew with an operable head. We needed to fix the head, and to do that we had to purchase parts, and if that meant using the 'wrong' kind of money to do it, well, that was unavoidable. Too bad!

"Here we were, American sailors on an American ship, in fact the ship is even named USS *America*, and we all serve the US Navy and our country. Now on this Navy ship, USS *America*, they have toilets that will fit over the holes in the deck, but we can't get them because we don't have the right kind of money? I've just never seen so many things we couldn't do for our troops because of all the regulations, incompetence, and stumbling blocks."

Against the advice of his supply officer, Hawk authorized the purchase of all the necessary equipment and material. With the energetic supervision of the second class in charge, the "SHIT Team" hung curtains, painted the space, replaced mirrors and toilets, and unclogged every urinal. When they were finished, the Black Lions' head may have been the only fully functional head on the entire ship, and one of the few that had solved the riddle of making piss run downhill.

It was a small triumph for the Black Lions, but it made a large impression on the troops. They understood that there was someone willing to go to bat for them, and that understanding helped unify them as a team. Together, and against all odds, they realized they could make things happen.

Although the Black Lions SHIT Team was making vast strides in habitability and conditions of their assigned spaces, the situation was going decidedly south for the air wing. On April 11, two VA-195 "Dambuster" A-7s collided during a low-level training sortie 130 miles south of Naples. Both aircraft were lost and a family home was destroyed by the debris, but fortunately there were no injuries to the inhabitants or the pilots. Lt. Mike Talcott and Lt. j.g. Bob Lowe were recovered after the ejections and returned to the ship.

Port Visits

America steamed into Palma and dropped anchor on April 14. On April 16, one of Hawk's best friends and his first fleet pilot joined the air wing; in fact, he took over the air wing.

VAdm. James Watkins, C6F, attended the change-of-command ceremony, during which Phillip R. Wood was relieved of the duties of commander, Carrier Air Wing 11, by Jack "Stinger" Ready.

Hawk was elated. Although he thought highly of Cmdr. Wood, he was ecstatic that Cmdr. Ready had taken command. Maybe their luck would change, and maybe the supply system and response to material and condition discrepancies would now improve.

Unfortunately their "luck" was something that just wasn't destined to change, at least in the near term. On April 26, a third Corsair was lost when it flamed out just prior to recovering aboard the ship. The pilot, however, was rescued by one of the ship's SH-3s. This was the third aircraft lost on a cruise that had just begun. The only consolation was that no lives had been lost.

America entered the Adriatic Sea on the third of May. On the fourth of May, she dropped anchor near the city of Split, Yugoslavia. America rolled out the red carpet, and thousands of Yugoslavian government officials and citizens toured the ship. It was as if the Barnum and Bailey Circus had come to town. By all accounts the guests were simply in awe of the immense size of the ship and the number of aircraft on board.

It was at this time that the Naval Investigative Service (NIS) began to tighten their investigation on the mess officer concerning allegations of larceny and theft of government property. That officer, feeling the heat, decided Yugoslavia was as good a port as any to jump ship. He couldn't have been more wrong. Sometime later, he was apprehended, tried, and convicted of criminal violations under the Uniform Code of Military Justice and sentenced to Fort Leavenworth Military Corrections Complex.

America pulled out of Yugoslavia following a very successful port call and cruised into the Ionian Sea. The America battle group took part in Dawn Patrol, a NATO exercise involving British and Italian forces with assistance from the US Air Force. Following that exercise they steamed north into the Adriatic Sea for a six-day port call in Venice, followed by an eight-day port visit to Trieste, Italy.

At each port, there seemed to be as many visitors coming aboard America for tours as there were sailors venturing off the ship for liberty. In fact, to many sailors, there seemed to be a carnival-like atmosphere, and America was the main attraction. The ship's staff went so far as to organize a Sunset Parade on June 8, while in Trieste for a group of distinguished guests, the American consul general, and several senior military officers. All the PR overtures and "showboat" notoriety was interesting, but Hawk was hungry to get back to sea and into a cockpit again.

Bombing under the Flares

On June 12, *America* pulled out of Trieste and headed south into the Ionian Sea. She was scheduled to take part in a surface surveillance and antisubmarine warfare exercise with three Italian vessels on June 14 and 15. On Friday night, June 15, tragedy struck. VA-195 lost their fourth A-7, and this time, the life of one of their pilots.

Lt. Michael Talcott crashed 130 miles east of Catania, Sicily, during a night-bombing training sortie. According to the mishap investigation, the pilot was believed to have become disoriented during a practice bombing run while operating under Mk. 45 parachute flares.

Bombing at night is a mission ripe with risks, but bombing at night under parachute flares is a whole different snake pit. The flare is initially released by one of the bomber aircraft above the pullout altitude of the bombers. Initially this is similar to the position of the primary light source, the sun, during day visual bombing. The light is above the aircraft as the pilot commences his dive delivery and 4 g pull-up to his pattern altitude. As the parachute flare continues to fall, however, it may descend below the pullout altitude. Despite the warnings placed on this condition, inexperienced pilots sometimes unwittingly key off the light source as a point of reference for their pull following the weapon release instead of transitioning immediately to their instruments. If they don't maintain a positive scan of their instruments, there is a tendency for the pilot to roll the aircraft so that the light source, as in the daytime, appears above the aircraft. In this condition, the pilot is actually pulling toward the light source and therefore toward the water.

Although the mishap board did not have enough evidence to prove this was the cause of Lt. Talcott's accident, there were enough similarities in the observed sequence of events and ultimate outcome to suspect this was the cause of the mishap. This was Lt. Talcott's second mishap in two months. He was one of the pilots involved in the midair collision that caused the loss of two A-7s on April 27. It was a painful loss and hit the "Dambusters" and the entire air wing hard.

At this point, *America*'s Med deployment should have been a busy but relatively safe peacetime cruise. The Vietnam War was over, and while there was an occasional flaring of nostrils and incendiary intonations in the Mideast—the standard international buffoonery and fist-shaking by Qaddafi, there were no military hostilities. Yet in less than three months, four aircraft had been destroyed, another two severely damaged, and the life of a pilot had been lost. These incidents hearkened back to something carrier aircrew have known since the first carrier rolled off the rails: naval aviation—even in the best of times—is a terribly unforgiving line of work, and not for the dull witted or weak of heart.

Land of Camel Herders and Fighter Pilots

On June 18, *America* sailed into Alexandria, Egypt. This was something of a historic event. It was the first visit by a US carrier since Nasser closed the Suez Canal in 1958. Although for years there had been a certain political tension between the two nations, the people of Egypt treated *America*'s sailors with great courtesy and genuine warmth. During the six-day port call, over three thousand servicemen completed bus tours of the ancient city, visited the pyramids, and gawked at the sphinx. In return, the crew of *America* hosted visits for Egyptian diplomats, government officials, military leaders, and staff of the American consul general.

One of the many officers to come aboard was a US Air Force colonel assigned to the US embassy in Egypt. Hawk had met him while he was at TOPGUN and the colonel was stationed at Nellis Air Force Base (AFB). Hawk recognized him immediately and joined him at the top of the brow.[14] After pleasantries were exchanged, the colonel asked Hawk if VF-213 would host a small contingent of Egyptian fighter pilots for a tour of the ship and a presentation of the capabilities of the Tomcat. Hawk quickly accepted.

The next day, a dozen Egyptian fighter pilots came aboard. Hawk and several of his officers greeted the Egyptian officers, and the colonel made the introductions. He explained that all the Egyptian pilots had flown either the MiG-17s or MiG-21s in combat against the Israelis during the October 1973 Yom Kippur War, a war in which the Egyptian air force lost over two hundred of its frontline fighters in twenty days. That piece of news, indicating that the Egyptian pilots defiantly went toe to toe with the Israeli air force (a vastly better-trained force), significantly elevated their stature in the eyes of the Navy aircrew.

The Black Lion escorts provided a tour of the ship that included the hangar and flight deck, arresting gear, catapult engines, the ready rooms, and mess decks. Following the tour, the Egyptian pilots were treated to a formal briefing on the F-14 and were then allowed to inspect the Tomcat.

The senior Egyptian pilot, a lieutenant colonel with steel-blue eyes and a dark complexion, was a MiG-23 pilot who had been trained in Russia. He was asked how he liked the MiG-23 compared to the MiG-21, and his response initially puzzled most of the Tomcat crew.

He claimed that he preferred flying the MiG-23 Flogger over the MiG-21 Fishbed. His reasoning was sound. The Flogger was a swing-wing design similar to the Tomcat, but unlike the Tomcat it was cursed with a heavily loaded wing and a poor turn rate. More importantly, however, was that it accelerated like a scalded dog. At one time the MiG-23 was reputed to be the fastest-accelerating airplane in the world. Navy TACAIR pilots were aware of the 23's acceleration capability, but this was, in their minds, more than offset by the problems associated with the weapons system, departure characteristics, and embarrassing turn rate.

The MiG-21, on the other hand, had a respectable turn rate, and though it was supersonic, its acceleration rate and top speed fell well short of the Flogger's. The lieutenant colonel explained that a Flogger could hold the Fishbed off and stay out of his weapons envelope, but when the Fishbed attempted to disengage, the Flogger could simply chase him down and kill him.

This illuminated an interesting alternative combat discipline—one that few Navy fighter pilots consider—*patience.*

The tour was a smashing success. To show their appreciation, the Egyptians reciprocated by extending an invitation to tour their airfield. Hawk jumped on the offer like a duck on a June bug.

The USAF colonel coordinated a tour at Inshas Air Base near Cairo. Craig "Tweety" Honor, Ed "Bull Dog" Allen, Chuck "Sneakers" Nesby, Hawk, and seven other Lion and Aardvark aircrew signed up.

The following day they scrambled on a helo lift from Alexandria airport to Inshas airbase. There they were escorted through the underground intelligence bunkers, where they were allowed to view the Egyptian surveillance logs and photographs from reconnaissance flights over Israel. As soon as Hawk saw the reconnaissance log, he sucked in a big lungful of air. *Could this be a mistake?*, he wondered.

In 1978, the Egyptians and Israelis signed a nonaggression accord spearheaded by President Carter. Under that agreement, both nations agreed to honor one another's sovereign airspace. At that time, the pact was holding. What Hawk and the rest of the group were being shown was a gallery of overhead imagery showcasing Israeli military structures, facilities, and aircraft parked on runways, which, according to the documentation, featured five different Israeli air bases.

It was a bit of a mystery how the Egyptians got the overheads and how they avoided getting shot down. But what completely baffled Hawk was why they were allowing US Navy fliers to view them. Intelligence, surveillance, and reconnaissance data, especially overhead imagery, were usually so closely guarded that only the intel weenies were allowed access, and even then a "need to know" condition had to exist. It was completely mystifying to Hawk that the Navy fliers were allowed to view this material.

The tour continued with a bus ride around the field to a large, semisubmerged concrete bunker and below-desert-level hangars with bombproof doors.

The Navy contingent was amazed at the immensity of the bombproof hangar doors. "The hangars looked to be made of reinforced concrete sunk into the desert floor and covered with sand. The doors, also reinforced concrete, were set on steel wheels that rolled on iron rails similar to railroad tracks. It looked sophisticated, but when the Egyptian troops were told to open the hangar doors, instead of the loud whir of electric motors powering the doors open, several personnel ran to the doors with pry bars and literally manhandled the giant doors across the tracks. It wasn't an easy job, and it took several minutes to fully open both doors."

Inside the hangars sat two MiG-21C fighters. Hawk and company were allowed to closely inspect these and even given the opportunity to sit in the cockpits.

The group then filed back on the bus and was driven to the base of the tower. When they exited the bus, the Egyptian colonel explained, "We will now demonstrate our Alert Three launch for you."

A three-minute alert? If they could do that, Hawk thought, *it'd be better than anything I've seen in the Navy.*

The Navy fighter and attack crews routinely stand Alert Fives when the ship enters overflight zones, but it is not unusual to take up to ten minutes to get the ship pointed into the wind and fire the first aircraft off the deck.

"When," Hawk asked politely, "are you going to launch the alert?"

"Whenever you say, 'Launch,'" the colonel smiled and replied.

"You mean you want me to say, 'Launch the alert fighters,' and you'll start the clock?"

"That is correct. Whenever you say 'Launch,' we will start the clock."

Hawk could barely believe they were staging this show for them. *What a great opportunity.* "Okay . . . Launch 'em!"

The colonel turned to one of the controllers standing atop the tower, and yelled something in Arabic. A controller raised a flare gun and fired a round nearly straight up. Even before the flare began its decent, the unmistakable wailing of a turbojet winding up reverberated across the desert floor.

"We could easily hear jets starting up, but sand dunes and the sunken hangars prevented us from seeing them. Well inside two minutes, the first MiG-21 taxied to the hold-short area and initially appeared to be waiting for his wingman. We didn't hear or see a second jet initially, and the solo MiG-21 taxied toward the runway. Without the customary flight control and engine checks that we do religiously before launch, the Egyptian pilot firewalled the throttle and began his takeoff roll while he was still taxiing onto the runway. We'd have been keelhauled for that.

"It was June, so it was hot, and it took awhile for the MiG-21 to get airborne, but he did a low transition on takeoff, and it was a nice one. Not long after he took off and climbed out over the end of the runway, the second MiG-21 taxied toward the runway and started his takeoff roll. He also made a low transition. It must be an Egyptian air force thing, but this guy was so low he occasionally disappeared behind the dunes separating us from the runway. Sometimes all we could see was the tail moving swiftly down the runway like the dorsal fin of a shark.

"We fancy ourselves as pretty good pilots, pretty shit hot when it comes to unsolicited air shows, but this guy's low transition was so low, you could only tie the record—you just couldn't get lower. And it didn't end there. We were so locked on to the wingman's low transition we completely forgot about the lead MiG-21.

"From above and astern of the wingman, the lead MiG reappeared, and, so help me, I've never seen a better, 'shit hot' high-speed rendezvous from a low transition. The flight lead came back to make a perfect high-to-low conversion on number 2 just after he got his gear up. Extraordinary closure control! Perfect timing! Incredible execution!

"They continued to put on the best low-altitude air show you could imagine. There was no margin for error. They were absolutely in the sand. They did a section loop that started in the weeds and completed the maneuver just as low. It was so low we were positive the wingman was going to die. There was no separation and no movement between airplanes on the top of the loop. I mean the wingman looked like he was just painted onto the other airplane.

"It wasn't any 4 g pullout on the backside of the loop either. They had to be pulling 5 to 6 g's. Anything less and they would have would have created a smoking crater at the end of the runway. After a few precarious seconds when no one was sure they were going to make the pullout, they finally leveled off at perhaps 10 feet above the sand dunes and raced across the desert floor with at least 500 knots.

"It was simply amazing and disputed every assessment that the MiG-21 was a piece of junk. It was an incredible exposition of airmanship and demonstrated some serious trust between the wingman and his flight lead. More than that—it blew the socks off assessment reports that surmised they couldn't fly jets!

"They returned for a section landing, popped their drag chutes together, rolled to the end of the runway, and taxied back.

"When the show was over, we all looked at each other and seemed to all be thinking the same thing: *Did we just see what we thought we saw?*"

"I don't know what kind of combat fighter pilots they were, but I wouldn't want to have a low-level fly-off with those two!"

Shortly after the MiGs landed, a third MiG-21 appeared in the break. He landed and taxied to the base of the tower. The engine was still unwinding when the pilot crawled out of the cockpit and strode over to the colonel and the Navy fliers. He was an Egyptian air force major. The colonel introduced him to the Navy pilots. He was polite and spoke excellent English, and though he allowed the Navy contingent to walk around his jet, they were not allowed access to the cockpit.

Hawk had seen several MiG-21s, even fought a few in classified programs in the desert, but this one was different. It was a brand-new MiG-21F and dressed out in a lizard desert camouflage scheme. The glass panels on the side and nose of the aircraft gave it away. It was a photo-recce variant, and presumably the type that had taken the overhead shots of the Israeli military facilities that the group had just seen. Hawk couldn't help but wonder where this particular photo-recce MiG-21 had just come from and what kind of hair-raising stories the MiG pilot might share.

The tour ended with a lavish lunch and a friendly exchange of aviation stories. The Navy contingent thanked their host and boarded the helo for the trip back to Alexandria.

It was an amazing tour, and unlike anything Hawk had expected. It dispelled all the rumors about the performance of the MiG-21 and the MiG-23, but more alarmingly and perhaps more tactically significant, it countered the reports about the airmanship of Egyptian pilots.

America sailed out of Alexandria toward Souda Bay, Crete, on June 25. As soon as the ship broke into open water, Hawk's group gathered together to consolidate thoughts and observations and to review the photos they had taken of the buildings and the equipment at Inshas. They drafted a field intelligence report, which addressed aircraft performance, facilities, defensive weapons emplacements, intelligence-gathering capabilities, and descriptions of the hangars and command and control bunkers. They didn't embellish their assessments of the Egyptian fighter pilot's airmanship—they didn't need to.

CVW-11 released the report to the chief of naval intelligence. Within days, via secure channels from ComSixFleet, the chief of naval intelligence responded with a communiqué praising ComSixFleet and *America*. He declared the report "the best field operational intelligence of its kind and the type of information Navy intelligence should receive regularly from the fleet."

Independence Day in the Med

The Fourth of July is a particularly special day in the US military and is celebrated with proper respect and exuberance. This holds true even at sea. As *America* steamed toward a training anchorage in Pollensa Bay, Spain, she began Independence Day celebrations with a twenty-one-gun salute to the nation and her namesake. Tables were set on the flight deck and loaded with cold cuts, BBQ'd meats, baked goods, sweets, fruit, and refreshments of every variety that rivaled any picnic back home.

The festivities continued through the day and well into the evening. CVW-11 aircraft dropped parachute flares, and, as the sun fell in the west, USS Arthur *W. Radford* and USS *King* fired star shells and sailors lobbed bottle rockets into a cobalt-black Mediterranean sky. Aside from the fact that they were far from home, all hands enjoyed the break, the chow, and the fireworks show.

For most aboard *America* that day, for the hundreds of sailors from all walks of life, cultures, ethnic backgrounds, and economic strata, this coming together, this sharing of an immaculate moment, would remain exquisite in the memories of the crew and would likely be what they most remembered of their cruise. And for that moment, there was even a near bonding between the ship's crew and the men of CVW-11.

As uplifting and exciting as the experience was, Hawk couldn't get his mind off *America's* next port visit—the midcruise stand-down, his reunion with Miss Jenny, and the change of command.

CHAPTER 4

I Relieve You, Sir!

In Hawk's mind this incident solidly reinforced one of the primal LSO rules: "Never trust anyone to fly the ball. Treat everyone like a nugget. In fact, expect them to do the craziest, most unpredictable, stupid-ass things imaginable, and at the worst possible moment!"

—John "Hawk" Smith, *Roger Ball!*

Command

On July 9, 1979, *America* navigated southwest around the Balearic Islands, east of Spain, and dropped anchor at Palma de Mallorca. While some of the ship's crew and air wing took leave and returned to the states, several of the wives made the trip to Palma to join their husbands. Miss Jenny had organized a trip from San Diego to Palma for a pride of Black Lion wives. She had made a single trip to the Med during Hawk's 1969 deployment, which somehow qualified her as the Black Lion Wives Club tour guide and travel agent.

Hawk boarded the first liberty launch available and double-timed it to the hotel where the Black Lion wives had reserved rooms. He found Miss Jenny sitting with several of the wives at the hotel sidewalk café. The instant he saw her, those big blue eyes and impish smile, the cruise frustrations and stress seemed to magically vaporize. After fourteen weeks of separation, Hawk and Miss Jenny were together again. All else, for a time, was fluff.

Aside from this most significant event, their reunion, there was one other celebration tied to this port call—the Black Lions' change of command.

For generations, naval officers in command (O-6 or below) of an operational US naval surface ship, submarine, air squadron, or other designated operational command are entitled to wear the Command at Sea pin.[1] It is a gold device the size of a dime, with six small stars clustered around a larger star affixed above an anchor. The small stars are symbolic of the first six vessels of the United States Navy: USS *United States*, USS *Constellation*, USS *Constitution*, USS *Chesapeake*, USS *Congress*, and USS *President*, commissioned and launched from 1797 to 1800.

The Command at Sea pin, a.k.a. the "Texaco Star," is worn above the name tag, a quarter of an inch above the right chest pocket on the uniform shirt and uniform jacket.

The Command at Sea pin is awarded to naval officers selected and groomed for command, and testifies to the special trust and confidence that senior naval leadership holds in such officers. It embodies the tradition of, and the authority granted to, selected officers for command at sea and acknowledges the tremendous accountability and responsibility intrinsic in that authority.

On July 14, 1979, VF-213 personnel assembled on the hangar deck of *America* in their freshly pressed liberty whites. Emily Applegate, the CO's wife; Miss Jenny; and several other Black Lion wives were seated near the podium. The outgoing commanding officer, Cmdr. T. B. Applegate, made his remarks and introduced the guest speaker, CAG[2] Ready. As was typical of CAG Ready, his delivery was both pointed and poignant. He didn't mince words and didn't engage in drawn-out oratories.

Nearing the end of his address, he called Cmdr. Applegate and Hawk to the podium for the traditional reading of orders, at which time command was officially passed to Hawk. Cmdr. Applegate and Hawk saluted one another, and Hawk responded, "I relieve you, sir!" Cmdr. Applegate then pivoted to CAG Ready, saluted, and announced, "I stand properly relieved!"

Hawk, at that exciting moment, was the new commanding officer of the Black Lions and was identified by his Command at Sea pin affixed above his name tag on the right side of his uniform. His first order of business was to address his command.

The distinguished visitors and guests took their seats as Hawk stepped to the podium. "CAG Ready . . . during another change of command some fourteen years ago, the public address system screeched, wailed, and then finally failed. Standing at parade rest in ranks was then Lt. j.g. Jack Ready, who whispered to an Ens. Hawk Smith, 'Hawk,' he said, 'there are three things the Navy will never get right—audiovisual systems, public address equipment, and close-order drills.' Well, sir," Hawk continued, "you'll notice that the Lions have first-rate audiovisual equipment in the ready room, the public address system is operating perfectly, and, with time and practice, I'll bet we master close-order drills without wounding any of our troops."

With those closing remarks, Hawk gave his first official order and a favorite of both the new commanding officer and his guests: "Company Commander, take charge and carry out the plan of the day!"

The plan for that day was a scheduled "all hands" change of command reception at the local hotel bar in Palma. There was no grumbling in the ranks—a rare thing!

By all accounts the reception was a complete success. The Black Lion wives dressed in lion costumes complete with twin tails (replicating the two vertical stabilizers of the Tomcat) and, on an impromptu stage, performed their version of the Tomcat Can-Can.

The following day the officers and troops joined forces on the beach and "baptized" all new Black Lions and their guests in the balmy Mediterranean Sea.

Miss Jenny became the center of attraction for many of the squadron personnel. She was a down-home Virginia girl, and though she had always been knockout gorgeous, she never let it go to her head. She'd already made a few involuntary trips into the water and was sitting comfortably soaked on the beach conversing with several sailors. Many just wanted to be near her; she had always been a good listener, genuinely interested in what others had to say, and very easy on the eyes.

For a moment, Miss Jenny was taken aback and at a loss for words when one junior enlisted man, with all sincerity, asked her, "Miss Jenny, what school did they send you to?"

"Ah . . . I'm sorry. What school do you mean?"

"You know, what school did they send you to so you could learn to talk with enlisted people?"

It was obviously surprising to several junior enlisted men that a senior officer's wife could be so down to earth, so easy to talk with, so easily approachable, and genuinely interested in what they had to say. But that was just Miss Jenny.

July 16 was a big day aboard *America*. The new executive officer of the ship, Cmdr. Welch, reported aboard and relieved Capt. Fredrickson. A few hours later, *America* hoisted her anchor and steamed out of Palma de Mallorca to Barcelona for two days of rest and relaxation.

Weeks earlier, the ship's commanding officer had agreed to allow the wives to make the one-day sail to the new anchorage. Air wing representatives spoke with the mess chief petty officer and requested a special meal—something savory to impress the wives.

That afternoon, "surf and turf," lobster tails and steaks, was served in the chief petty officer's mess. For the officer wives, however, the big "Welcome Aboard" luncheon in the officer's mess was beans and franks.

"It was simply one more 'gotcha' in a whole long list of other 'gotchas' on the worst carrier in the Navy," Hawk remembered, "and this special dinner they cooked up seemed an awful lot like a jab in the eye of the air wing officers. Things aboard ship were slowly and perceptibly getting better . . . but it wasn't happening overnight."

America steamed slowly into Barcelona and set the anchor. Hawk and Miss Jenny had two more wonderful days to spend with one another. Two days left to shop, sightsee, and act as the tourists they were.

It was July 18, and they strolled through the small shops and markets that lined the main street near the port. Two gypsy girls dressed in brightly colored, traditional garments, and looking every bit the part of gypsies portrayed in the travelogues, greeted Hawk and Miss Jenny warmly. They were friendly, cute, and vivacious, and Hawk couldn't help but buy Miss Jenny a bunch of overpriced flowers. The gypsy girls thanked Hawk and continued their sweep through the marketplace.

Hawk and Miss Jenny strolled arm in arm down the cobbled road to an ice cream stand. It was a hot afternoon, and ice cream sounded just right—after all, it was Miss Jenny's birthday. Hawk, using his best southern-drawl Spanish, ordered two ice cream cones and reached into his pocket for his money, only to discover his wallet was missing. He'd been relieved of $150 and didn't even know it!

He knew in an instant what had happened. He'd been pickpocketed. His first instinct was to be angry, but one look at Miss Jenny, those clear blue, luminous eyes, and the only emotions he felt were true and total love and the sense of profound fortune that had been visited upon him. He would let nothing ruin what little time they had left together.

In spite of the Barcelona misadventure, Hawk and Miss Jenny squeezed the most out of every second of their time together. They joined up with Chief and Denise Anderson for dinner and dined on escargot and other Barcelona specialties and drank several (too many) glasses of sangria. Late in the evening they rambled down the Ramblas arm in arm, singing country tunes.

It seemed surreal. The time flashed by and five days were over before they realized it. The Black Lion wives, with some remorse, boarded a train and disappeared down the tracks headed for parts north. Hawk shook himself out of his reverie, put on his war face, and boarded *America*.

Harpoon Shoot

America steamed out of Barcelona on July 23, headed for the Ionian Sea. Her next mission was to take part in National Week XXVII, a complex four-day exercise that would begin on July 26. It involved several different war-at-sea scenarios and training exercises. One of those was an open-ocean, live-missile shoot or MissilEx.

The missile shoot exercise area was vast and encompassed part of the Gulf of Sirte (Sidra). Although by international law the Gulf of Sidra is outside 12 miles from land and in international waters, Muammar Gaddafi declared all waters south of latitude 32°30' "Libyan territory." He made routine blustery threats that any ships or aircraft operating in those waters were in violation of Libyan sovereignty and would be dealt with accordingly.

Although no one familiar with Qaddafi's modus operandi expected him to go toe to toe with US forces (that just wasn't the way he worked), Soviet MiG-fighter aircraft flown by Libyan pilots were located at airfields in northern Libya and within easy strike range of the *America* battle group. Just to be sure Qaddafi would not have an unexpected surge of courage, most TACAIR assets carried a combat load-out, and alerts were manned twenty-four hours per day throughout the exercise.

On July 28, under the umbrella of *America* fighter patrols, a live firing of the new Harpoon antiship missile was conducted from USS *Arthur W. Radford* at a target hulk, the former USS *Lansdowne*, nearly 60 miles away. Considering the critical nature of this first test fire and the possibility, however slight, of disruption by Libyan forces, everyone was on high annoyance level.

Not far away, two Russian AGI intelligence-gathering trawlers patrolled the waters, hoping to record video and telemetry data. Occasionally, exercise directors purposely allowed the Soviets to "view" the results, in order to "get the word out," but this wasn't one of those occasions. The exercise controllers wanted the AGIs as far away as possible both from the shooter and the target ship; it would require considerable maneuvering to set up the geometry.

Test engineers and technicians from the Pacific Missile Test Center (PMTC) coordinated and controlled the exercise. A brief was conducted by PMTC representatives on board *America*. Attending the brief was the commander of the battle group, his staff, representatives from the shooter ship, and the two missile chase crews: Hawk; his RIO, "Bull Dog" Allen; and, in the second Tomcat, Mike "Weasel" Forchet and his RIO.

All elements of the missile shoot were addressed. The weather forecaster announced that a thin overcast layer at 1,000 feet would remain in the area but was not expected to interfere with the mission. The PMTC briefer addressed the parameters and profile for the chase birds. He explained that the chase aircraft should orbit overhead the shooter ship at 3,000 feet. When the range went "hot," the controllers would commence a countdown from sixty. At "T" minus zero (T-0), sixty seconds after the commencement of the countdown, the chase aircraft should be abeam the shooter ship, pointed in the direction of the Harpoon launch corridor, at an altitude of 50 feet and an airspeed of 500 knots.

The briefer emphasized the importance of good photo coverage by the chase crew from launch all the way to impact. He cautioned that the chase crew should be prepared for the Harpoon's terminal "pop-up" maneuver. Just prior to impact the Harpoon would pop-up from its cruise altitude of 50 feet and climb a few thousand feet. During the terminal portion of the profile, the missile would dive and, it was hoped, hit the ship.

The briefer unnecessarily added, "It would be surprising if the fighter chase crew could capture any decent footage. In the past they had trouble arriving at the proper position at launch time and just couldn't seem to be able to stay up with the missile as it navigated to the target. The A-6 chase teams, added the briefer, "seemed to produce much-better photo coverage."

This footnote may have been tossed in as bait, it may have been a true statement, or it could have been both, but it was an unwelcome input, especially in front of the admiral and the commanding officer of the Black Lions. At that moment, the briefer, unknowingly, made the highest-quality photo coverage ever recorded a personal mission for Hawk.

Weasel made a smooth join-up on Hawk and Bull Dog as they navigated toward the firing ship. They checked in with the exercise controllers and set up a racetrack pattern 3,000 feet overhead the firing ship. One delay followed another as the shooter positioned and then repositioned them to keep the AGIs as far away from the firing corridor as possible.

When everything appeared to be ready, the controller commenced the countdown from T minus sixty.

Masks were snugged up, visors lowered, harnesses locked, and recorders punched on. Bull Dog checked and rechecked his camera, and Weasel took a comfortable tactical wing formation on Hawk. Hawk adjusted his airspeed and radius of turn to be abeam the ship at exactly 50 feet and precisely at 500 knots punctiliously at T minus zero. Everything was working out perfectly.

At T minus twenty-five seconds the controllers announced a one-minute suspension of the countdown. Hawk exhaled deeply, eased off his turn, and headed for a point overhead the ship that would allow him to be in position when the countdown resumed. A minute later the countdown began again, this time from T minus twenty-five. That was the first surprise.

Fifteen seconds later the controller announced a second one-minute suspension of the countdown. Hawk again turned to reposition his aircraft to continue, but ten seconds later, not the minute that they had announced, the countdown resumed and this time there was only ten seconds to go to for T minus zero and missile ignition. Surprise number 2!

No wonder these morons had so much trouble getting good photo coverage, Hawk thought. *The other Tomcat chase crews weren't given any time to maneuver to the right position when the Harpoon came out of the tube. I guess the controllers don't understand that a suspension of the countdown doesn't magically freeze all the chase aircraft in place. They still had to continue to maneuver and adjust their position.*

"Ten . . . nine . . . eight . . ."

Hawk was at 3,000 feet and at 350 knots and headed nearly opposite the direction of the firing corridor. It was nearly an impossible position to complete any acceptable turn to maneuver to their designated position by launch time.

"I can still make this work," Hawk muttered to himself. "Weasel, pull up and right. Stay clear and keep me in sight," Hawk growled over the radio. And to Bull Dog he said, "Hang on to your camera. I'm coming around hard!"

With that, Hawk thumbed the maneuvering flaps down, rolled inverted, and heaved the stick back in his lap. He initially squeaked off a handful of power to get the nose to tuck under, but as soon as the nose completed 90 degrees of pitch, as soon as it was through the vertical and arcing back to the opposite horizon, he stuffed both throttles into full afterburner.

He put over 5 g on his airplane and dipped slightly below an altitude of 100 feet, at the bottom of the oblique split "S" maneuver. He lost over 100 knots in the maneuver, but a heartbeat later, when the thunderous blowers kicked in, his Tomcat had catapulted through 480 knots. He expertly modulated the throttles to stabilize at 500 knots and about the same time comfortably settled at an altitude of 50 feet. Miraculously he had his Tomcat perfectly abeam the ship. *If they're actually on time this go-around, this is gonna work out!*

He checked aft of his wing and was happy to see that Weasel had anticipated the maneuver and was in a comfortable loose-deuce position.

To the casual observer aboard *Radford*, it may have looked like a well-rehearsed air show. The Tomcat, with not a whole lot of altitude to begin with, rolled inverted and pulled toward the water, skimmed within a few feet of the ocean, and leveled off at 50 feet.

Hawk's Tomcat was exactly abeam the ship, pointed in the direction of the firing corridor, precisely at an altitude of 50 feet and spot-on 500 knots. No sooner had Hawk come alongside the ship than a tremendous orange ball of flame erupted aboard the ship, and a long white pipe, having all the features of a telephone pole, emerged. The solid-propellant booster motor pushed the missile out of the tube and to the profile altitude and velocity just seconds after firing. Then the Teledyne booster jettisoned from the missile as it began a gentle arc toward the sea. Less than two seconds later the turbojet fired and accelerated the 12.5-foot missile to 500 knots.

Hawk quickly glanced in his rearview mirror to see how Bull Dog was handling the rollercoaster ride. Bull Dog, without a peep, filmed the entire launch. To Hawk's complete amazement, he had the camera steadied and trained on the missile as it breached the tube.

"Weasel, how ya doin'?" Hawk asked.

"Half a mile in trail, Hawk. We're good!" Weasel reported.

"Roger!"

The Harpoon cruised at 500 knots under the cloud layer as it made small heading and altitude corrections during the 50- mile run to the target. The cruise portion of the profile was uneventful. The missile was stable, and Hawk easily maintained position on the Harpoon, allowing Bull Dog to keep the camera rolling. Hawk was alert to the thin overcast layer the weather guesser spoke of at 1,000 feet, but it wasn't "thin." It turned out to be a broken layer about 500 feet thick. That could be a problem during the missile's terminal pop-up maneuver.

The Harpoon continued to the target on altitude, on airspeed, and on course. A few miles from the hulk, the Harpoon, as advertised, made an abrupt pitch-up. Hawk announced on the radio, "Weasel, the missile's popping. Give me some room." Hawk eased back on the stick while holding position on the missile as he followed it through the overcast. Without leveling off, the Harpoon hit the apex of its trajectory, then began to arc downward. Rather than push the stick forward, which would have left both Hawk and Bull Dog hanging in their straps, Hawk made a gentle canopy roll around the missile as it descended. This gave Bull Dog a clear shot at both sides and the top of the missile in its final dive—something the PMTC controllers had never dared hope for.

Hawk followed the missile through the cloud layer. As the missile continued its terminal attack on the target ship, Hawk broke away.

The missile continued its dive through a broken section of clouds. Bull Dog recorded the final seconds of the missile flight as it contacted the masthead and then bounced off the superstructure and disintegrated, showering the surrounding sea with scores of missile parts.

"Baby green!" Hawk announced on the UHF, signaling a good hit. "Baby direct green!" he repeated.

There was no immense ball of flame, no concussion wave, and no frag pattern. The Harpoon, in this case, was loaded with a practice warhead. Had it carried a live warhead, the surrounding water would quickly have become a large, frothy oil slick covered with debris, and likely caused sufficient damage to send the hulk to the bottom of the sea.

Hawk's section returned to the ship. The four aircrew climbed out of their cockpits and made their way to the debrief. They knew at once it was a good photo shoot, a very successful mission for PMTC, but it wasn't until the exercise director, now in his crow-eating mode, announced, "That was a great job, Skipper. And the photo coverage . . . well, despite the cloud cover, it was the best photo coverage we've ever had. Thanks to you and your team."

"On behalf of the Black Lion team," Hawk replied, "glad we could help. It's a pleasure to serve."

Hawk, sensing the debrief had concluded, turned and led his three aircrew back to the ready room.

Not a word was spoken among the aircrew. There was no need. There was quiet personal jubilation as they reveled in their accomplishment.

During the three-day open-ocean MissilEx, not a single flight of Libyan aircraft was reported anywhere near the exercise area, nor were there any further chest-beating announcements from the Libyan dictator.

National Week XXVII was hailed a tremendous success. All tasks were completed and there were no international incidents, mishaps, or fatalities. *America* brought her helm north for a port call to Marseilles, France. As it turned out, this would be the only port visit to a French city during the deployment.

MAYDAY from Bad Bob

It was late August when Hawk received a letter, an impassioned MAYDAY call, from one of his star instructors at TOPGUN, Dan "Bad Bob" McCort. Bad Bob explained that after completing a demanding but successful three-year tour at TOPGUN, he had received orders to a Phantom squadron aboard USS *Midway*, home-ported in Japan.

Orders to a Phantom outfit as a department head could cause terminal consequences to an officer's career. In order to remain competitive and keep command opportunities open, fighter crews needed to stay in the Navy's frontline fighter—the Tomcat.

Bad Bob explained that while most of his contemporaries had joined the swelling exodus from the Navy to chase lucrative airline careers, he had decided to stay in. The only reason he didn't leave the Navy was due to Hawk's inspirational leadership while he was skipper of TOPGUN. Although Bad Bob had arrived at TOPGUN later in Hawk's tour, clearly Hawk had made an indelible impression on Bad Bob.

And Bad Bob was not alone. Hawk had made a long-lasting impression on many of his junior officers during those dark days when TOPGUN was under the constant bombardment by the then-current fighter wing commander, RAdm. Fenner. Fenner was no fan of the distinguished and preeminent TOPGUN. Many of those who knew RAdm. Fenner surmised that he was narcissistic enough to believe that TOPGUN was sucking the oxygen out of his command, and acrimonious enough to do something about it. After failing to develop any traction following a half-dozen judge advocate general (JAG) investigations directed at Hawk and TOPGUN, the admiral believed he had stumbled upon a possible serious violation of the Uniform Code of Military Justice (UCMJ) in the then-famous Christmas card fiasco. The admiral gleefully and vigorously pursued this incident. The rest is history.

Bad Bob was new to the command when this miscarriage of justice took place, but like all the TOPGUN instructors, he joined the cabal, putting his naval career on the line in a supreme act of loyalty and personal sacrifice.

In regard to his current dilemma, Bad Bob remembered the TOPGUN Christmas card debacle and turned to the man for whom he held the highest respect—the one man he knew who would put his shoulders into righting a grave wrong.

Upon reading Bad Bob's letter, Hawk recalled at once what a tactical powerhouse and exceptional professional this young naval officer was. The Navy had invested a great deal of resources in this officer, and in return, Bad Bob had repaid the Navy and the nation many times over. Hawk immediately went into action.

In a hand-penned letter to the new commander of the fighter wing, RAdm. Paul T. Gillcrist, Hawk scripted an ironclad case to reassign Lt. Cmdr. McCort to a department head position in a Miramar-based "Tomcat" squadron.

"Dear Admiral Gillcrist," the letter began, "please allow me to introduce myself. I am the proud commanding officer of VF-213 and recent CO of TOPGUN. Lt. Cmdr. Dan McCort has asked for my assistance in requesting reassignment to an F-14 squadron. I can testify that he is an extremely safe, tactically proficient fighter pilot, imbued with exceptional airmanship skills and devotion to the Navy. In short, he is an extraordinary naval officer and a superb fighter pilot in all respects.

"He has recently received orders to a Phantom squadron aboard USS *Midway*. In my mind, this is a waste of talent and patently wrong for the Navy. The F-14 community is in dire need of competent fighter pilots to continue the bloodline. His tactical skills and ability to instruct in the fighter mission should remain with the most advanced fighter commands in the Navy—the Tomcat squadrons. I respectfully request flag intervention to correct this. I appreciate your assistance in this matter, sir. Very respectfully, John M. Smith, commander, USN."

Hawk then attached Bad Bob's letter to his own and mailed it.

Hawk wrote a second letter to Bad Bob: "Badly, I received your letter and enclosed it with one of my own to Adm. Gillcrist requesting flag intervention for your F-14 orders. Currently, I'm at sea on the worst ship in the Navy and there's not much else I can do for now. Keep your knots up! Keep the faith. Keep the pressure on and don't let up! Hawk."

Although Hawk had never met RAdm. Gillcrist, he'd heard much about him. By all reports he was a straight shooter, a fair-minded officer, and a fighter pilot through and through. Hawk believed he would be willing to step into the fray. Now it was all up to the admiral.

The Far Turn

On August 8, *America* steamed out of Marseilles and headed south around Sardinia and promptly ran into a spectacular summer storm. According to the *America* Command History submission for 1979, the storm was "the roughest that *America* experienced during the entire deployment."

It rocked and heaved the 1,000-foot ship like a toy duck. The less nautically conditioned sailors completed a full operational checkout of all the ship's heads.

America arrived in Genoa, Italy, on August 13 for a brief stay. The prospective commanding officer of *America*, Capt. Rene "Sam" W. Leeds, came aboard and commenced turnover briefs with Capt. Meyer and the ship's department heads.

Heading to Augusta Bay to conduct Phase II of National Week XXVII on August 18, *America* passed through the Strait of Messina for the last time during the cruise. She anchored in Augusta Bay on August 21, where exercise officials conducted briefings aboard USS *Independence* in preparation for the exercise.

On August 23, ship's company and air wing personnel, decked out in their glimmering dress whites, assembled on deck for *America*'s change of command. Capt. Meyer turned his ship over to Capt. Leeds and then debarked to report to his new duty station: commander in chief of US Naval Forces Europe, in London.

Hawk hadn't given it much thought initially, but in the course of two months most of the officers in the highest leadership positions on the ship had been replaced: the air boss, the XO, the supply officer, and finally the CO of the ship. These were key positions aboard an aircraft carrier, and one would expect that a massive turnover in leadership would have an equally massive effect on morale and efficiency of the ship—and it did! The situation improved markedly.

It may have been a complete coincidence, but by Hawk's account, "Suddenly nothing was too hard. Since the mess officer had jumped ship in Yugoslavia, the mess ran far smoother and the chow was better. Since the new XO had come aboard, ship's company was more eager to repair habitability discrepancies. And since the new air boss had taken over, suddenly, mysteriously, the elevators seemed to operate just fine."

But the most spectacular change came after the replacement of the ship's supply officer. "When Cmdr. Ralph Parrot came aboard, inexplicably, the ship had all types of equipment and material. Aircraft parts were miraculously discovered, and often without the assistance of Senior Chief Bernie Mo or Nat Craig.

"The changes took awhile, but they were colossal. Scores of material discrepancies were slowly whittled down, aircraft availability skyrocketed, and, after a barrage of captain's masts convened by the new captain, there was a new wave of respect and discipline that swept over the ship. *America* began to function and look like the man-of-war she was. All of a sudden we were back on a Navy ship. The ship's company and air wing personnel began to pull together as a team. People were responsible, accountable, responsive, and respectful. This was extremely important and completely lacking under the old management."

Phase II of National Week XXVII began on August 24. On that day, the air wing commenced flight operations and flew around-the-clock for thirty-six hours without a break. It was tough for the flight crews, but it was even tougher on the plane captains and flight deck personnel. The aircrew could catch short combat naps between sorties and watches, but the plane captains and flight deck crews were expected to be at their post for as long as flight operations continued. "Those kids were amazing," Hawk commented. "They ran their asses off day and night. They took short naps between launches and ate sandwiches brought up from the mess when they could. Most amazingly, they never bitched, never whined, never failed to do their job, and never failed to take care of their shipmates. If these guys were any other kind of government employees or unionized labor, there would have been a strike and national outcry that would make headlines across the nation. You just can't find kids like these outside the military. They are absolutely something special!"

The exercise was completed on the afternoon of August 27. *America* anchored in Augusta Bay on August 28 for the debrief. By all measures, National Week XXVII was a complete success and the last exercise the *America* battle group would be involved in during the deployment.

That afternoon she weighed anchor and steamed around the south end of Sicily, through the strait of Sicily, and then turned to the west toward her last two ports of call: Valencia, Spain, for some well-deserved rest time, and then through the Strait of Gibraltar to Rota, Spain. From that point, she would head west—bound for home.

Convertible Tomcat

There was limited flying en route to Valencia, but during one night of carrier operations the LSOs highly recommended sending a Black Lion F-14 to the beach. It wasn't a particularly bad night for Weasel Forchets, but it was his turn in the barrel. In LSO parlance, "he was looking ugly on the ball!"

"He had a hell of a time getting aboard," Hawk remembers. "No tankers were available, and with no indications that his night approaches were improving. He was sent to the nearest suitable bingo field, Palermo, Sicily."

In an amazing example of everything going wrong that could go wrong, Weasel's misadventure unfolds.

Weasel and his RIO landed safely at Palermo, but their Tomcat was loaded with one Sidewinder, a Sparrow, and the world's most sophisticated and highly classified missile: the AIM-54 Phoenix. They discovered that the pins for the missiles and the magnetic hood for the Sidewinder were not aboard the aircraft. To add to the problem, there were no US military units available to provide security for the aircraft or missiles. The supersecret Phoenix was not something that was left hanging around on an airplane without dedicated, armed security.

The soup thickens!

Armed with pencil flares and shroud cutters, Weasel and his RIO spent the entire night on the flight line guarding their airplane and the Phoenix.

The next morning, Weasel discovered that Palermo had start carts but no JP-5. Weasel passed this information back to the ship. This represented a problem, but Hawk offered a simple solution: VA-95 could launch a KA-6 tanker, have the refueling system checked "sweet,"[3] then fly to Palermo. Meanwhile, Hawk would fly to Palermo on a HS-12 helo and, with what fuel remained in Weasel's Tomcat, take off, hit the tanker overhead, and return to the ship with the tanker. Problem solved!

It was a perfectly sound solution and promoted the least chaos. CAG Ready accepted the plan. Capt. Turk, the admiral's chief of staff, rejected it. He had another, slightly more complex plan.

A fuel truck would roll to Palermo and fuel the Tomcat. The ship's COD would fly a new crew into Palermo with the missile pins and the Sidewinder hood and bring Weasel and his RIO back to the ship. So far so good—but then the plan diverged into an area of many uncertainties. Since *America* was still trying to out-chop according to the cruise schedule, she was steaming west, and no flight operations were scheduled until she completed her port call in Valencia. The replacement Tomcat crew would therefore fly from Palermo to Rota. When the ship pulled out of Valencia and made for open sea, they could recover aboard the ship.

The first part of the plan proceeded without a glitch. A COD flew to Palermo, and Weasel and his RIO were replaced by Tom "Rookie" More and Bob "Ranger" Feist. With the Tomcat refueled, they launched out of Palermo for the long trip to Rota. Meanwhile, CVW-11 staff fired a message to Naval Base Rota, requesting armed Marine security for the Tomcat upon arrival.

Rookie and Ranger arrived at Rota without incident. They installed the missile safety pins and Sidewinder hood and assisted in servicing the aircraft. A young Marine was *volunteered* as a security guard. When he arrived at the airplane, armed and enthusiastic, Rookie and Ranger explained the significance of the three missiles, especially the big ugly one, the Phoenix. The aircrew departed for the BOQ just as night fell, and, with the Marine watching over their airplane, all was well . . . for a time.

The early September evenings in the Med couldn't be considered cold, but the young Marine, taught to "innovate, adapt, overcome" and make best use of available resources, realized it would be far cozier in the cockpit of the F-14 than outside, and from there, he reasoned, he could still provide security. There was only one impediment to the plan—gaining access to the cockpit. The resourceful Marine surveyed the outside of the cockpit area and discovered a small panel with stenciling. He couldn't quite make out the words in the poor light but realized it had something to do with the canopy. Not to be thwarted by the details, he thought it was the control to raise the canopy—and it was—but only once.

The Marine opened the panel, grasped the handle, and realized it was connected to a very long lanyard. That should have warned him that it was not the prescribed device to open the canopy. It should have, but it didn't.

The Marine backed away from the Tomcat, uncoiling the lanyard as he went, farther and farther until he hit the end of the lanyard. An ever-so-slight tug on the handle and, as advertised, the canopy opened.

KABLAM!!!

The explosive cartridge fired and sent thousands of dollars' worth of canopy twirling end over end, narrowly missing the tail section of the Tomcat.

Message traffic sizzled over the airwaves between Rota, the ship, and Washington, DC. In response to Rota's message describing the situation, "Marine guard inadvertently jettisoned canopy from VF-213 F-14A. Missiles, AIM-7F (1), AIM-9F (1), and AIM-54 (1), aboard and intact."

Due to the sensitive nature of the subject and to avoid offending other parties that might be on distribution, key explanatory text within the message was encrypted in "aviator acronyms"—"GF," YGTBSM," WTFO," and "HS," and other coded exclamations were liberally salted throughout the narrative.

Because a Phoenix missile happened to be on board the Tomcat, the message precedent was elevated to "FLASH," and that precedence gave it automatic distribution to CNO's watch team at the National Command Center. There it gained considerably more attention than anyone had anticipated, and also prompted action on a second front. The unencrypted acronyms caught the eye and elevated the angst of National Command Center, which demanded an explanation from the CNO watch team of the unusual and unlisted code acronyms. Try as they might, the watch team could not decipher the code words, so they fired off a tersely worded message calling for "plain language" wording.

Oops!

The message was received by the ship's comm center and immediately routed to the CO of VF-213. There was no way to soft-peddle the wording. The response from *America* back to CNO and NSC reluctantly explained the codes: "GF"—Great fuck; "YGTBSM"—You've got to be shitting me; "WTFO"—What the fuck, over; and "HS"—Holy shit.

The embarrassment was indescribable and captured far more attention in places high up the military and national chain of command than the actual canopy-jettisoning incident ever would have.

On September 10, *America* pulled into Rota, Spain, and dropped anchor. The Black Lions' convertible Tomcat was barged from the beach to the ship and then craned aboard.

"It was a rough and angry sea that day," Hawk recalls. "And a sad sight to see our Tomcat swaying back and forth under the crane. By this time there wasn't one thing that could have gone wrong that hadn't, and I was fully prepared to watch our Tomcat slip the cables and turn into an artificial reef. I was very relieved, even surprised, when my Tomcat was gently set down on the flight deck! That was one of the first things that hadn't gone wrong. I just couldn't believe all the high-level attention this got, but it was just par for the course on this cruise."

America Turnover with *Nimitz*

America pulled out of her last overseas port on September 12. She plowed into the Atlantic on a westerly course, making good speed that would have them back in nine days.

Two days later, a section of Black Lion Tomcats were launched to intercept two Tu-95 Bear Ds attempting to locate and surveil the *America* battle group. Shortly after the Bears were intercepted, they turned back to the north without ever having come within visual range of any of the battle group.

USS *Nimitz* joined *America* as she steamed west to conduct an underway, blue-water turnover on September 15. Shortly after the turnover, the battle group received a farewell message from VAdm. W. N. Small, commander of 6th Fleet: "As an extremely successful Mediterranean deployment draws to a close, you are deserving of special recognition. By playing host to ambassadors, flag officers, mayors, and countless distinguished visitors from the US and foreign nations, you have once again extended *America*'s hand of friendship and have helped people understand the importance of the US role in keeping world peace. As the *America*/CVW-11 team returns home, you can be confident in your abilities and secure in the knowledge that you have succeeded in your mission. Well Done!"

Aside from the initial frustrations of the supply system, habitability, condition of the ship, discipline of ship's company, and the loss of too many lives and aircraft, it was a successful cruise.

Adm. Small's plaudits and high praise were right on point. But to Hawk, it would always be remembered as the worst cruise of his life on the worst ship in the Navy.

CHAPTER 5

Homeward Bound

*"Mom, when I grow up
I want to be a Navy fighter pilot."
"Son, make up your mind—you can't do both."*

—Source unknown

Animal House

The *America* battle group still had a seven-day voyage ahead of them following the turnover with USS *Nimitz* on September 15. Hawk, and by now the great preponderance of the crew, half-expected something catastrophic—a major event aboard the ship or a military flare-up in the Atlantic—to erupt, which would cause a major delay in the crossing schedule. Remarkably, nothing did.

As the days to their out-chop from 6th Fleet ticked down, tension and edginess among *America*'s crew were supplanted by a phenomenon well known since men went to sea in wooden ships—*channel fever*. It was a condition characterized by unaccountable restlessness, excitement, anxiety, and great relief after surviving a long period at sea and in anticipation of coming home.

Throughout the ship, a resurrection of zeal, joy, and positive attitudes was measurable. And even those once-sour relationships between the air wing and ship's crew were now almost collegial. Men dreamed of holding their wives, children, and loved ones, of returning to their normal, humdrum lives. Even the simplest acts of home life—mowing the lawn, taking the dog for walks, fishing, barbecue, and driving—began to occupy their thoughts all through the day and night. And there was no inoculation known for this insomnia and nocturnal wanderings. Home now was not such a distant thing, and all was good.

These symptoms were perhaps even more prevalent within the Black Lion crew who had something of a head start in the buffoonery department. But from the perspective of the Black Lion skipper, Hawk couldn't have been happier with the conduct of his team. Through it all, the JOs' perpetual, effervescent, and unsinkable wit made the best of a bad cruise. The humor, camaraderie, innovation, and eternal spirit were best epitomized in their attitude around the ready room, and nothing gave the JOs a better opportunity to express themselves than during the nightly movies.

"You want to talk about something memorable," Hawk explained, "the ready room demeanor was just great. The guys were always getting into something. Great flicks and world-class shadow images on the projector screen. They had model aircraft that flew through the projector light, and Spike Prendergast treated us to his stupid, dog-finger puppet show. No matter what movie was showing, suddenly this shadow dog would pop up from nowhere and start sniffing some girl's butt or chasing an aircraft shadow across the screen. It would just break you up.

"One night during a cowboy movie, a pair of boots fell out of the overhead right in the path of the projector light and just sat there dangling. No one claimed them; no one took any notice of them. They just hung there in the flickering projector light until the end of the movie. You just never knew what these guys were going to do.

"When I look back on it, I realize it was pretty silly, but at the time, considering what we were going through, it was just the levity and the departure from reality we needed. It was the best medicine. That kind of foolhardy, crazy rambunctiousness kept our heads on straight and kept us focused on what was important. It was one of those unexplainable cruise phenomena. No one can describe the importance of those little bright spots in maintaining balance and holding the fellowship together. The talent in the squadron—the grab-ass, slapstick humor; joviality; and originality . . . was limitless and very necessary."

On September 21, 1979, six-days after *America* out-chopped, the Med was thousands of miles in her wake. It was the night before the fly-off. They had completed the last of the Bear alerts, and channel fever had an unholy grip on the crew.

It was getting late on the evening before the fly-off when Hawk packed the last of his gear in two parachute bags and strolled down to the ready room. "What's the movie tonight?" he asked the duty officer

"Don't know, Skipper," he chirped.

Don't know? That's strange. One of the primary responsibilities of the duty officer was to be on top of the nightly movie, Hawk considered. *What's even stranger is that no one is even here, and it's almost time to roll the flick. Something's up!*

"Where is everybody?"

"Don't know that either, sir. Let me make a call." And with that, the duty officer picked up the phone, dialed a couple of numbers, and mumbled something into the mouthpiece. Two minutes later, the ready room door flew open and the JOs started filing in wearing black horned-rimmed glasses and white sheets stripped from their bunks. The serpentine-column filed into the ready room, and the chanting began: "Toga! Toga! Toga!"

Well, that was the answer to both of the skipper's questions. The JOs had been lying in wait until he arrived to make a proper entrance, and the movie for the night was *Animal House*.

Animal House (1978) had ascended to the reigning position of best of the cruise flicks, and no wonder—the similarity between the antics in the movie and the events of the cruise were not lost on the Black Lion crew.

As soon as the movie rolled, shadow airplanes chased frat rats across the screen and finger-dog-sniffed Dean Vernon Wormer's wife's posterior, all movie lines were repeated by a chorus of faithful *Animal House* cult members, and, on cue, John Belushi's famous "Guess what I am?" scene took on exciting new realism with the help of the entire ready room.

"It was a night to remember, and it was incredible. The guys were rowdy and having a great time. We were all celebrating getting off that friggin' boat and making it to the end of cruise . . . alive. And even though only fourteen guys were going to fly off the next morning in the seven airplanes we had up, everybody was happy for them and joined in the celebration."

Chaos at Cannon

As hard as the maintenance team had worked, three of VF-213's ten Tomcats were still hard down. But barring an engine simply falling out of the engine bay and onto the flight deck, the jets on the flight schedule were going to launch. Airplanes headed for home never go down.

The remaining seven Black Lions' jets and those of the Aardvarks were shot into the sky early on the morning of September 21 for the cross-country trip to their home base, NAS Miramar. The Black Lions and Aardvarks made their first stop at NAS Oceana for fuel and to "decarrierize"[1] the tires.

While six of the Lions' Tomcats departed for their next two refueling stops—Little Rock AFB followed by Cannon AFB—Hawk enjoyed a long-awaited but short reunion with his parents.

Hawk said his goodbyes, then he and chief mounted up and launched for Cannon to link up with the rest of the squadron.

It was dusk, and a large rain shower had just swept through Cannon when Hawk and Chief started their en route descent. The weather was clear overhead, but there was standing water on the runway—breaking could be a problem.

As soon as Hawk switched from center to the tower frequency, he sensed something was amiss at Cannon. The Cannon tower controller, speaking to another Navy airplane, was clearly agitated. He was trying to divert that jet to another field, and apparently without much success. "Dragon four-zero-seven we have an aircraft off the runway at the intersection with blown tires. I say again—the runway is closed!"

Whoa! This ain't good! Dragon? That's the Golden Dragons of VA-192! They're not supposed to be here. They were going to stop over at NAS Albuquerque. What the hell?

"Cannon tower, Dragon four-zero-seven, be advised I've just made a weather divert from Albuquerque. I'm emergency fuel and I need to land—NOW!"

"Dragon four-zero-seven, understand your situation; however, the runway is closed. You can't land here!"

Oh, oh! If the runway is closed, we're in a bit of a predicament ourselves.

"Tower, Bravo Sierra.[2] I've got nowhere else to go. I'm landing here! Dragon four-zero-seven is abeam, gear down, full stop."

Silence from the tower replaced the normal "Cleared to land" announcement.

Several seconds later, the silence was suddenly shattered by a disturbing interrogative from the tower: "Dragon four-zero-seven, do you need assistance?"

"Hell yes, I need assistance. I just blew my tires!"

Just inside 10 miles away, Hawk could just make out the runway, and it appeared that there were two aircraft clobbering the runway.

Hawk, still several miles from the runway, announced his intentions: "Cannon tower, Black Lion two-oh-three, single F-14, 8 miles for the overhead."

It may have been that Cannon tower had finally realized the full impact of the problem the weather had caused, or, more likely, they may have just given up any hope of "controlling" Navy aircraft. Whatever the reason, Hawk and Chief received clearance to land.

"Black Lion two-zero-three, roger. Caution the A-7 off the runway at the intersection and a second A-7 off the runway at the overrun. You're cleared for the overhead. Report base."

As Hawk approached the runway, he spotted the A-7 at the intersection. He looked farther down the runway, in the overrun area, and was shocked to see something indistinguishable sitting in the middle of a large charred area, an area that appeared to have been the center of a very hot fire. For just a moment it took Hawk's breath away. *Did one of the Dragon's A-7s catch on fire on the runway? Impossible! I would have seen the flames and smoke.*

Hawk switched his attention to the task of getting his 20-ton jet stopped and avoiding the A-7 hulks on the side of a very wet runway.

Hawk squeaked his Tomcat onto the concrete and aerobraked the 63-foot jet to minimize the hydroplaning effects of standing water on the runway. They passed the first "World-Famous Golden Dragon" leaning awkwardly to one side at the intersection. At the end of the runway he was very relieved to see that the second Golden Dragon, stopped in the middle of the charred area, was not the source of the singed concrete. Luckily, the A-7 simply came to a stop in the center of a charred area after the main mounts blew. Hawk was also happy to see the other six Black Lion aircraft sitting safely chalked and chained in the transient line.

Hawk and Chief secured their jet and made a high-speed run to the officer's club to link up with their team and discover what had happened.

As Hawk and Chief entered the O Club, it was obvious that a party of sorts was in full swing. The Lions and a few Golden Dragons were whooping it up, but the skipper of the Dragons, Cmdr. Tom Latendresse, was not partaking in the festivities, and he wasn't alone. He was huddled at a small table against the wall with a US Air Force full bird colonel, reported to be the base safety officer. Both the skipper and the colonel looked grim.

Hawk mingled with the other fliers and gathered the facts. The Golden Dragons diverted to Cannon when a squall line ripped through their original destination, Albuquerque. They had not depressurized their tires, which significantly reduced their effectiveness on wet fields and often led to blowouts under the control of heavy-footed pilots. One Dragon blew a main mount and came to rest at the intersection of the runways. Another Dragon blew both main mounts and came to a stop in the center of an area where, the night before, an F-111 caught fire and burned to a crisp.

The tower controllers became annoyed when the first Corsair fouled their runway, but they became absolutely incensed when the second A-7 landed without clearance and blew both main mounts.

It is an age-old dictum that shit rolls "downhill" (it's a gravity thing), but first an "issue" must be created and then ascend "uphill." There it is transformed into "shit" so it can then roll or, in this case, fall heavily "downhill."

The Cannon tower controllers complained to the tower supervisor (issue creation and ascension), who complained to the base safety officer (issue transformation), who lambasted the Golden Dragon skipper (shit free fall to impact).

Hawk observed the mannerisms and body language of the two officers. Hawk had had his own run-ins with staff pukes in the Air Force and the Navy. He knew from experience that if it was approached incorrectly, one could win the fight but lose the war. There was going to be a big "to do" about this, all right, and Skipper Latendresse wasn't going anywhere, fly-off or not, until the incident was fully investigated, evaluated, and reported—in triplicate! Hawk decided then and there that *this boy needs some high cover!*

"Tom wasn't restricted to quarters. The safety officer didn't have that authority, but he did have the authority to impound all the Corsairs pending a full investigation, and therefore nothing starting with an "A"—as in "A-7"—was going to depart from Cannon AFB for a while.

Budley to the Rescue

Cmdr. Bud Ore, call sign "Budman," was assigned to commander, Light Attack Wing Pacific, at NAS Lemoore as the operations officer. As soon as he got wind of the problem at Cannon, he went into action. He quickly made contact with a VA-147 JO at Cannon to determine what was needed to repair the A-7s. He then requisitioned a Corsair, had three main mounts bolted to the bomb racks, and launched from NAS Lemoore, bound for Cannon AFB. He arrived in the evening, not long after Hawk had landed.

Bud, "Budley" to his friends, and Hawk had been squadron LSOs on USS *Saratoga* during the 1969 Med cruise. They were good friends and had maintained that friendship through the years. Hawk's meeting with Budley was certainly an unexpected welcome, but it was primarily a rescue mission from God. Budley's task was to rescue a wingman and bring the A-7s of the "World-Famous Golden Dragons" home.

Hawk, with all the smoothness and grace of a career statesman, grabbed Budley and Chief and rolled in on the base safety officer.

They casually wandered over to the table and asked to join them. When the colonel invited them to sit down, the three officers pulled up chairs and squeezed in. Hawk began the conversation by respectfully explaining that they were coming off a long, hard cruise. He mentioned that they hadn't seen their families in almost seven months, and bought the colonel a drink.

The colonel was polite but remained aloof. Hawk articulated the significance of their deployment, the worst in Hawk's recollection, explained their long-awaited trek to the West Coast, recounted the fly-off, and bought him another drink.

Hawk explained the issues with the weather at their original destination and detailed the problems with carrier-pressurized tires. Another round of drinks materialized. The colonel softened.

Bud and Chief were there for top cover. They provided well-timed "Ah-men!" exclamations, and one could almost hear the Baptist chorus in the background. There were plenty of well-placed affirmation head nods to verify that everything Hawk chronicled was gospel.

Another round of adult nectar.

Through it all, the colonel quietly weighed all the information and savored the gratuitous libations. He wore wings, silver, not gold, but clearly he sympathized with their predicament. He listened intently.

Hawk laid the story before him. Some of the grimness began to fade from his face. As Hawk's delivery came to a crescendo, supported by vigorous and well-timed head nods from Bud and Chief, the colonel looked sternly at the four officers. His eyes dropped to his hands, cupped around his cocktail, and he was deep in thought. When he again looked at the officers, much of the tension had been replaced by understanding. It was clear he had made a decision. There would be no violation, no investigation, no report, and the Golden Dragons could depart Cannon the following day.

Hawk, Budman, Chief, and Tom Latendresse were ecstatic. They had turned the tables from vanquished to victorious! In Hawk's words, "We'd just saved a brother. We were at the peak, the very pinnacle of self-actualization. We couldn't be happier. We couldn't be taller, or louder, or smarter, or richer, or better looking. We bought the entire bar a round; in fact we bought several, as I remember. We weren't prisoners on USS *America* anymore. We had just won an engagement, a small one by any measure, but it was a titanic victory for us. We just saved a brother, and we were all headed home!

"It was a great night. We spent a lot of money, but it was cruise money, and you just can't spend all your money during cruise. The safety officer turned out to be a great guy and really helped us out—especially Skipper Latendresse."

Home Is the Sailor

It was a one-leg flight from Cannon to Miramar and, compared to the previous day's events at Cannon, uneventful. Hawk had all seven Tomcats together in a single flight. The weather was VFR[3] at cruise altitude and was forecast to remain so at their destination.

"Black Lion One, Los Angeles Center," the center controller transmitted, "we'll start you down from altitude, but we'd like to break your formation up to facilitate entry into Miramar airspace."

"Negative, center!" Hawk immediately retorted. "Just give me headings and altitudes. We'll keep the formation closed up tight and will be right on the numbers. All you'll see on your screen will be one return."

"Ah . . . roger, Black Lion. We can do that. Thanks! And welcome home, Black Lions!"

Los Angeles Center minimized the vectors, brought them down from the jet route structure, and turned them over to San Diego Approach.

Hawk could see Miramar 30 miles away. He and his boys were now just minutes from home, moments away from the warm embrace of family, loved ones, and good friends.

"Let's get them into the break formation, Chief."

"Roger, Skipper!"

Chief passed hand signals from both sides of the cockpit, and the flight of seven F-14s began to transform into two formations: a four-plane arrowhead formation in the lead, stepped down and followed closely by a three-plane wedge formation.

"Miramar tower, Black Lion One with seven, approaching the numbers," Hawk transmitted over tower frequency."

"Roger, Black Lion One; you're cleared to break. Wind 2-7-zero at 12 knots."

Seven enormous Tomcats streaked inbound and thundered into the break. They flew tight over the runway, above the cheering spectators clustered below. From the ground, it was an exquisite formation and a welcome sight.

Hawk signaled for the break execution, and, just as he had briefed, the three aircraft in the wedge formation executed a break in three-second intervals. Three seconds after the third aircraft had broken, the left wing of the diamond formation broke. The interval continued until all seven Tomcats had turned downwind in near-perfect interval.

The F-14s landed, cleared the duty runway, and taxied to base operations. When all aircraft had been chocked and pinned, Hawk keyed the radio and, per the brief, transmitted, "Lions, cut . . . now!" At that instant, the thunder of the TF30 engines was replaced by the whine of the turbine sections and the "clackity-clack" of the compressor blades as fourteen engines were shut down, followed by the lifting of seven canopies in unison.

Hawk and Chief exited the cockpit and strode toward the base of the tower, where the guests had gathered. Hawk easily picked out Miss Jenny and young Jack at the front of the crowd. Hawk was making good speed to Miss Jenny and his son when he was abruptly intercepted midstride by Capt. Huiseman, operations officer for FitWing. Hawk stopped when Huiseman stepped in front of him.

One of the very few advantages of being on cruise was avoiding the daily aggravation and politics of fighter wing, Hawk thought. *I know he isn't here to greet us on our return; that's just not his style. So just what game is he playing?*

"Welcome home, Skipper," Huiseman said.

This is a surprise. Maybe I had this figured wrong. I was sure he was here to rub my nose in something. "Thank you, sir! It's good to be home."

"Adm. Gillcrist couldn't be here. He had to go to DC. I just wanted to let you know he isn't going to be able to do anything about Lt. Cmdr. McCort's request for orders to a Tomcat outfit."

Ah . . . that's why he's here. Welcome home, Hawk! Is it just this guy or is there a conspiracy in the staff ranks not to give a shit about our people?

Hawk hoped that somehow Huiseman had his information wrong.

"Well, that's not good, Captain. Bad Bob's an extraordinary naval officer and a hell of a fighter pilot. He's sacrificed a lot to make our community better. It'd be a shame to lose him."

Huiseman's mouth came open. He was about to form a witty reply when Hawk stepped around him and continued his march to his wife and son.

Ten seconds after Hawk had his arms wrapped around Miss Jenny, her fragrance wafting up to great him, with little Jack hugging Hawk's leg, he had effectively compartmentalized the whole incident.

Home is the sailor, home from the sea.

CHAPTER 6

"On the Beach"

When I was young, I was completely caught up in building and racing anything with wheels. There was nothing I couldn't tear down and rebuild and make it even faster. It had been a longtime dream of mine to own a junkyard. Just imagine all the engines, drivetrains, and other parts you could have all in one place. Just think of all the cars you could redesign and rebuild!

—Capt. John Monroe "Hawk" Smith

Forging Alliances

Hawk drove to the squadron late in the morning the following day. He linked up with his new prospective XO (PXO), Cmdr. Jim "Comet" Haley.

Cmdr. Haley had reported aboard and took over the beach det a few months before the Black Lions returned from cruise. It was Hawk's plan to keep him on the beach rather than have him report aboard *America*, and it was a sound approach for several reasons. Not only did it give Hawk's senior lieutenant commander, "Crash" Zahalka, an opportunity to test his steel in the very demanding position of acting XO, it also allowed Comet to organize the beach detachment, commence training of the newly assigned sailors, and ready the hangar spaces for the squadron's return.

It began as a beautiful day and only got better as the day progressed. Hawk was comfortably seated in his freshly painted office, an office comparatively small for the CEO of a company with nearly half a billion dollars in assets, but the appropriate size for the commanding officer of a Navy fighter squadron. There was another perk, however, that few company leaders could afford: the office was sitting just a few hundred yards from the runway of a master jet base with a ramp full of Tomcats and other Navy jets. Hawk wouldn't trade it for the world.

Hawk was in the midst of a pass-down brief with the PXO when he received a call from Bad Bob. It was good news. No . . . check that . . . it was great news. Bad Bob had received verbal orders to an F-14 squadron at Miramar. Bad Bob was ecstatic, and Hawk quietly let out a sigh of relief. And it was all because Hawk and RAdm. Gillcrist had campaigned to make it happen.

That's why the admiral wasn't at the fly-in, Hawk mused. *He was in DC, in part, to put pressure on the detailer to get orders for Bad Bob. The system worked, and it cost me only the price of a stamp.*

The second part of this news was that it made Capt. Huiseman look shallow. That revelation would, however, remain a closely held secret. Hawk would never lower himself to divulge such prattle in public.

Later that morning, Hawk's phone rang. "Good mornin'—Black Lions commander Smith speaking, sir."

"Hey, Skipper, Dick Scharff; I know you're probably pretty busy, but if you've got a few minutes, I'd like to come and shoot the shit with ya."

Cmdr. "Hard" Richard Scharff was the supply officer at Miramar and was reputed to be, in most circles, the best supply officer in the Navy. Hawk had heard of him.

"Dick, good morning. Sure, come on over. See ya soon!"

"Aye, aye, Skipper!"

Though he was in high regard at Fightertown, Hawk learned long ago to make his own judgments on the character of people; too often their reputations fell short of Hawk's expectations. He had to meet this guy in person.

Dick found his way to Hawk's office and politely tapped on the doorframe to get Hawk's attention. "Dick, come on in." Hawk stood to greet him.

Dick was a big guy, not too tall but nearly as wide as the doorframe. He had a big, genuine smile and was carrying a little more weight than he probably needed, but he was still well padded with the kind of muscles shaped and hardened as an athlete.

Hawk extended his hand and thought that he inadvertently stuck it into a walnut crusher. "Grab a seat, Dick."

Dick found a seat to his liking, sat down, and threw a beefy leg over the arm of the chair. He seemed completely trusting and quite at home with Hawk, a man he had never met. Hawk had become something of an expert at judging human nature, and this man before him he liked at once.

There was the customary small talk about recent events in Fightertown and questions about cruise, and finally Dick came to the subject of his visit.

"How're your airplanes, Skipper?"

"Well, Dick, it's like this . . ."

Dick lifted the floodgates and Hawk held nothing back. For the next hour, Hawk discussed parts issues during cruise, supply system issues, and pressure from fighter wing encouraging cannibalization actions, and detailed the inherent design flaws of the Tomcat that made it the most labor-intensive tactical aircraft in the Navy. Dick said hardly a peep, but he was leaning forward in his chair and locked on to everything Hawk said.

In the end, Dick said something important that indicated a larger problem at work. "Skipper, things have changed since RAdm. Gillcrist took over. We've got much more response from the wing when we need their support, but there are still big problems in the supply chain and parts support. There's a lot I can do, but I'll need the fighter squadron skippers and maintenance officers to come forward and tell it like it is so we can fix some of these problems."

Pay dirt!

"Dick, you need anything from me . . . anything . . . all you gotta do is ask!"

The rumor mill might be right for once—Dick Scharff might be the best aviation supply officer in the Navy.

Stand-Down

Ten days after the fly-in, the bulk of the Black Lions personnel, plus the tools, test gear, parts, manuals, ground support equipment, and servicing systems, had arrived back at Miramar.

The Black Lions were, again, back in the starting blocks, perched for another all-out lap on the turnaround cycle gridiron—and not much had changed since their last turnaround.

Hawk, Cmdr. Haley, and the department heads and chiefs had a delicate balancing act to perform. The troops had just returned, they were exhausted, but they were supposed to have thirty days for the customary postcruise stand-down to catch up on seven months of home repairs, car servicing, and family issues. The airplanes were beat, and along with their sister squadron, the Aardvarks, they were tail-end Charlie on the parts and supply chain—again! Unfortunately, to meet the long-range schedule, aircraft corrosion control inspections were in full swing, and an administrative and material inspection (ADMAT) was right around the corner. Unfortunately, the troops wouldn't be getting much time off—not yet.

By November's end, through a combination of solid leadership, focused commitment, and a titanic effort by the troops, the Black Lions completed a long list of postcruise maintenance inspections, but the next hurdle before them, and looming large, was the command ADMAT inspection by the fighter wing staff.

ADMAT Inspection

ADMATs, as do most inspections and reviews by higher authority, always cause a certain level of anxiety and concern, similar to a prostate exam by a former pro lineman turned doctor. In this case, over a dozen experienced chiefs and senior petty officers and several midgrade maintenance officers spent a week inspecting, reviewing, accounting for, and generally probing all the command written policies, records, and procedures. No pragmatic and experienced officer or chief petty officer takes them as "friendly" visits, nor should they. The inspectors come bearing gifts and grand smiles, but they are there to discover wrongdoing, procedural violations, and mishandling of funds.

This particular inspection went well . . . up to a point.

The official ADMAT inspection results were presented during the command inspection debrief. RAdm. Gillcrist, CAG Ready, his staff, all the wing inspectors, and the Black Lions' officers and chief petty officers were gathered in the ready room for the debrief. The inspectors praised the Black Lions officers and supervisors for their commendable efforts and courtesies. The grades reflected their hard work.

The upbeat tone of the comments suddenly took a left turn when the wing supply chief petty officer inspector came to the podium.

"Gentlemen," he began, "during my inspection in the supply department, I have discovered a violation of the ADMAT guidelines and what might become a major violation of the command's fiduciary authority."

This chief seemed to be relishing his moderate level of importance and perhaps had taken his own significance a bit too far.

"I have discovered that squadron funds have improperly—and without authorization—been used to purchase ship's equipment. According to my inspection, we have uncovered an unauthorized purchase of toilets, urinals, mirrors, and other equipment!"

The supply chief studied the crowd, measuring the impact. The inspector had just solved the mystery of the "Great Train Robbery," or so he acted.

But the chief never finished the delivery. He almost choked on words unsaid as Hawk rose slowly to his feet. He had had enough bullshit.

The ready room became deathly quiet.

"I think I know what you're referring to, Chief, and I think I know where this discussion's going, so before we go too far down a road I know none of us want to travel, let me explain how we got here."

"Admiral, let me say it like this . . . we weren't embarked aboard *America*; we were captured and imprisoned on the ship. It was the worst ship and the worst cruise I've ever been on. As a naval officer responsible for keeping my men healthy, safe, in reasonably good spirits, and with all the habitability facilities normally afforded to Navy personnel on a naval vessel according to Navy regulations, I took it as my solemn duty to provide those appropriate sanitary and habitability conditions the ship couldn't or wouldn't.

"Yes, we purchased the hardware and provided the labor to fix the head we were assigned. Between the two squadrons, we had nearly two hundred sailors who used one head. Less than half the shitters, urinals, and mirrors they were supposed to have actually worked. There were no toilet paper hangars and no shower curtains. My troops—US Navy seamen—had no privacy and were afforded no dignity in the course of their normal bodily functions. The ship simply refused to fix the problems.

"Frankly, sir, it was a goddamn embarrassment to me as a career naval officer that this condition, on a US Navy ship, was not only allowed to degrade to such a state of ill repair, but that it was not fixed after numerous attempts to bring these problems to the attention of ship's company per Navy procedures. To me, it was a sad and shameful statement reflecting the give-a-shit attitude that *America* leadership held for our sailors.

"Yes, sir, I used our funds to purchase toilets and other equipment, and yes, sir, I signed the requisition for all those items. And if that's a major discrepancy, if that's an unauthorized purchase, then fine, it's my fault; I'm the guy that authorized it and I'll take full responsibility.

"Admiral, I can explain this to you in detail later if you like. If anybody else has any more questions, ask me later."

Hawk sat down. For a moment it was as quiet as deep space.

The admiral stood and scanned the room. "Ah, um. Thank you, Chief. Anything else?"

The supply department inspector, now the color of a freshly cooked lobster, clearly had a number of rehearsed points to divulge, but he looked as though he just got his johnson caught in his zipper. "No, admiral" was all he said as he returned to his seat.

The rest of the inspection debrief went smoothly. Comments were succinct and full of praise.

When it was the admiral's turn to speak during the closing comments, he thanked his inspectors, the skipper, and the Black Lion team for their hospitality and their stellar inspection.

To the Black Lion chiefs and officers, this was a "stand-tall" moment, and as seen through the eyes of the Lions, it was a daring risk their skipper took on behalf of the squadron. Rarely did anyone cross swords with an inspection team leader during an ADMAT debrief, and certainly not in the presence of the admiral. At that moment, surrounded and outnumbered by the pagans, Hawk was their white knight standing ground and proudly holding their colors high.

Professionalism and decorum prevented any Black Lion member from demonstrating the slightest sign of admiration for their skipper, but inwardly there were many victory cartwheels.

Not a word was ever again spoken of an *unauthorized purchase*.

Hitting the Wall

Come December 1979, Hawk hit a morale low-water mark that rivaled his days in Indoc during Aviation Officer Candidate School (AOCS). Interestingly, his aggravation was caused by the confluence of three separate but related circumstances: the material condition and readiness of his aircraft, the perceived lack of high-level Navy leadership in light of the fighter community's downward spiral, and, finally, his own uncertain naval career.

It had been three months since they'd returned from cruise, and Hawk saw an exact duplication of obstructions and man-made tragedies that perpetuated the time compression problems and forced all the "just-in-time" scrambling that had made preparation for the previous cruise so difficult and stressful for his troops.

The Black Lions were short over 30 percent of their manpower. They were either reassigned to other commands or attending schools. Fuel was at an anemic level. But the biggest knee knocker wasn't fuel—it was, once again, aircraft parts. They were last on the supply priority list for parts. Only time would change that, but time was not something they had in surplus.

The Navy, like all the services, had finite funds, and everything seemed to be accomplished on a shoestring budget. There was only so much money to purchase so many parts, and those few parts were designated for the squadrons who needed them most—those already deployed and those in the last several months of preparation for deployment.

Hawk understood the system, but that didn't make it any more palatable. This practice, by design, pushed the great bulk of the training and aircrew certifications to the last few months of the turnaround cycle. It was an inefficient way to prepare for cruise, and, in Hawk's mind, it needlessly jeopardized the lives of his aircrew, the well-being of his men, and the material condition of their airplanes.

Although RAdm. Gillcrist and Dick Scharff were clearly in their court and exerting Herculean efforts to change the process, even they had come up against an apoplectic Navy embalmed by convention. Hawk, from his perch in the CO high tower, saw little to be optimistic about.

Finally, Hawk's many battle scars had weakened his resolve. He'd been in too many dogfights with the odds too often stacked against him, and had too few victory splashes on his canopy rail for the indignities he had suffered.

By Hawk's assessment, up to this point he was an accomplished man. He'd done everything he had ever dreamed of, and he had gone far further than a South Carolina country boy had a right to expect. In Hawk's mind he had finally ascended to the very pinnacle of his potential as a career naval officer, and his only concern was the terrible free fall that followed command and flying.

In his words, "I'd been the CO of the best squadron in the Navy and also the CO of one of the most lethal fighter squadrons in the world, and now . . . the end of my tour was in sight. My flying days were pretty much over, and there were only a few jobs that held any magic, any attraction, and any wonder for me.

"Being a CAG would be optimum," Hawk said in a moment of reflection. "Becoming a carrier skipper was beyond my imagination and, based on the TOPGUN Christmas card catastrophe, simply an impossible dream.

"Don't misunderstand—I mean, I cared about my men and our tactics, naval aviation, and my country, but as for climbing the flag ladder, I couldn't care less about schmoozing or politicking!

"When I was young, I was completely caught up in building and racing anything with wheels. There was nothing I couldn't tear down and rebuild to make it faster. It had been a longtime dream of mine to own a junkyard. Just imagine all the engines, drivetrains, and other parts you could have all in one place. Envision all the cars you could redesign and rebuild!

"Well, my junkyard dream was looking better and better."

Miss Jenny's Fire

For two weeks in December, Hawk cogitated on the state of his squadron, his Navy, and his life. On Christmas night 1979, he and Miss Jenny slid into their jacuzzi under a blanket of sparkling stars limned against a black-velvet sky.

Hawk was dark and solemn, and Miss Jenny sensed his burden. "Hawk, what's wrong with you? You hadn't peeped twice this whole evenin'?"

I'm not sure she wants to hear this. I'm not sure I even want to say it, but she asked, so here goes!

Hawk took a deep breath, scanned the night sky, then lowered his gaze and met Miss Jenny's ocean-blue eyes.

"Miss Jenny, I'm finished. I'm fed up with all the bullshit. Screw it! I'm going to resign my command. The last four years have been one damn gong show after another.

"The Navy doesn't care if we have a squadron or not. They don't care if we have airplanes or not. Nobody gives a shit about real readiness, or troop morale, or retention, or combat capability, and I'll be damned if I'll stand by and watch my squadron fall apart and my people broken.

"By falling in line, by standing quietly by and doing nothing, I'll become part of the problem. I'll be endorsing the lunacy of all this, and that's nuts. I just don't want to become part of the problem.

"I don't want to be part of it anymore, Miss Jenny. I'm going to resign from my command so I can blow the whistle and tell somebody what's goin' on!"

Hawk's resolve was known throughout the fighter ranks for having the hardness of blue-tip tool steel, but on this evening he met his match.

There was, at first, a moment of quiet, deliberate tension as Miss Jenny digested Hawk's comments and formulated her own.

Miss Jenny started off slow, then, with the growing inertia of a locomotive, she began.

"Hawk, I know we've had some hard times. Hell, Hawk, life is made up of a string of hard times, one after another. Now ya just got home from cruise, and I know things are tough, what with another cruise starin' us straight 'n the eye an' all, but you've got a lot of young 'uns lookin' up to you and dependin' on you.

"Now you may be down on the Navy right now and down on yourself, but right now you're thinkin' 'bout yourself—not about your people, and that's no way for a leader to think.

"If there's somethin' wrong, fix it! Hell, Hawk, you fixed everythin' else in your whole life; now fix this!"

"Miss Jenny, I can't fix lack of parts. I can't fix lack of fuel. I can't fix lack of funding. I can't fix lack of people. I can't fix the give-a-shit attitude of our leadership."

"Then go after the source of the problem and fix that, Hawk. And don't you dare say you can't fix sumthin' till you tried, and don't you dare quit until you're beat, and Hawk, you've never been beat yet.

"Hawk, you've never quit anythin' in your life, and people are countin' on you. What kind of example does that set by you quittin'? You're in a position of leadership, and true leaders don't quit when things aren't goin' their way. They don't walk off the field and leave their team behind. And you absolutely will not quit while people are followin' you and dependin' on you."

"Yeah, but Miss Jenny . . ."

"Hold it. I'M NOT DONE YET!"

"Hawk, the most amazing thing 'bout you is you have no sense of what you cannot do. Everythin' you set your mind to, you did. You quittin'—well, that's just crazy talk, Hawk. That's just selfish talk comin' out of you, and that's just not you. My Hawk's no quitter—never was—never will be. Now, I'm not gonna hear any more talk 'bout this!"

Whatever pithy comment Hawk had attempted to insert in the middle of Miss Jenny's delivery was wisely left unsaid.

Hawk leaned back in the jacuzzi, his head resting on the edge of the tub, and cogitated over Miss Jenny's sage words.

The stars were dazzling and still sparkled against the indigo sky, but the water temp had dropped significantly.

Epiphany

Hawk returned to work the following Monday. He stepped into his office, tossed his cover on his desk, positioned his briefcase on a nearby chair, and closed the door. For the next thirty minutes he mused over the state of affairs. He replayed everything Miss Jenny had said. He'd had an earful, and rightfully so. Miss Jenny was right, absolutely right . . . about everything.

Miss Jenny was a paradox. Her dazzling looks and brilliant azure eyes beguiled her clarity of vision and sagacious grasp of the heart of the problem. *She's right, of course,* Hawk admitted. *I can't leave, even if I wanted to. There's too much to do. Too many people are depending on my staff and me. I don't care about my career. I've done everything I ever wanted to do, but our next leaders are here, and I won't leave them high and dry.*

When he really analyzed the situation, he realized that he, like every other fighter squadron skipper in Fightertown, was dealing with the same issues, the same problems, and the same institutional rigor mortis.

Internally he was suffering from two conflicting emotions: embarrassment and frustration. Hawk contemplated the situation, and the more he did, the more his embarrassment and frustration were morphed into energy, which was then channeled into the inception of a plan.

TARPS Mission

High on Hawk's evolving plan was a need to convince his less visionary JOs that a new Tomcat mission, the Tactical Airborne Reconnaissance Pod System (TARPS) mission, was the wave of the future for fighter squadrons.

The TARPS mission sprang from the intelligence requirements of the Cold War with the USSR, when reconnaissance and surveillance of Soviet ships and maritime activities were in high demand. To ensure continued fleet coverage of ISR—intelligence, surveillance, and reconnaissance data—Naval Intelligence and other agencies envisioned improving the data-gathering capability vested in the RF-8 Crusaders and Marine Corps RF-4 Phantoms by uploading a TARPS pod on a new platform. The pod itself carried a suite of different lenses, cameras, and other intelligence-gathering sensors, but what a monster—the pod was 17 feet long and weighed nearly a ton. It required a brute of an airplane to haul it, and that airplane needed enough thrusties to get through the target area (always at a location that did not respond kindly to American flyovers) without getting shot down. The Tomcat was the perfect match for the TARPS mission.

The Navy began outfitting selected F-14 squadrons with TARPS pods in 1980. The F-14 TARPS birds were to be tasked for several missions, including mapping, pre- and poststrike bomb damage assessment, standoff oblique photography, and maritime ship surveillance.

Hawk had earlier proposed that the Black Lions be designated as the CVW-11 TARPS[1] squadron. Initially the JOs were resistant. Anything that interfered with the sovereignty and purity of the fighter mission was an aberration and not to be embraced. It was standard fighter drivel, but Hawk, part clairvoyant and part optimist, saw the universal good in the mission and the operational mandate for growth and refinement.

TARPS was just coming online when Hawk explained the following to his aircrew, "the current NAVAIR plan is to designate one of the two F-14 squadrons in each CVW as the 'TARPS' squadron. Each TARPS squadron will get three brand-new aircraft right off the Grumman production line. Additionally, that squadron will receive two additional crews, more funding, and the latest ECM gear, and—since the new mission requires more training and certification in low-altitude nav sorties—the TARPS crews will be required to fly a bunch more flight hours to maintain their quals. And . . . here's the deal clincher . . . the crews flying the TARPS mission will be the first in and the last out on combat missions."

By the time Hawk had finished laying out the other side of the issue, the JOs' heads were bobbing up and down like a bunch of dashboard hula dolls.

The first TARPS birds were delivered in January 1980. Side number 216 arrived with a factory-fresh coat of paint, that thirty-million-dollar new Tomcat bouquet, and a stray plastic fuel line cap adrift in the main fuel line, something that was missed during final construction of this particular Tomcat.

In the first weeks of operation the plastic fuel cap migrated into the main fuel line, and their brand-new TARPS Tomcat became a very expensive, brilliantly shiny, static display.

Call to Action

Throughout January the number of down aircraft and the awaiting parts list continued to grow. The "Lions" were out for five engines, several wing airbags, fuel pumps, brakes, and six main mount wheels.

In order to identify good wheels from bad, maintenance procedures called for painting the retrograde wheels red. This gave the Tomcat a somewhat humorous resemblance to a Flexi Flyer.[2] What was not funny was that on any given day in January, the entire flight schedule was written for only three out of twelve aircraft assigned,[3] and on some days fewer than that actually made it into the air.

Hawk wasn't flying much, and that gave him time to think. That was always dangerous.

Hawk wondered just how well the East Coast fighter community fared for F-14 parts. He called his longtime friend Cmdr. Moon Vance, CO of VF-101, the F-14 FRS at Oceana.

"Cmdr. Vance, VF-101. How can I help you, sir or ma'am?"

"Moon, Hawk; how are ya?"

"Hey, Hawk. Doing great. Heard about your cruise aboard *America*. How ya doing?"

"Been better, Moon."

After a few moments of pleasantries, Hawk came to the point. "Moon, we've got nine airplanes in the barn; six of them are down and awaiting parts. You won't believe this, but I'm out five engines and five wing airbags. There's a backlog for portside wing airbags at Miramar a mile long, and we can't even get ahold of brakes or wheels. Moon, you mind if I ask you a few questions?"

"No, Hawk. Shoot!"

"Moon, I need to know how many aircraft you have and the status of your aircraft. I need to know how many parts you have back-ordered and all the aircraft that are SPINTAC.[4] Before you say anything, I've got to tell you—I'm going to put a message together and send it to RAdm. Gillcrist. It might get hot around here. Now, can you give me that information?"

"Oh yeah, Hawk. No problem. I've got the daily aircraft status report right here. We've got twenty aircraft in 'A' status,[5] and all of them are up. NORS aircraft[6]—none, and SPINTAC aircraft—none. And as for parts, we don't have any big issues that I'm aware of."

Jesus. Unbelievable. How do they do it?

"Moon, I can't thank you enough. I'm going to quote you, with your permission, in this message. Sure hope it doesn't come back to bite you."

"No problem, Hawk. Good luck!"

The disaster within the supply system was a Navy epidemic brought on, in part, by budget cutbacks following the war. Further, the East Coast air wings chopped to the western Pacific (7th Fleet) were gobbling up parts allotted for West Coast squadrons, with no reallocation and no payback of parts returned to the West Coast squadrons. In other words, the East Coast fighter squadrons were receiving both East and West Coast parts.

And there was another aspect to the parts problem. A problem that should not have existed but, in the world of the "can do" spirit, was alive and thriving—cannibalization maintenance actions.

Under the previous fighter wing commander, Capt. Huiseman and maintenance personnel on the fighter wing staff attempted to direct squadron maintenance policies to reduce SPINTAC aircraft statistics through reporting trickery and cannibalization actions, which entailed pulling parts off a good aircraft to fix a down aircraft.

By Hawk's assessment, that approach was flatly wrong. It often resulted in broken parts, it was patently unsafe, and it caused twice as much work for his maintenance team. He felt his boys were already plenty overworked. Hawk simply refused to comply with the fighter wing's policy. This position did not endear him with the ComFit staff.

When Huiseman discovered that the skipper of VF-213 refused to follow unwritten guidance, he was ready to pop kittens. He couldn't actually order Hawk to cannibalize his aircraft, but Hawk just wouldn't take the hint.

It was amazing to Hawk that the wing invested so much time in micromanaging the squadrons, making strong "recommendations" on how to conduct daily maintenance, and how little time they actually invested in going after the core problems. There may have been a strong effort in doing just that, but if there was, it was the best-kept secret at NAS Miramar. What aggravated Hawk the most, and that which exacerbated the dilemma on the West Coast, was the lack of leadership.

RAdm. John Disher, commander of ComFit at Oceana, had taken an aggressive and proactive role in getting his supply department stocked as well as possible. The dichotomy between the East and West Coast fighter communities appeared to come down to the lack of concern or effort of the previous West Coast ComFit commander and his staff.

The worst of it was that the problem had existed for so long that the leadership accepted it as status quo. It was analogous to a group of people hanging by their thumbs. It hurt like hell, but since everybody was in the same painful fix, it was accepted within the group culture.

Hawk huddled with Crash, his maintenance officer, and Habib Schwartz, the assistant maintenance officer. Hawk recapped the conversation with Moon and passed the data on to Habib. Hawk explained that he intended to launch a message to the wing, and he warned them that "this message is going to be radioactive—it'll probably get me fired."

"Now," Hawk leaned forward and whispered, "write me a message that will bring the walls down!"

That afternoon, Habib presented Hawk with a "Personal for" message to RAdm. Gillcrist. It struck at the heart of the problem and said, "Under the current supply system, VF-213 cannot meet NATOPS monthly minimums and is unable to complete turnaround schedule training events. The command has an adequate number of trained maintenance personnel but is plagued by a growing list of outstanding aircraft parts."

The message finished with a general-quarters alarm: "Currently, VF-213 is 'not mission capable.'"

It was focused and well written, provided objective critical analysis of the problem, and addressed the systemic nature of all the Miramar squadrons' aircraft availability issues. It was accurate, irrefutable, and long overdue.

Hawk sat quietly in his office. He read, paced, and then reread the message, making small changes to the text. He tried to imagine the blowback, the fratricidal damage the message might cause to his people, his command, and other fighter squadrons. He was a long way from caring about what happened to his own career, but the careers of others, those who would shoulder the burden of leadership for the next fighter generation, were on the line, and he had to make sure they would not be in the frag pattern. The last time he launched something like this, he nearly destroyed the best squadron in the Navy—TOPGUN.

He thought long and hard on this decision and thought about Miss Jenny's impassioned words: *Fix the problem!*

This may not fix the problem, he thought, *but it is about to get a whole lot of attention.*

On a Friday evening, after most of the people at Miramar had secured for the weekend, Hawk released the message.

Gator's Big Push

The Monday morning All Officer Meeting (AOM) had hardly begun when Hawk was informed by the administration officer that he had an urgent call from RAdm. Gillcrist's staff, which requested a return call. Hawk got out of his chair, excused himself, walked to his office, took a long and deep breath, and returned the call.

At Navy Fighter Weapons School in March 1977, Hawk explains the fighter performance characteristics of the YF-17, prototype of the FA-18 Hornet, to a class of TOPGUN students following Hawk's sixth flight in the airplane. *J. Monroe Smith*

One of Hawk's greatest attributes was to bring a certain sense of mirth to any situation. While at VX-4 as the F-14 Tomcat program officer, that attribute was a very helpful trait, considering the constant pressure on the program team from the higher-ups. *J. Monroe Smith*

The first F-14 Tomcat arrived at Point Mugu for its initial operational test and evaluation in September 1972. In the spring of 1973, Lt. Cmdr. Hawk Smith and Lt. Bruce Peeper, the two primary program aircrew at VX-4, are shown standing in front of their operational evaluation F-14 during the joint evaluation team project. *J. Monroe Smith*

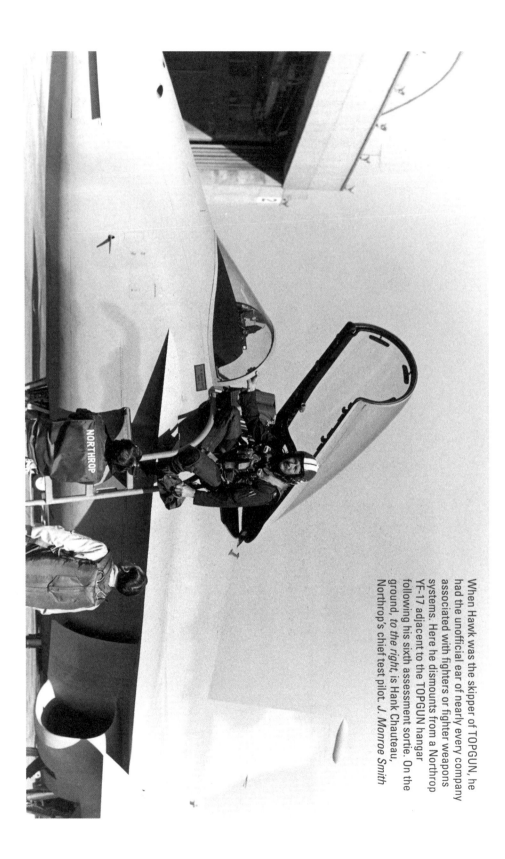

When Hawk was the skipper of TOPGUN, he had the unofficial ear of nearly every company associated with fighters or fighter weapons systems. Here he dismounts from a Northrop YF-17 adjacent to the TOPGUN hangar following his sixth assessment sortie. On the ground, *to the right*, is Hank Chauteau, Northrop's chief test pilot. *J. Monroe Smith*

Lt. Gordo Fast and Hawk in the cockpit of a VX-4 Tomcat at NAS Point Mugu. *J. Monroe Smith*

DANGER DANGER DANGER
EJECTION SEAT

DANGER DANGER DANGER
EJECTION SEAT

PITOT STATIC PROBE

VF-103 Navy F-4 Phantom, flown by Hawk, escorting an intercepted Iraqi Tu-16 Bison, a Soviet-built, long-range strategic bomber. *J. Monroe Smith*

October 1, 1993: Miss Jenny kissing Hawk a final time as Capt. John Monroe "Hawk" Smith. At the end of the side boy formation, he returns to the civilian world, a little older, slightly battered, but with a new mission in life. *J. Monroe Smith*

October 1, 1993: former Blue Angel and commander of Naval Air Forces Atlantic, VAdm. Anthony A. "Tony" Less officiating the retirement ceremony of Capt. John Monroe "Hawk" Smith and Miss Jenny after thirty years of service to the Navy. MCPO Bernard stands behind and to the right of Hawk. Farther to the right is RAdm. Ed "Bulldog" Allen, Hawk's longtime friend and a guest speaker at the ceremony. *J. Monroe Smith*

Lt. j.g. Hawk Smith, in khaki dress uniform, with classmates upon completing the F-4 RAG program at VF-101 at NAS Oceana in 1967. *J. Monroe Smith*

F-14A in the vertical. The 42,000 pounds of thrust made a significant impression on the aircraft it was designed to fight. This tail stand does not begin to impress one of the raw power of the mighty Tomcat.

VF-213 Tomcat coming aboard USS *Enterprise* (CVN-65)

VF-213 F-14s providing fighter escort for an A-6 Intruder

An unlikely duo; Black Lion
F-14 in climb-out with
TOPGUN F-16 Viper

Three Black Lion F-14s in right echelon

F-14 with wings extended, forming compression vapor off heavily loaded wing and fuselage

Black Lion F-14, gear down, hook down, flaps down, and a little low over the ramp

F-14 turn to a very short and final approach

Black Lion F-14 off the waist cat in an impressive early port-clearing turn

An F-14 making its own cloud due to high vapor compression as the aircraft is at or nearly at supersonic flight

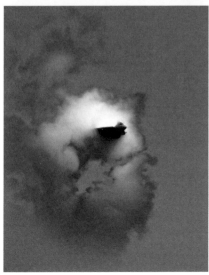

F-14 off the cat with good end speed

Rotation off the waist cat with possible flare jettison

A section of VF-41 F-14s on section climb out near NAS Fallon, Nevada

Dead six o'clock on a F-14D just off the waist cat; notice the gear is still down

F-14D hooked up and squatting on catapult 2, awaiting launch

Fight's on! Merge pass of a TOPGUN F-16 with a very fast swept-wing Tomcat.

Hawk with Black Lion helmet, looking for the bad guys

Silhouette of an up-sun F-14 on a nearly cloudless day

A VF-213 F-14D over Iraq, looking for a fight

"This is Cmdr. Smith returning Adm. Gillcrist's call."

"Hold on, sir!" the admiral's secretary politely responded.

"Hey, Monroe."

Hawk steadied himself. "Good morning, Admiral."

"I want to say that was the best damned message I ever saw."

Deliverance!

"I tell you what—that took a lot of research to identify the problem, and a lot of guts to put it on paper. That's the kind of detail we need to get to the bottom of this problem, and we definitely have a problem, no doubt about it. We'll get this thing fixed, Monroe, and I'm going to use your message to help get it resolved."

Who's speaking, please? Is this the same Navy it was last week? Hawk wanted to ask, but instead he said, "Sir, I appreciate your support on this. It's a big problem, and it affects all your fighter squadrons, sir—not just the Lions. I'll do anything I can to help you on this."

"I just might need your help, Monroe. I may call on you for more on this issue, but I'll keep you posted on our progress."

Hawk was shocked. The leadership turnaround was incredible. Salvation was at hand, and it appeared that it took only one message to one true dedicated leader to get the ball rolling.

RAdm. Gillcrist's promises were not idle boasts. Cmdr. Dick Scharff and other key staff members were summoned by the admiral for an urgent strategy session. Not long after, Adm. Gillcrist marched over to COMNAVAIRPAC to brief the three-star admiral on the disparity between the East and West Coast fighter wings and the effect it was having on his fighter squadrons. To drive his points home, he referred to the statistical analysis embedded in the Black Lion message.

Hawk's Junkyard Dream

It was during this first glimmer of a sea change when Hawk received a phone call from his friend Jim Stevenson.

In 1975, when Hawk was assigned as the CVW-14 senior landing signal officer aboard USS *Enterprise*, Jim came aboard to gather data for his book on the F-14.[7] It was at that time he had met and interviewed Hawk. Their paths crossed again when Hawk was at TOPGUN and Jim published the *TOPGUN Journal*. In 1980, Jim was working with Dave Marash of ABC's *20/20* documentary team.

Jim was developing a story on aviation readiness of all the services and led the *20/20* group to Miramar on a fact-finding trip. They had been given permission from CNO Public Affairs Office to speak with people on base, but for obvious reasons, there weren't many people willing to meet with the *20/20* crew. Their proclivity to bias, in some cases completely skewing stories to better align with their *agenda*, was well known within the services.

Jim recalled that Hawk was now one of the F-14 squadron skippers and asked Hawk to meet with them. Hawk, somewhat reluctantly, agreed to speak with them "off the record."

Hawk met Jim and the film crew as soon as they arrived at the security gate. He greeted them warmly and escorted them to the hangar. Jim started off with several benign questions about their mission, squadron size, number of aircraft—things that anyone could get out of the library. Hawk noticed that Jim's questions gradually became more pointed. Hawk finally asked, "Jim, is this off the record?"

"Ah . . . off the record. Of course. No cameras. No recorders. No nothin'!"

"Okay. Well, Jim, you know the situation in the F-14 community sucks! I'll walk you around and show you what we're up against."

Hawk guided the *20/20* team out to the flight line. There on the tarmac sat three Tomcats, all on bright-red wheels and looking all the part as expensive Soap Box Derby coasters. Through the creative genius of an anonymous star maintenance technician, stenciled in large, proud letters on one of the intake nacelles was *"Reusable Container, Do Not Destroy."* That got a chuckle out of the camera crew.

"Jim, parts availability for the F-14 is simply horrible. The F-14 is complex and hard to work on and requires an exceptionally skilled team of maintenance people. Consequently it has the highest maintenance man-hour-per-flight-hour ratio in the fleet; in fact, in the Navy. Our airplanes require sometimes over a hundred hours of maintenance to get them in the air for one hour. Jim, we have brake problems, wheel problems, and engine problems; poor reliability is inherent in the airplane; and the reliability of the replaceable parts and subcomponents is also poor."

"Skipper, would you say this on camera?" Jim asked.

"I most certainly will not!" Hawk snapped.

"Well, why not?"

"Jim, I don't need you! I don't need *20/20*. What I need is parts, and trained technicians, and fuel. Now, you don't have parts, you don't have technicians, and you don't have fuel. What you have an abundance of is trouble. Now, you know, Jim, I don't need any more trouble. I've already enjoyed as much as I can stand. My only goals are to lead the Lions, maintain a low profile, have up jets so we can fly, and train, and fight, and get my guys ready for the real world. That's all I want to do. I don't have time for any bullshit, and I sure don't have time for any more trouble."

"Well, what would it take to have you talk to us on the record?"

"Somebody way up the food chain would have to give me a direct order to talk to you guys on the record. I'm just not going to do it otherwise."

"Will you talk to us if someone up there tells you to?"

"Well, hell, I'll be required to . . . if someone directs me. But you have to know, I ain't anxious to do it."

"Okay. Fair enough, Skipper."

Hawk bid Jim Stevenson and Dave Marash a good day and headed back to his office. *That should have convinced them not to ask for an interview "on the record,"* Hawk happily thought.

The phone rang the next day. Hawk answered, "Black Lions, Cmdr. Smith speaking, sir!"

"Sir, please hold the line for Adm. Gillcrist," the yeoman responded.

"I'll hold." *Holy cow. What now?*

"Monroe, how are you?"

"Fine, Admiral. Thanks for asking. And how may I be of service to you, sir?"

"Monroe, I'd like you to do a favor for me. I'd like you to interview with those *20/20* folks. You know, they're on base and they asked to interview you by name."

"Admiral, you don't want me to interview with these people. They already know too much about what's wrong, and they're asking tough questions."

"You can do it, Monroe. Interview with them. Make it happen and make it positive!"

"Admiral, you can't make it positive with these people. They ask questions like 'Why is your brother in jail?' And if I said, 'Why, I don't even have a brother,' they'll say, 'Well, don't get defensive, just answer the question!'

"I can't make my answers positive and tell the truth. It's impossible. There's nothing positive about our current readiness."

"Monroe, I've got great confidence in you. You can do it. If anyone can tell the truth and make it sound positive, it's you! Now, go ahead and talk to them."

"Aye, aye, Admiral."

Jim Stevenson, Dave Marash, and the *20/20* team showed up the next day. Hawk welcomed them into his little office. He was ready for them. He had learned a lot about speaking the truth plainly, avoiding trick questions and minefields, and framing clear responses to avoid contextual misrepresentation.

After the preliminary niceties, Dave burrowed in and began asking the hard questions. Hawk methodically assembled his answers. He spoke the truth but avoided divulging information that might be embarrassing to the Navy. Hawk responded to Dave's technical and performance questions, taking care to keep his answers in the *Unclassified* realm. Hawk explained the vast air combat superiority advantage of the Tomcat over all possible threat aircraft.

Clearly, Dave and the rest of the team were impressed. The tone of Hawk's responses changed noticeably in regard to the Tomcat's reliability, maintenance requirements, and logistic support, but he was careful to keep his answers as positive as he could within the lifelines of the truth.

The interview was almost over. Hawk had been doing well, holding his own, and then Mr. Marash popped one last question that Hawk readily fielded: "Cmdr. Smith, how do you like being the commanding officer of one of the first F-14 Tomcat squadrons?"

By now, Hawk was relaxed—maybe too relaxed.

"Well, sir, when I was younger I wanted to be either the skipper of a fighter squadron or the owner of a junkyard, and now it seems . . . I'm both."

Renaissance

The *20/20* interview aired in April 1980. High marks go to Dave Marash for a balanced and intriguing interview. It stirred no national outrage with the American people, and it was not a "breaking news" headliner, but it did raise the situational awareness of COMNAVAIRPAC leadership.

RAdm. Gillcrist was summoned to COMNAVAIRPAC to explain the errant actions of one of his wayward commanding officers. Cmdr. Lee Tillotson, COMFIT ops officer, was tasked to write a rebuttal article for the *San Diego Union Tribune* explaining the logistics support prioritization as it applied to the turnaround cycle.

Lee provided comprehensive clarification of the several stages of cruise preparation, and the supply and manpower prioritization system as it supported the turnaround cycle. It was well written and all-inclusive, but from any angle it looked just like what it was—damage control.

In late April, a curious thing happened. Mystically, the prevailing situation for both the Black Lions and the Aardvarks began to change.

There was not an overnight rejuvenation in the supply system, but gradually, over the course of a few weeks, parts began flowing into Miramar, and from there they trickled into all the Tomcat squadrons.

This appeared to be the confluence of several events that seemed to simultaneously converge. In the course of a few weeks, replacement wheels, engines, airbags, brakes, and equipment of every description slowly began to materialize. To install those new parts and repair aircraft, technicians and supervisors began to return from schools and report for duty. And, as if God had suddenly given grace for their suffering, VF-213 received two additional, "fresh off the Grumman assembly line" TARPS, Block 105 Tomcats.

Something had happened, or, rather, somebody high in the pecking order had caused something to happen. Bafflingly, somebody seemed to care about readiness. It might have been the unified assault of RAdm. Gillcrist and Cmdr. Dick Scharff upon the hallowed halls of COMNAVAIRPAC, or it may have been flag intervention by VAdm. Robert "Dutch" Schoultz, COMNAVAIRPAC, or it may have been the *20/20* interview. Whatever the cause, Hawk was asking no questions.

For his part, what small tremor or contribution his "Personal for" message and the *20/20* interview may have caused, he suffered neither official condemnation nor commendation, and he cared not. At this point, he was satisfied in the belief that true leaders had, at last, taken control of a system long in need of a major overhaul.

CHAPTER 7

Hardening of the "Lions"

It's always the guy you don't see that will kill you.
—Robin Olds

The Young "Lions"

The squadron began a recovery period in early spring 1980. Hawk now had both the time and the assets to attend to the most important aspect of the turnaround cycle—training the young Lions to be the leaders in the fighter community and the cold professional predators that was their calling.

In Hawk's sixteen-year naval adventure, he had many times conjured up the image of the perfect fighter squadron. It would be staffed with innovators, the tactical elite, throat-ripping fighter crew—but above all—professional naval officers and leaders unburdened by political baggage or ostentatious inclinations. His image was based on TOPGUN, and the engine of his model was the people—always the people.

Hawk believed, deep in his core, that people properly disciplined, properly empowered, and fired by a common vision could achieve nearly anything.

Little by little, at every opportunity—quarters, all-hands functions, AOMs, CPO leadership training, inspections, awards ceremonies, promotion gatherings, even at captain's masts—Hawk energized and challenged his people to divine a vision of the great *could be*.

The innovators, leaders, and explorers stepped to the plate. Like young lion cubs, the most adventurous, the most inquisitive, and the strongest climbed the tallest trees, explored farthest from their den, were the swiftest afoot, and fought the hardest. Hawk believed that success bred success, and not just for those who accepted the challenge but also for those inquisitive enough to watch and learn from the masters who made things happen.

Slowly, over the course of several months, the character of the Black Lions began to take new form. Gradually the Lions became a squadron of pioneers, trailblazers, and achievers, and from those, leaders grew. Little by little, small objectives were attained, and each achievement sparked a desire for another challenge, another mission.

The Lions wrote the first ever Tactical Squadron Operating Procedures (T-SOP) manual for the F-14. The F-14 already had a NATOPS manual, but the T-SOP built upon the operating procedures and detailed the "why" and the "how." It covered everything that would take place in the course of a routine fighter mission: radio discipline, taxiing, takeoff, formations, and return-to-force procedures. When a brief was given, the flight leader said, "The flight will be conducted in accordance with NATOPS and the Black Lion T-SOP. Are there any questions?" Each member of the flight understood exactly what would transpire. This allowed the aircrew to briefly address aircraft lineup, weather, and safety and then focus on the most-important aspects of the sortie—mission objectives and tactics.

The Black Lions were also one of the first F-14 squadrons to be organized around three perma-nent flight divisions consisting of four airplanes and eight aircrew per division. The three most-senior pilots—the skipper, XO, and Lt. Cmdr. Charlie DeGruy—were designated as division leaders. The next-most-senior pilots, three senior lieutenant commander department heads, were designated as "section leaders," flying in the number 3 position of each division. Flying in the number 4 position in each division were the next-senior pilots. The number 2 position of each division was slotted with the most-junior pilots in the squadron. The division leaders were responsible for the training and standardization of all those in their division.

In a similar way, the most-experienced RIOs were teamed with the least experienced pilots and were additionally tasked with ensuring that all the RIOs in their respective division were trained and standardized.

The arrangement of each division was standard fare for naval aviation squadrons, but the Black Lions made these divisions more durable. While the assignments were more or less "fixed," because of the strict adherence to standardization, pilots and RIOs could be reassigned to meet other tasking and the evolving schedule.

Tactical All Aircrew Meetings (T-ACM) were a standard training protocol of the Black Lions, and the opening event each Monday morning when based ashore. This helped ensure that the minds of the aircrew had made the transition from the fun and folly of the weekend to the very serious job of flying fighters on Monday morning.

Leading off the weekly event was a general AOM with all officers in attendance. Following the general AOM, the three division leaders convened a T-ACM. The subjects were, as one might guess, strictly "tactical." Training and discussions might include radar intercepts, weapons employment, defensive maneuvering, formations under different threat conditions, engaged and free fighter responsibilities, air combat maneuvering techniques, weapons parameters, and lessons learned.

This was a time for total focus on the fighter mission. Anything noteworthy could be briefed and reviewed for possible inclusion into the T-SOP.

One of many ideas that migrated from the T-ACMs to become a standard Black Lion tactical procedure was the use of maneuvering (main) flaps and slats in ACM.

The Science of Maneuvering Flaps

The Tomcat was a beast, and a complex beast at that. But the Grumman engineers were very successful in designing a fighter/interceptor that, despite its size, could turn with the little, first-generation jets and still sprint to supersonic airspeeds. They did this by maximizing the development of lift from as many surface areas and lifting devices as possible, and fitting the Tomcat with thunderous engines.

At nominal and high angles of attack, such as those conditions encountered in ACM, the undersurface of the airplane generates a massive lifting force—in fact, about half the total lifting force is produced by the airframe. The 63-foot, high-aspect-ratio wing (when swept forward) and the ingenious design of variable slats and flaps greatly added to the lifting force generated by the airframe. In effect, the Tomcat built lift from the underside of the airframe, the tapered variable-geometry wing, and several lifting devices on the wing, which changed the effective chord[1] and camber[2] of the wing.

The flap system had two primary modes: landing/takeoff and maneuvering. Further, the maneuvering mode had two types of operation: automatic and manual. In the automatic-maneuvering flap operation, the Alpha computer controlled the position of the flaps and the slats. Data inputs to the Alpha computer included airspeed, altitude, wing position, and angle of attack. In this mode, the maneuvering flaps were positioned on the basis of the amount of force the pilot placed on the control stick. In response to that demand (and the other data inputs), the Alpha computer positioned the flaps and slats.

While it was "automatic" and took much of the guesswork out of the equation, it did not provide for full throw of the flaps, nor did it achieve full optimization of the flaps and slats.

There were a couple of other snags with the automatic mode: the time delay between demand and actual positioning of the flaps and slats, and the turbulence over the tail surfaces generated by the auxiliary (inboard) flaps.

In the "automatic" mode, the Alpha computer made flap and slat adjustments on the basis of data and pilot input supplied at that moment in time. It did not have the prescience to adjust flaps for aerodynamic demands that were about to happen; it could not divine the pilot's future configuration needs. The pilot, of course, could. By using the "maneuver flap and slat thumbwheel" located on the left side of the stick grip, he could override the "automatic" feature. In effect, by toggling the thumbwheel the pilot could position the flaps and slats early, in anticipation of future needs, and avoid the inherent lag time associated with computer-controlled maneuvering flaps.

The turbulence generated by the auxiliary flaps presented a different problem and required a different solution.

The auxiliary flaps were positioned inboard, close to the wing root and upstream of the horizontal and vertical stabilizers. During slow-speed maneuvering at a very high angle of attack, disturbed, turbulent air created by the auxiliary flaps flowed over and around those surfaces, reducing their effectiveness and pilot controllability.

Aircrew who had experimented with cutting the auxiliary flaps out of the circuit—keeping them from deploying by pulling the auxiliary flap circuit breaker—discovered that slow-speed, high-angle-of-attack controllability was greatly enhanced.

So, by manually deploying the maneuvering flaps and slats and deselecting the auxiliary flap circuit breaker, the pilots were able to vastly improve high-angle-of-attack, slow-speed maneuvering and controllability in three key areas: full mechanical throw of the maneuvering flaps, pre-positioning of the flaps and slats for future needs, and reduction of the turbulent airflow around the tail surfaces.

"Technically" it was a small thing, but in terms of maximizing the performance envelope of the Tomcat, it gave substantially better pitch and roll authority, rudder control, and general "pointability," enhancing handling characteristics in the dogfight arena.

The tactical innovations and procedural initiatives developed by the Black Lions were not "close hold" secrets to be released only to those with knowledge of a secret fraternal-order handshake. These refinements were disseminated to all Tomcat squadrons in order to improve the breed and the mission effectiveness of the entire community.

Innovation and pioneering efforts were not limited to aircraft-maneuvering protocols. Hawk was adamant about maintaining section integrity throughout the flight. It chafed him mightily that the Navy's foremost fighter was the only tactical aircraft not authorized to make section takeoffs.

During the 1979 F-14 NATOPS conference, the Black Lions submitted a change proposal to authorize section takeoffs[3] for the Tomcat. "We [Navy]," Hawk wrote, "have the best and largest tactical fighter in the world, but the only fighter restricted from tactical section takeoffs. It's important to initiate policy to maintain section integrity during the takeoff and throughout the flight, especially during conditions of poor weather. VF-213 hereby submits a change proposal to the F-14 NATOPS to prescribe tactical section takeoffs in order to enhance section integrity and safety."

The change proposal was accepted without counterargument (a rare thing) and was incorporated into the F-14 NATOPS manual. This was a small but important victory for the Tomcat community, and a feather in the Black Lion warbonnet.

Scopes for the Fleet

When it came to honing the "fighter edge," Hawk was not too proud to borrow ideas from other organizations, even other services. The Air Force F-15 Eagle pilots used Redfield six-power riflescopes attached to the heads-up display (HUD) to increase the visual identification range of the adversaries during the intercept phase. The value of this technique was first vividly demonstrated during ACEVAL/AIMVAL in 1976.[4]

During the 1979 deployment aboard USS *America*, when the Navy supply system tried to satiate the Black Lions with a score (144 pair) of black plastic reading glasses (clearly a product of the Navy's birth control policy) instead of the riflescopes they ordered, Hawk asked his father to purchase and send him a 3 × 9 variable-power Weaver riflescope. Since there were no F-14 HUD-mounted scope brackets in the supply system, Hawk designed one. With the help of Petty Officer Vergara in the Lions' airframe shop, a handcrafted bracket was machined and mounted to the right side of the windscreen frame.[5]

The Black Lion pilots completed a tactical assessment that found that against a MiG-sized target, the VID range was extended from an average of 3 miles to over 7 miles. This was significant in that it allowed the fighters to launch missiles well before the merge, thereby improving both the probability of a kill and survivability in an attack.

Hawk approached Dick Scharff with an idea that would allow all the fighter squadrons to purchase riflescopes. Dick saw the benefit of the proposal but explained he couldn't order the scopes without approval from ComFit. This was an unusual "open" purchase; in fact, it was a first-time-ever buy, and expensive to boot. Dick, for this one, needed guidance from on high.

Hawk expected this and already had a plan on the drawing board that would bypass the normal torpid supply chain decision process. He'd fly RAdm. Gillcrist on an intercept sortie that would demonstrate the power and the tactical significance of the riflescope.

Joe "Crash" Zahalka, Black Lions' senior and most experienced RIO, flew with RAdm. Gillcrist while Hawk and Chief served as the bogey during an intercept hop over the Pacific just southeast of San Clemente Island.

They flew slow-speed intercepts at 20,000 feet—slow speed to maximize the admiral's time to "tweak" the riflescope. The intercepts began at 30 miles. When Crash called a radar lock at 20 miles, Hawk made a 90-degree turn to put his aircraft perpendicular to the admiral's flight path and then rolled the aircraft to provide a planform view of all 63 feet of the Tomcat. The admiral made the transition from the HUD to the riflescope at a whopping 20 miles and was at once amazed to clearly identify the bogey as an F-14.

The crews returned to Miramar and debriefed in the ready room. The admiral was brimming with accolades concerning the Black Lions' tactical breakthrough but was puzzled as to just what Hawk wanted him to do.

"Monroe, I'm completely impressed, but what do you need me for?"

"Admiral, it's simple, really. I'd like you to endorse the system and give all your fighter squadrons approval to purchase the scopes."

"That's it? That's all you need?"

"That's it, sir!"

"Well, consider it done!"

And with that, all Miramar fighter squadrons had approval and, surprisingly, funding to purchase riflescopes.

Have Drill

Some years before the F-14 came to the fleet, the services realized that the F-4 Phantom, for all its brute power and technology wizardry, was not the fighter all had hoped for. Therefore, an effort was mounted to try to determine how to improve tactics against enemy aircraft and also how to mitigate the rules of engagement with which US TACAIR pilots had to contend.

In the 1950s, when the Cold War face-off between NATO nations and the Soviet Union was the most pressing threat to world peace, a highly classified program was begun in an effort to acquire and evaluate several of the then-current Soviet Union's frontline fighters. Under US Air Force management and governed by the Tactical Air Command, several fighter pilots were selected to assess the flight characteristics of three Mikoyan aircraft: the MiG-17 Fresco, MiG-21 Fishbed, and MiG-23 Flogger.

At this same time, the US military was of the initial belief that two new state-of-the-art air-to-air missiles were our ace in the hole. But tacticians and weapons experts had put too much credence in the notion that the AIM-9 heat-seeking missile and the AIM-7 radar-guided missile would have a high probability of killing an airborne opponent at great distances, sometimes even beyond visual range of the aircrew. While they "could" destroy airborne opponents at long range, one knee knocker stood in the way—they could also kill friendly aircraft.

In the early years of the Vietnam War, on the basis of the ROE, fighter crews were required to have positive visual identification or two electronic-identification confirmations to verify that an unknown aircraft was indeed a bad guy before the fighter aircrew were given a *weapons-free* call. With erratic radar coverage over much of Vietnam, the identification of an unknown aircraft therefore relied primarily on the eyes of the fighter aircrew. This ROE all but eliminated the benefits of the new missiles, put the US fighters in visual range of the MiG pilots, retrograded the air-to-air advantage of US aircraft, and resulted in a gun battle in which the more nimble MiG aircraft too often won.

To complicate matters, in the mid-1950s and 1960s the Navy and Air Force were so confident in the capabilities of the air-to-air missiles that minimal close-in tactics and dogfighting training was accomplished. Air combat skills withered; ergo, the air war over Vietnam in the early years was a catastrophe for US fighter aircrew. In testimony to this problem, our (USN, USMC, and USAF) exchange rate in the early years of the war was about 2.5:1 compared to the years of the Korean air war at over 10:1.

To discover both the core problems and identify solutions to this quandary, Capt. Frank Ault was commissioned by the chief of naval operations to conduct a study.

In November 1968, Capt. Ault submitted the "Report of the Air-to-Air Missile System Capability Review" to the chief of naval operations.[6] The "Ault Report," as it became known, was a 480-page document that analyzed air-to-air performance of Navy aircraft, weapons, and aircrew in the early stages of the Vietnam air war. Capt. Ault stated, "Almost 600 air-to-air missiles have been fired by the Navy and Air Force pilots in about 360 engagements in Southeast Asia between June 17, 1965, and September 19, 1968. Performance in combat indicates a probability of achieving one kill for every ten firing attempts in any engagement where air-to-air missiles are employed in an environment similar to that of Southeast Asia. This is well below expected or desired levels." Capt. Ault continued, "[The Navy] has grown into a combat philosophy where we were placing more reliance on the machine than on the man."

The Navy, according to Capt. Ault, had not sufficiently improved tactics and training to exploit the full lethal effectiveness of modern air-to-air missile systems in the high-g dogfight environment.

The Ault Report included 242 recommendations. At the top of the list was the recommendation to establish a postgraduate-level school to improve expertise in the fighter missions. This recommendation provided the impetus for the inauguration of the US Navy Fighter Weapons School—what would become known as TOPGUN.

The Air Force had a different approach. In the late 1960s, under the aegis of the Tactical Air Command, a number of highly classified projects were initiated.

Have Drill, the MiG-17 project, and the related program, Have Doughnut, the MiG-21 project, were developed to first test, assess, and evaluate operational capabilities of the MiG airplanes against US fighters, and then to exploit any weaknesses.

There were other black programs that took advantage of the technical data and lessons learned from Have Drill and Have Doughnut. The Navy began a very interesting program that attempted to develop defensive maneuvers for the F-4 against the MiG-17. This was to be a joint Navy and USAF effort using the MiG-17 against a navy VX-4 F-4 Phantom. To pilot the Phantom, VX-4 turned to their resident F-4 rock star, the then lieutenant commander Ronald "Mugs" McKeown.

Mugs McKeown: To Kill a MiG

Generally, a squadron is filled with junior and midgrade officers with similar backgrounds, experiences, skills, and interests. There always seems to be one or two in each command who are a bit more talented and serious than their peers, more focused on their warcraft, and a few who are clear standouts. Lt. Cmdr. Ronald "Mugs" McKeown was one of those.

Mugs was somewhat intense, a bit rough around the edges, but he knew a few things about airplanes and a lot about fighter tactics, and for those who could tolerate his "forget the carrot" teaching technique, he was an extraordinarily gifted air-combat-maneuvering instructor and tactician.[7]

In 1967, Mugs was fresh out of the US Air Force Test Pilot School. He was quickly recruited for VX-4 by the CO, Capt. Nella Perozi. Although Mugs originally had his sights set on test pilot projects, he was not disappointed by the VX-4 assignment or in the projects that he became a part of.

His test pilot status and reputation opened a few doors—one, in particular, was an extension of the Have Drill project. Under this project, Mugs and Lt. Cmdr. Tooter Teague[8] were instrumental in developing offensive and defensive fighter tactics against the MiG-17 and MiG-21, including the Elliptical Energy Egg.[9] But Mugs was also heavily involved in developing a last-ditch, defensive maneuver for the Phantom.

If a Phantom crew came under gun attack by a MiG, the normal pilot reflex was a break turn[10] into the threat. Against the MiG-17 and, to a lesser degree, the MiG-21, that was precisely the wrong maneuver.

Mugs and Lt. Cmdr. Duke Johnson worked diligently to come up with the right maneuver. With Tooter Teague in the MiG and Mugs flying an F-4B, they developed a maneuver that, although hard both on man and machine, consistently resulted in neutralizing a gun attack—by anything.

The maneuver was started from a canned setup with the Phantom at 400 knots, in afterburner, and 1,000 feet in front of the MiG. When ready, Mugs commenced a turn into the MiG. Tooter rolled his aircraft to match wing position and then pulled back on the stick to maintain a tracking solution on the Phantom. Mugs then initiated the maneuver by pushing full-forward stick and feeding in bottom rudder.

Early MiGs had many ergonomic design flaws. One of these was restricted visibility, especially through the center windscreen over the top of the intake. The maneuver caused the Phantom to disappear under the nose. The MiG pilot's natural response was to roll 180 degrees, reverse the turn, and reestablish visual contact.

Tooter's reversal was Mugs's cue to reef back on the stick and stomp on the top rudder. Forward stick and bottom rudder followed quickly by full-back stick and opposite rudder was the right combination of flight control inputs to cause high divergent yaw and pitch rates, which resulted in a maneuver described as an end-over-end "tumble." This was a very disorienting and uncomfortable maneuver, but not nearly as uncomfortable as getting shot.

As soon as the Phantom tumbled (departed), Mugs quickly fed in forward stick and neutralized the rudder controls. In the three seconds it took to complete the maneuver, the Phantom was pointed straight down and had converted 400 knots of horizontal velocity to 200 knots of pure vertical velocity.

It was a difficult maneuver for the MiG-17 pilot to follow, and often the attacker swapped roles and became the defender.

It was a bright and brilliant morning, and 2.5 miles above the desert floor, several miles north of Nellis AFB, Tooter Teague guided his MiG-17 into gun position 1,000 feet behind a VX-4 F-4J flown by Mugs with Lt. Cmdr. Pete Gilleece, a veteran Phantom RIO, in the back seat. Mugs had practiced the maneuver many times in an F-4B, with very favorable results, but on this day, the first time he attempted it in an F-4J, there was a startlingly different outcome.

With a "Fight's on!" call, Mugs initiated the *last-ditch maneuver*—a hard pull into Tooter followed quickly by full-forward stick and bottom rudder. Tooter rolled the MiG into a turn in the opposite direction to keep sight. Mugs, on cue, tugged the stick back in his lap and reversed the pressure on the rudder pedals. As Mugs expected, the giant Phantom "tumbled." But then something happened that Mugs didn't expect—*BOOM! BOOM!* Both engines flamed out—first the left engine, then the right. In the midst of the mayhem, the Phantom continued to tumble and, in short order, developed into a spin.

Mugs[11] wrestled for control. He tried to relight both engines while he struggled with antispin controls. It was difficult to judge the elapsed time, considering the nature of the combined emergencies. The Phantom came out of the spin just as the engines slowly began to wind back up . . . but they were still headed downhill at an eye-watering speed.

Pete keyed the ICS: "Mugs, you wanna get out?"

"No. I've got the engines coming up," Mugs responded.

Mugs struggled with the stick, feeling for that perfect pressure point between best pitch rate and another departure. He was making progress, but the big jet's nose was still well below the horizon, and they hadn't started climbing.

A pause. "You wanna get out now?" Pete repeated impatiently.

"No! The nose is coming up."

"The cactuses are getting pretty fucking big, Mugs! How 'bout now?"

It was decision time, and finally Mugs relented, "Yeah. Let's get out." He got only the "Yeah" out and Pete was gone. Mugs was a second behind him. The chute had just blossomed when Mugs smacked into the ground. He hit hard.

Tooter had raced past the Phantom early in the defensive maneuver. He couldn't follow Mugs through the maneuver and wouldn't have even if he could. He saw the Phantom depart, which is what he expected. What he didn't expect was to see the Phantom hit the ground. Initially, Tooter didn't see any chutes. He circled low, slow, and close aboard for a better look. He saw Pete and finally picked up Mugs. As he passed, Mugs gave him the finger—Navy sign language for "All is well."

A short time later a project helo picked up Mugs and Pete and rushed them back to the project headquarters, deep in the desert. The flight surgeon completed a quick but thorough examination, then asked them if they wanted anything. Mugs promptly replied, "Yeah. I'd like a beer." The medical staff laughed.

"I'm not joking, I'd like a beer."

"That sounds like a winner. Give me one too!" Pete said.

The staff looked at them incredulously. When they realized Mugs and Pete were perfectly serious, cold beer was delivered.

The senior project officer loaded them (and their beer) into the helo for what Mugs and Pete thought would be a ride back to Nellis. They were very surprised at the helo's next stop—the crash site.

"Okay, get out," the special projects officer barked.

"Get out? We were just here!" Mugs needlessly explained.

"You have to be rescued."

"Rescued? Well . . . what was that we just did?"

"That? Well, we can't talk about that."

Mugs ordinarily would have put up a better fight, but he was sore, stiff, and tired, and the crew lured them out of the helo with a cold six-pack. Mugs and Pete sat down, leaned against the hulk, sipped their beer, and waited for the real SAR helo from Nellis to arrive.

An hour and a half later the Nellis SAR helo touched down in a swirl of sagebrush, dust, and flying lizards. The timing couldn't have been better—they were completely out of beer.

At Nellis, another USAF flight surgeon looked them over. When the flight surgeon asked for blood, Mugs said, "Nope. You're not taking any blood!"

"What?"

"You're not taking any blood."

"Why not?"

"Naval aviators don't give blood. It's against the rules. Sorry!"

"All right, we need to take some x-rays. Then we need you to wait here until we're done reviewing the film."

Mugs and Pete agreed to the x-rays, but not the directive to wait in the receiving area. "We're going to the bar," Mugs explained. "We're not flying anymore today anyway. Call us there."

The ejection occurred about 0800. By noon they were in the bar. When they were paged, Mugs and Pete returned to sick bay. Totally lacking any bedside manner, the flight surgeon read the x-ray report: "Gilleece?"

"Yo!"

"You're okay!"

"McKeown?"

"Yeah."

"You've got a broken back!"

Mugs had crushed a vertebra but didn't know it. He recalls that he was stiff but didn't hurt too bad. The flight surgeon grounded Mugs for six weeks.

At this time, the project team was running five tactics hops per day, per pilot. They flew from the crack-of-jack well into the evening. They needed all the pilots on the team. Mugs pleaded his case with the flight surgeon. The flight surgeon was honest and straightforward: "Mugs, I can't let you fly. If you eject again, you're really going to hurt yourself."

"Well then . . . I guess I just won't eject," Mugs calmly replied.

Six days after the mishap, Mugs was back in the air.

Despite the setback, Mugs and others in the black programs delivered a phenomenal amount of data and lessons learned to the TACAIR pilots of all services. When Constant Peg[12] extended training opportunities to all frontline fighter, strike, and attack aircrew, their probability to complete the mission and return, unscathed, following an air-to-air encounter skyrocketed.

In March 1968, President Nixon called a halt to bombing in North Vietnam. On March 3, 1969, a year after the bombing halt and only four months after the submission of the Ault report, TOPGUN conducted its first class. Fighter crews graduating from the four-week course were hungrily assimilated by Navy frontline fighter units. These TOPGUN graduates returned to their squadrons with a new comprehension of tactics, weapons systems employment, airmanship, and teaching skills. From these core educators, fighter squadrons improved their war art. Air operations over North Vietnam resumed in early 1972. By the end of that year, in testimony to the effectiveness of TOPGUN, the Navy's kill ratio rocketed to 12.5:1. When one fighter pilot returned from a combat mission that earned him a MiG kill, he was asked what his engagement was like. He responded, "It was just like training at TOPGUN, but these guys weren't half as good!" The hard lessons from the Ault report and the incorporation of Constant Peg and programs like it made monumental improvements to the fighter black arts.

Constant Peg

Perhaps one of the most significant training achievements of the Black Lions was facilitated by their foresight and flexibility to take advantage of Constant Peg.[13]

Constant Peg was a derivative program of Have Drill and Have Doughnut. While the Have Drill (MiG-17) and Have Doughnut (MiG-21) programs provided invaluable information on the MiG-series aircraft and identified some aircraft performance handling deficiencies, only a very few of the TACAIR pilots of any of the services actually were able to train against them. Constant Peg changed that.

By 1977, the exploitation programs were expanding, with the intent of exposing as many TACAIR crews to the three MiG models as possible. Hawk had keen insight into the Constant Peg program on the basis of his TOPGUN and VX-4 experience and contact points. He was also aware of a significant learning point. Early in the air war, none of the TACAIR pilots who had engaged the MiGs ever won their first engagement. It was a no-brainer to conclude that the first time the fighter pilot came up against a MiG-17 should not be in an actual dogfight.[14]

Participation in the Constant Peg program required a "Top Secret" clearance and an "in-brief." Sorties were scheduled for as many tactical squadrons as possible, but there were only so many MiG sorties available, and many aircrews were vying for the training.

Having full knowledge of Constant Peg and realizing that not all of his aircrew would likely reap the benefits of the program, Hawk requested top-secret clearances for all his aircrew during the '79 cruise. Shortly after returning from that cruise, Hawk arranged for the entire squadron, including the new aircrews, to receive the highly classified Constant Peg "in-brief."

The Black Lions had their fair share of regularly scheduled Constant Peg sorties, but they also took the unprecedented step of becoming the perpetual "on-call" squadron for all the sorties that were aborted by squadrons that, for any number of reasons, could not meet the schedule.

The Lions established a working relationship with the Red Eagle[15] controllers at Nellis AFB and designated one Black Lion crew to be on the flight schedule as the go team to respond to short-notice Constant Peg pop-ups. A canned round-robin flight clearance to the Nellis range complex with a return leg to Miramar was always at base operations, ready to file into the system. When a regularly scheduled crew canceled their Constant Peg sortie, the Lions were called, and a crew could race to the Nellis target complex and be ready to fight within an hour.

In 1980, the Black Lions had more engagements with MiG aircraft in the Constant Peg program than any other Navy squadron. Experience and training benefits resulting from this initiative became vividly obvious during air combat training and competition later that year.

Pride Runs Deep

By early 1980, through their tireless participation in Constant Peg and several tactical innovations, word had reached the US Air Force at Nellis AFB that the Black Lions were the rising pros from Dover[16] in the fighter world.

The 64th and 65th Aggressor Squadrons[17] conducted several instructor certification courses each year to train USAF tactical pilots as aggressor instructors—similar to TOPGUN's adversary courses for Navy and Marine pilots. In support of this training, the aggressor squadrons invited other USAF, Navy, and Marine squadrons to Nellis to fly against the student and instructor aggressors.

For two weeks in April 1980, the Black Lions would pit their Tomcats against the F-5Es in multiple aircraft scenarios of up to eight aircraft. It was some of the very best training the Lions and the USAF aircrew would ever receive. The Lions tested their evolving formations, tactics, and fighter maneuvers against small, supersonic, radar-equipped aircraft simulating Soviet fighters. In return, the USAF aggressor instructors and students fought some of the toughest Navy aircrew in the fleet.

In addition to the unique joint training, Ordnance Chief Petty Officer Blake Crowley, the Black Lions' gunner,[18] finagled an opportunity for the Lions to carry and evaluate the brand-new AIM-9M, the latest in the Sidewinder missile series.

Chief Crowley had supported the Navy contingent during the ACEVAL/AIMVAL tests at Nellis in 1976 and had made several productive contact points with the Air Force. Through his Air Force ordnance cohorts, he had discovered that an F-15 fighter squadron at Nellis had been tasked to conduct evaluation flights on the AIM-9M—still in operational evaluation by USAF. Progress, however, had been slow. Chief Crowley hinted that the Black Lions might be able to provide evaluation flights in conjunction with aggressor training missions. Chief Crowley briefed Hawk on the opportunity, and Hawk jumped on it.

For nearly two weeks, each of the Black Lion aircraft carried AIM-9Ms. In that short time they flew more missions and produced more evaluation reports than the assigned Eagle squadron had in the previous four months.

The Air Force was pleasantly dazzled with the positive assessment and the enlightening recommendations for AIM-9M's operational employment. The Black Lions, at the same time, had a very rare opportunity to gain experience with the next-generation heat-seeking missile.

Feedback on the results of the air combat training gradually made its way to the Black Lion troops. The Lions were shredding the aggressors. Using riflescopes for long-range VIDs, the F-5s were generally getting hammered prior to the merge. Those that actually made it to the merge found the prospects of tangling with the Tomcat chilling.

According to unsolicited USAF reports, the Tomcats were being flown unusually well. They were using tactics and formations the aggressors had not seen before, and the close-in maneuvering by the behemoth Tomcats was simply dazzling. The slow-speed, high-angle-of-attack work, something that most Tomcat pilots avoided like warm beer, was taking a heavy toll on the F-5s. This was quite contrary to the experiences the aggressors had with other F-14 squadrons.

Pride and professionalism are epidemic, and it quickly took hold of the Black Lion plane captains. Early in the detachment, the troops began to launch and recover their Tomcats as though they were trained by the Marine Corps Silent Drill Team. They marched to the flight line as a squad, peeled off in front of their assigned aircraft, stood at parade rest until arrival of their aircrew, launched their aircraft, stood straight as pool cues to salute their departing aircrew, formed up, and then marched back to their line shack as a squad. Returning flights received the same pageantry.

As Hawk recounts, "All the aircrew were impressed with our plane captains. Hell, all our line people looked like the Blue Angel plane captains, and they did it all on their own.

"The line division is usually staffed with the most-junior personnel in the command, and there's just no way you can suddenly order them to march to and from the flight line and put their hearts into it. Nobody told them to do it. They came up with the idea themselves, and they did it because they were proud of their squadron and believed what they were doing was important. It was their outlet to show their pride, and it was infectious.

"I got a big kick out of the Air Force plane captains. They studied our boys. They watched in utter amazement, but it wasn't something they were going to pick up. That kind of performance comes from the heart."

The Nellis Det was a boon to the esprit de corps of the Lions and a tactical treasure trove, but the climb to the top was never a sure thing and had to be earned each step of the way.[19]

Fastest Gun in the West

Two months following the Nellis Det, the Black Lions were prepping for their annual air-to-air gunnery detachment (Gun Det) at El Centro, California. The frustration in preparing for the detachment solidly fortified the saying "Nothing worth doing is ever easy," but this experience begged an addendum: "Things worth doing are never easy, but they don't have to be stupid too."

By Hawk's account, "Air-to-air gun quals were required events for certification, but everything connected with that detachment was simply too hard. First, there weren't enough TAD[20] funds, and then there weren't enough rooms available for the aircrew and enlisted personnel. We cut the detachment personnel to the absolute bare minimum to meet the billeting restrictions and solved that problem. Then we were told there were no banner-towing cables available, then no paint for the bullets, and no gun camera film development services at El Centro. And, oh yeah . . . we may not have enough fuel funds to complete the detachment. To listen to the people, supposedly there to support us, there was just no way anyone could get anything done . . . there was just no way this mandatory gun det could happen. It was as if a gun det of this magnitude had never been done before. It was impossible!

"At the predetachment planning meeting, the Black Lions reviewed what seemed to be an endless list of impossible tasks. The JOs and enlisted folks hit the ground running. They formed teams and took responsibility for each and every item on the list. They accepted the tasks primarily because the jobs needed doing, but also because our guys had the attitude that nothing was too hard once they had their minds set on it."

In the course of several days, bolstered by the unrelenting steel resolve of key chief petty officers and JOs, the complexion of things began to improve. ComFit came up with funds, NAS El Centro billeting discovered that there really were several more rooms available, bullet paint was purchased on the open market, banner-towing cable and attaching hardware was ferreted out, and the gun det was suddenly, miraculously, a doable thing.

"For my part and that of our senior leaders, we made sure our enlisted leadership understood their responsibilities, had the authority they needed, and then simply got out of their way and let them work. It made you smile!"

T-ACMs preceding the gun det focused on air-to-air gunnery training and stressed safety, pattern interval, altitude, airspeeds, ranges, angle-off, gunsight symbology, and precision marksmanship. In order to get his team completely energized for the mission, Hawk invited the father of modern air-to-air gunnery, Gene Tye,[21] to speak to the squadron.

Gene had lectured on air-to-air gunnery while Hawk was at TOPGUN in 1977. He was an exciting speaker and knew his subject matter cold. Gene delivered an informative and inspirational presentation on the fundamentals and techniques of successful air-to-air gunnery training and real-world gun engagements.

On June 16, 1980, the Black Lions flew their Tomcats to Naval Air Facility El Centro. For the next eleven days, they conducted air-to-air gunnery training on towed aerial banners. The results were spectacular. The Black Lions expended more ammunition (32,923 rounds) than any other Miramar fighter squadron in the same period[22] of time. They racked up six century (100 hits) banners,[23] six double-century (200 hits) banners, and a record-breaking 400 rounds in one target. One of the Lions' pilots established an all-time record for air-to-air gunnery record with the Tomcat: Lt. Greg "Mullet" Gerard scored an incredible 52 percent hit rate.[24]

These accomplishments came on the heels of the "High Noon" air-to-air gunnery derby competition conducted the month before, in which the Black Lions took first over all other Miramar-based fighter squadrons. Their achievements set a new benchmark in the fighter community for air-to-air marksmanship.

Hawk was exceptionally pleased with their performance, but what elevated his pride even more was that his Lions devised a solution for each and every obstacle thrown in their path. He was simply astounded by the resolve and never-say-die commitment of his Black Lions.

The Training Carousel

The next deployment was scheduled for April 14, 1981, aboard USS *America*—again on the East Coast. Before the ship sailed, there remained several major training events in the turn-around cycle. In competition with these was the first-ever Miramar Fighter Derby.

The highly anticipated Fighter Derby was the single most important competitive exercise in Fightertown. It was the "Super Bowl" of Miramar-based fighter squadrons and would define the pecking order and stature of each.

As important as the Fighter Derby was, it was not part of the turnaround training cycle and took secondary precedence to those that were.

In August, just prior to the Fighter Derby, CVW-11 squadrons spent two weeks aboard USS *Kitty Hawk* for carrier qualifications. The objective of this period was to qualify the crews for carrier ops—day and night. This couldn't have come at a worse time, since it prevented any squadron-level tactics or ACM training in preparation for the Fighter Derby.[25] The Fighter Derby was a "come-as-you-are" competitive exercise, but most of the other fighter squadrons at Miramar had been practicing for weeks.

The Lions came off the ship on Sunday, August 24, and began the Fighter Derby on Monday—no stand-down, no maintenance time, and no time to train for the big match.

So the Black Lions sucked it up and put their collective heads down for the charge into the Fighter Derby. Where there was exhaustion, they had grit; where there was loneliness for family, they had comradery; and where there was confusion, they had leadership. But was this enough to bring victory to the Black Lions in the approaching Fighter Derby?

CHAPTER 8

A Clattering of Sabers

Victory has a thousand fathers, but defeat is an orphan.

—Count Caleazzo Ciano

Fighter Super Bowl

The 1980 Fighter Derby was a first for the fighter community. For two weeks, each of the several Miramar fighter squadrons competed in a real-world training scenario. They were pitted against professional adversaries: TOPGUN instructors flying F-5s and VF-126 adversary pilots flying A-4s: the Mongoose (A-4E), the Super Fox (A-4F), or both. The engagements included a section of fighters against a section of bogies, but without prior knowledge of the type of bogies, F-5s or A-4s, the fighters were facing.

All engagements took place on the Yuma Tactical Air Combat Training (TACTs)[1] range, a fully instrumented air combat range just east of MCAS Yuma. Points were awarded on the basis of the effectiveness of radar intercepts, VIDs,[2] premerge AIM-7 Sparrow and AIM-9 Sidewinder shots, section integrity, air combat maneuvering, and bogey kills. Points were deducted for bad IDs, ROE noncompliance, and the big one—kills on the fighters.

Fighter load-out for the Tomcat was full 20 mm ammo with two AIM-9Ls and two AIM-7Fs. The Phantoms, with no internal gun,[3] simulated a combat load of two AIM-9Ls and two AIM-7Fs. Bogey load-out included guns and two simulated Soviet Atoll (AA-2) missiles, similar in performance to the AIM-9D.[4]

Computer-driven electronic range telemetry, within the perimeter of the TACTS range, evaluated all shots to determine if range, angle-off, altitude, and airspeed dynamics were within the parameters of the weapon's envelope. The TACTs range even factored in the sun position in order to better evaluate heat-seeking missiles. To inject realism (and frustration) into the exercise, all simulated missile firings were subject to Monte Carlo rules. The Fighter Derby judges, led by Lt. Cmdr. "Eggs" Benedict, applied a "risk factor" to each missile shot, which statistically simulated system failure probabilities. Each missile firing that was computed to be "in parameters" by the TACTS range telemetry computer was then subjected to a Monte Carlo determination by a roll of the judge's dice to determine kill probability.

To further enhance mission realism, all fighters flew the 120-mile leg from Miramar to the Yuma range, engaged the bogies in a single fight, and returned to Miramar—nonstop. Fuel management was added to a long list of factors, just as it would be in real combat.

Hawk vs. Toado: Gunfight at the OK Corral

On one of the engagements early in the competition, Lt. Cmdr. JR "Junior" Davis and Lt. Cmdr. Jim "Nice Guy" Nise flew as number 2 with Hawk and Dan "Chief" Anderson. Though they didn't know it, they were scheduled to fight a VF-126 Scooter flown by Mike "Zonk"

Zoka and a TOPGUN F-5E piloted by Capt. Lennie "Toado" Buccho. Toado happened to be the Marine pilot assigned to TOPGUN when Hawk had pleaded his case for additional manpower with Col. Mike Sullivan, USMC, in the spring of 1977. Toado had arrived at TOPGUN after Hawk departed for the Black Lions, but the word was out, even then, that TOPGUN had inherited a spine ripper.

Toado, a Marine Phantom pilot, was one of those gifted aviators who could climb into the cockpit and immediately become a homogeneous component of the airplane. He was talented, a natural tactician, and had that "Damn the torpedoes" attitude common in aggressive fighter pilots. In an engagement against Toado, fledgling fighter pilots could usually measure their life expectancy by the number of turns it would take to be killed by Toado. In the cockpit of the F-5E Tiger, he was a thing to behold!

Hawk and his three teammates understood the significance of their Fighter Derby debut. Their performance would affect the cumulative point standing for the entire squadron. They were pumped, confident, and primed for the fight.

The engagement between Hawk and Toado that day had nothing of the marketing hype or bluster of the October 30, 1974, boxing match between Muhammad Ali and George Foreman, the famed "Rumble in the Jungle." But what it lacked in media coverage was most certainly compensated by the raw tension as Hawk and Toado matched skills, experience, tactical prowess, and steel resolve as two of the finest fighter pilots in naval service met on the electronic battlefield.

On a typical late-summer, azure-sky day, Hawk brought his section into an easy right-climbing turn after takeoff from Miramar and headed east toward the Yuma range. As they neared the range, Hawk glanced at JR and received a thumbs-up responding to Hawk's "combat check" hand signal.

Hawk contacted the range controller: "Yuma TACTs, Black Lion two-zero-zero, flight of two, in company with two-zero-six, 20 west at flight level 2-3-zero, checking in for the fifteen hundred range time."

"Lion two-zero-zero, roger, sir. Midnight[5] is your controller on this one. Your bogies are established on the east station. Call when ready!"

Hawk made a quick glance at JR, who gave him a final "thumbs-up." "We're ready to go, Midnight."

"Roger, Black Lion! Your bogies are 1-zero-5 degrees at 41 miles."

Now, it was the RIOs' turn to earn their money. "I have contact at 40 miles, composition two in a left turn through north at 22,000. Speed 300 knots," Chief transmitted on squadron tactical frequency.

"Concur," Nice Guy announced, then continued, "I show a trail formation with 1 to 2 miles' separation."

The radar work was flawless and typical of Chief and Nice Guy. Good as it was, they couldn't determine the aircraft type or by whom they were being flown. Both bits of information would have been helpful.

Although all the Black Lion pilots had undergone an extensive slow-speed, high-angle-of-attack maneuvering syllabus, their tactics were designed for the quick kill—establish a long-range VID, get missiles off the rails as early as possible, maintain section integrity for as long as feasible, and, if any of the bogies lived through the merge, either blow through the fight to reset the geometry or employ fighter maneuvers that maximized the performance margin against the type of aircraft engaged.

The "Lion" tactical rule of thumb was to optimize the Tomcat's enormous thrust-to-weight advantage by trying to engage the A-4 Scooter in an energy or vertical fight. With the F-14's eye-watering turn rate and nose-positioning authority, a different tactic was used against the F-5 Tiger. The Tomcat driver would try to sucker the F-5 into a turning or position fight—a good, old-fashioned street brawl. In either case, the Tomcat had wide, specific excess power advantages against both the Scooter and the Tiger.

Chief maintained a cadenced flow of pertinent information on the radio: "Bogies now at 22 miles, descending through 18,000 feet. Airspeed, 400 knots. Formation is, stand by . . . they've broken into a line-abreast formation about a mile apart."

"Roger, concur!" Nice Guy responded.

Hawk looked to his left. JR was holding a combat spread position to the north and had already anticipated Hawk's descent to match the bogies' altitude.

For as long as young men took to the skies to bring death and destruction to their enemies, the experienced raptor pilots were aware of, and used to their advantage, a natural atmospheric phenomenon. On clear days there is usually a narrow band of light gray hugging the horizon. The bogies are generally far easier to visually detect and identify in that band. If they were higher than the fighters, they would blend in with the darker-blue sky, and if below they would become difficult to detect against the multihued desert ground clutter. Hawk descended to the bogies' altitude.

"Bogies, composition 2, range 12, 15,000 feet. Airspeed now 450 knots. Formation appears to have changed. Leader is south. Wingman, 1 mile to the north, 1 mile in trail, and slightly low.

"Lead bogey has accelerated. I show him at 500 knots. I'm locking the lead bogey now!"

"Roger, I'm searching," Nice Guy said.

Hawk monitored his radar display and made a slight heading correction to place the aiming diamond squarely in the center of the HUD. At 10 miles he saw a tiny speck the size of a fly turd in the center of the aiming diamond. Hawk called out, "Talley ho," indicating he was padlocked on a bogey.

The F-5 was a tough airplane to see at any angle, but head on or tail on it had a smaller cross-sectional area than a Volkswagen, making it very difficult to establish a tally-ho at range. Hawk leaned forward to peer through the riflescope and discovered that the lead bogey was an F-5. He made a small turn and centered the scope on a second speck to the left of the Tiger—a Scooter. This was the worst of the three possible bogey combinations and, with near certainty, would force the fighters into two one-versus-one engagements. It would also likely degrade section integrity after the merge.

Hawk weighed in: "Lead bogey to the south is an F-5. I'll take him. Wingman is an A-4, level, 5 degrees left, a mile and a half in trail, and slightly low."

"Roger! Talley 2. I'll take the A-4," JR transmitted.

"Stand by," Chief announced. "Fox one on the F-5 at 6 miles!"

Five seconds later, the range had closed to 5 miles and Nice Guy called the second shot: "Fox one on the A-4!"

"Lion, both missiles scored as kills. Continue!" Midnight transmitted.

So far, so good! Hawk whispered to himself.

The radar work, early VID, and the fact that they had missiles in the air well before the merge were all point getters, but the shots did not *kill/remove* the bogies. The real fight was about to begin.

Hawk stole a quick glance at JR to his left. He had increased the distance from Hawk so he could bracket the A-4 to the north. *Good move*, thought Hawk. *Either way the Scooter turns, he'll be sandwiched between us.*

Hawk switched his gaze back to the F-5, which had made a slight turn to the south. Hawk plotted the geometry in his mind's eye and at once recognized that the F-5 pilot was trying to force him to turn south. "JR, I'll take the F-5 down the right side. I'll have to come right to engage. DO NOT LET THE A-4 SHOOT ME!"

"Roger, Hawk. Tally. Visual!"[6]

A half mile from the merge, the F-5 pilot did the unexpected. He went belly-up in a Godzilla left turn. The move surprised Hawk. *Why would the pilot transmit his intentions like that?*

As soon as the Tiger pilot made his move, Hawk thought he knew who might be flying. *That's ballsy. That's crazy. That has to be Toado!*

It was Toado, but he wasn't crazy. He was crafty, and sneaky, and deadly. And that was just the way the Marines liked their fighter pilots.

Toado wanted to get a turning fight going right off the bat. His hard port turn to the south would force Hawk to also turn south and away from the A-4. This, Toado hoped, might set up Zonk for a quick shot on Hawk as he exposed his tailpipes to the A-4.

Hawk had little choice. He could neither extend out of the fight to the east nor turn to the north. Either action could cause him to lose sight on the F-5. Loss of the tally on an F-5 was usually followed shortly after by the blood-chilling computer-generated "BEEEP" tone in the headset announcing a missile in the air.

The hair on the back of Hawk's neck bristled. He had to turn right. But by turning right, to the south, Hawk would expose his tail to the A-4. If JR did not engage the A-4 immediately, the A-4 could easily converge for a shot on Hawk.

Hawk watched Toado's F-5 for less than two seconds and reevaluated his countermove. The F-5 had at least 500 knots just before the pass. The hard turn that Toado had laid on had dissipated at least 100 knots, and that gave Hawk's F-14 a very distinct energy advantage.

Hawk pushed the throttles to the firewall. The blowers lit up like two steel foundries and puked nearly 36,000 pounds of thrust out the pipes. He pulled back on the stick and made a slight nose-high turn into the F-5. He was going high over the Tiger. The maneuver would allow him to do three things: avoid a shot by the A-4 if JR didn't engage him, maintain sight on the Tiger, and, most importantly, dictate the conduct of the fight. Toado clearly wanted the Tomcat to enter a horizontal-turning fight, especially since he had the initial positional advantage. Usually this maneuver was inadvisable, but this was Toado, and anything was possible.

When Hawk assessed how much energy the F-5 had bled in the turn, he realized the smart move was to try to push the fight into the vertical.

As soon as Hawk made his pull into the vertical, Toado eased off his turn, leveled his wings, and started a nose-up pull into Hawk.

"I'm engaged with the A-4. YOYO!"[7] JR announced.

"Roger!" Hawk responded. That was comforting news. JR was tangled up with the Scooter, which meant that Hawk could now concentrate on his most immediate problem, Toado.

Initially, the view from Toado's position must have looked appealing. He had this giant Tomcat treed in front of and a few thousand feet above him, and he still had respectable airspeed available to chase the Tomcat, but it was kind of like having a lion by the tail . . . *okay, now what do I do?*

Toado began his nose-high pull into Hawk. At this point, Hawk was unconcerned. He was fighting a one-versus-one against an airplane he had hundreds of hours in and knew intimately. As much as he respected the Tiger, he knew it could not match the vertical extension or the turn his Tomcat was about to perform.

As Toado continued his climb, Hawk studied him over his right shoulder and watched for telltale signs of energy depletion. What he saw next made him smile. The vertical closure had ceased, and the nose of the F-5 wobbled slightly, then began to fall back toward the horizon. That was the cue for Hawk's next act.

The Tomcat was nearly 4,000 feet above the Tiger. The nose of the Tomcat was nearly straight up, and the airspeed was under 150 knots. Hawk gently pulled the throttles back to military, then manually extended the maneuvering flaps and slats as he delicately caressed the stick to the right and aft to coax the nose through the vertical and back behind the Tiger. When the nose broke through the vertical and pitched toward the opposite horizon, Hawk began to program the stick forward, so as to allow his jet to extend farther into the F-5's extended six o'clock position.

Hawk and Chief were inverted, hanging in the straps and getting a God's-eye view of the Tiger below. Hawk double-checked the wing position—they had already programmed forward. He studied the relative position and energy of the two jets. When he calculated that he had enough horizontal and vertical displacement to complete the turn and converge on the Tiger, he heaved the stick all the way back into his lap.

At that instant, 32 feet of horizontal stabilizer fully deflected into the airstream and snapped the Tomcat's long nose straight down. The Tomcat pivoted rather than turned and completed over 150 degrees of pitch in the time it takes to take a deep breath.

When Hawk recentered the stick, the Tomcat's nose was just a few degrees behind Toado's F-5 and about 200 feet above him. The Tiger, at this point, was nearly ballistic, and the nose was dipping back to the horizon.

Hawk made the last minor nose adjustment, placing the aiming diamond precisely on the tail of the Tiger, and squeezed the stick trigger.

"BEEEP!" signaled another missile in the air. "Fox -two on the F-5 heading southeast," Hawk barked on the radio.

"JR, how ya doin'?"

"Had better days, Skipper!"

"Okay. Hang on. I'll be right there!"

Hawk stuffed the stick forward with his right hand to unload for maximum acceleration and with his left hand shoved the throttles forward. In just a few seconds he had regained considerable energy and, thinking the Sidewinder shot was valid, began a hard turn to the north to come to JR's aid.

The transmission Hawk heard next sent an ice-cold shiver down his spine: "Lion two-zero-zero, your shot was scored a miss!"

A miss? You've got to be shi—— . . . *No time to argue.*

"Roger, Midnight. Copy, miss! JR, hang on, son. I'll be with you in a second."

Thinking that he had killed the Tiger and, in an attempt to save JR, Hawk had handed a huge tactical advantage back to Toado. Hawk had turned left to the north and put the Tiger on his tail. When he did that, he lost sight.

Hawk quickly reversed, then made a hard, nose-low, energy-building turn to the right and back to the last known position of the Tiger. He scanned the area south of him and was quickly rewarded with a tally. The F-5 was south, in a left turn, still several thousand feet below Hawk but bringing his nose up to meet him.

Christ, he can't possibly want to go vertical again. How crazy is he?

In the last several seconds of the engagement, Hawk had bled down to less than 300 knots. He still had more airspeed than the Tiger, but once again the Tiger had a slight positional advantage.

Hawk turned into Toado to keep him in front of the wing line, then unloaded to build more energy.

As they closed for a right-to-right pass, Toado was in a nose-high right turn with about 45 degrees' advantage on the Tomcat. The Tomcat was in a level right turn. Toado reversed his turn just prior to the pass and continued to press Hawk. This would generally be considered a tactical mistake, but Toado had a plan. Toado's reversal would force three events: intimidate Hawk, cause him to commit to a one-circle fight, and force him to turn harder into him and thereby bleed airspeed.

The only bug-in-the-honey problem was that Hawk instantly recognized the setup from the fighter pilot book of dirty tricks. It was a move that Hawk had used dozens of times, and he wasn't about to bite this time.

Hawk had a countermove that Toado was not going to enjoy—he hoped.

Hawk lit up the blowers, reversed his turn to the left, and began a climb. He looked over his left shoulder and noted that Toado had continued his left turn, and now he had begun to pull his nose up. Hawk had redefined the geometry to force a two-circle fight.

It was an uncomfortable position for Hawk and Chief to be in. The Tiger was below and behind Hawk, and the Tiger's nose was only about 30 degrees below Hawk's jet. *If I'm reading the energy signs right, there ain't no way he can maintain this kind of aggressive pursuit for long. He's got to be out of airspeed. Watch this one, Toado!* Hawk whispered to himself.

Hawk leveled his wings and pulled to the moon—an audacious move considering his low airspeed. The Tomcat made a gigantic, nose-high arc over and behind the Tiger. As the airspeed indicator flirted with the 100-knot mark, Hawk gently eased the engines out of blower, slammed the main flaps down, and heaved on the pole. Almost instantly, the nose of the 63-foot Tomcat snapped through the horizon and pointed at the Tiger's extended six o'clock.

From Toado's cockpit, the turn must have looked depressingly like the previous maneuver, and it was no less sobering the second time.

Hawk converged on the Tiger from above and well aft. Toado, as talented as he was, struggled just to keep the nose of his Tiger up, but this time Hawk was leaving nothing to chance. He was going for another Fox-two shot and would follow that up with a gun kill.

Toado tried desperately to defend against the Tomcat, but with so little airspeed and no g available, all the rudder and stick input did was alter the attitude of the aircraft—it did nothing to its trajectory or track-crossing angle.

Twice now, Toado had watched as this Tomcat driver had completely reversed his advantage. Whoever this guy was, he had completed two exquisite vertical extensions; the fastest, most astounding high-pitch-rate turns over the top that Toado had ever seen; and then, in an awe-inspiring display of tactical acumen and airmanship, skillfully maneuvered to his extended six o'clock. By now, Toado was certain he knew who his opponent was—Hawk. And this time, for all the wizardry and tactical guile Toado was known for, this dazzling air show was about to come to an abrupt end.

Just as Hawk converged on the Tiger, much of the exuberance and a lot of his concentration were diminished with this UHF transmission: "Hawk, things are lookin' ugly here. We could use some help!"

"I'll be there in two, JR. Just stay alive!"

Hawk converted on the Tiger's six o'clock. "BEEEP!" "Fox two on the F-5!"

"Lion, that was scored as a miss!"

"Roger!" Hawk was incredulous but concentrated on his next shot. He pressed in for the kill on the hapless Tiger.

Approaching 1,000 feet and 30 degrees of angle-off, Hawk let the gun pipper[8] steady on the canopy and then marched it down the spine of the F-5. "Pipper's on. Tracking. Tracking. Tracking. Pipper's off! Now, if that's not a kill, I'm turning in my wings!"

Without waiting for a response, Hawk broke off the attack at 500 feet, lit the blowers, and made a hard turn to the north to save JR. Hawk was pointed nearly north when "BEEEP!" blasted over the radio. "Lion two-oh-six, that's a kill. You're out of the fight."

"Roger. Two-zero-six is out of the fight!"

"Skipper, I'm dead," JR announced.

"Roger, JR!"

Shit!

"Chief, you see the bogey out there?"

"I have a visual on JR's F-14, but no tally on the A-4."

Shit, Hawk swore to himself. *JR just got shot and we don't see the Scooter. There's only one smart thing to do.*

"Chief, we're lighting 'em up. Keep your eyes open!"

"Looking!"

As much as Hawk wanted to settle the score with the Scooter, he knew that it was a lot easier for Zonk to pick up the Tomcat than it was for Chief and him to get a tally on the Scooter. The prudent decision was to bug out of the fight and minimize the loss.

Hawk scanned the area north and east—no Scooter in sight. He checked the throttles all the way to the wall; brought the Tomcat around in a hard, nose-down left turn; and bolted for the western edge of the range.

Hawk checked the fuel gauge. They'd burned tons of JP-5. Passing through 560 knots, Hawk believed the A-4 driver was miles to the east. Hawk made a risky decision and pulled the throttles back to cruise setting. Fifteen seconds after he came back on the power and a mile from the edge of the area, the hair-raising "BEEEP!" blared over the range frequency. "Lion two-zero-zero, you're dead!"

"Roger!" Hawk acknowledged.

Hawk didn't bother to look back. Now he knew where the Scooter was—probably a mile at dead six. He just couldn't believe an A-4 had just run him down.[9]

Hawk was mightily disappointed in the way the entire engagement went in general, and in himself in particular. He had unfortunately relearned several ACM rules again. Foremost among them was to train as you would fight.

Lessons Learned . . . Again

In one two-hour ACM sortie, Hawk had broken several of the fighter commandments, flown one of the most horrific sorties of his life, and, worse, jeopardized the standing and the likely outcome of his team in the Fighter Derby.

It was not the fault of poorly written objectives or the Monte Carlo rules. The jet hadn't hiccuped, the sun wasn't in his eyes, and, Chief, Hawk's RIO, performed magnificently. Everything that had gone wrong was the fault of one person . . . himself. Hawk was smart enough to recognize that fact, and big enough to accept it.

"As I look back on that fight," Hawk recounts, "there was too much ego, too much bravado, and too little discipline. I felt like I was Godzilla when we took our vector to engage the bandits. It's hard not to when you strap on an F-14. We should have taken our shots premerge, and if we were directed to continue the fight, which we were, we could have kept the section together, blown through, opened up the separation to 10 or 12 miles, and made a nose-low, in-place turn so when we came out of the turn we'd have them visually highlighted in the gray horizon against the sun. I didn't relish the idea of outrunning a Tiger, and I sure didn't want to get in a turning fight with the Super Fox A-4[10] unless we had two tallies.

"On the second merge, I would have expected we'd have either Sparrows or Sidewinders in the air before the pass, and hopefully we would have killed at least one. Monte Carlo rules can't work against you forever! At that point we could kill the last bogey in a two-versus-one fight, which is a no-brainer, or, if things weren't looking good, we coulda bugged west, gone home, had a beer, and declared victory.

"The key is to maintain section integrity and provide mutual support. When that broke down . . . well . . . things just started to go to shit!

"The thing that bothered me most was what that hop did to our collective score in the Fighter Derby. It was my fault, my fault alone. We could still recover, but we were going to have to score some brilliant victories."

"I knew we had the right aircrew. They were innovative, tough-minded, competitive, and disciplined predators. In my mind, they were our all-star team. I had the highest expectations that, in the end, we'd do well!"

CHAPTER 9
Counting Coup

The fighter pilot is an attitude. It is cockiness. It is aggressiveness. It is self-confidence. It is a streak of rebelliousness, and it is competitiveness. But there's something else—there's a spark. There's a desire to be good. To do well; in the eyes of your peers, and in your own mind.

—Robin Olds, *Fighter Pilot: The Memoirs of Legendary Ace Robin Olds*

The Debrief

Hawk took small solace in knowing that he was not outflown. He had violated several tactical disciplines, a death sentence in the real world but only hugely embarrassing in this instance.

What bothered him most, however, was the fact that when the points were tallied up for Fighter Derby, the whole squadron would suffer the consequences—sadly, all the Black Lions would pay the price. It was a hard blow personally and professionally, and the experience ate at him for some time.

A few days later, however, one of his pilots performed so well in the competition that the significance of his own performance seemed inconsequential.

All Things in Competition

Happy hour at Miramar O Club on Wednesday night was the watering hole for Miramar aircrews. The ambiance was extraordinary, the drinks were cheap, and, although the tales of aviation exploits often explored the continuum from highly imaginative to the truly bizarre, the company was always entertaining.

Tactical aviators, by design, are highly competitive. Given nearly any activity from amusing exercises to daredevil stunts, aviators will turn anything into a test.

Due to the alarming rates of DUI citations being issued to Navy personnel coming off base in the evening, at some point the Miramar O Club management installed a breathalyzer machine. In addition to what was thought to be a warning device for their patrons, management reasoned, it was also a revenue generator.

Upon first assessment, the concept had no downside. In a normal setting, management would have been correct, but this was the West Coast Navy fighter master jet base, and the clientele was many standard deviations away from normal.

Set in a prominent location of the main bar, a patron could pay a measly twenty-five cents, insert a straw into a port on the machine, exhale into the straw, and get a readout on their blood alcohol level.

The breathalyzer sat relatively unnoticed until one competitive-minded aviator challenged another to a test to see who could get the higher reading. In no time the challenge escalated, and soon several other (many) competitors had joined the match. When lagging behind the field, a snort of a favorite strong spirit could boost one's readout to a more competitive level.

Late that evening, too many wives, girlfriends, and squadron mates were contacted to provide transportation for those competitors who placed high in the finals.

A short time later, the breathalyzer mysteriously and inexplicably disappeared. The winner of the contest was never identified, nor was the winning blood-alcohol reading. No one could remember either.

Happy-Hour Banter

Hawk and a number of aviators were gathered around the bar when the discussion turned to the relative performance capabilities of the Tomcat vis-à-vis the Super Fox.

The Tomcat's strong card lay in the very long-range interceptor role, and in that regime, it was the world's most lethal fighter. Yet, the F-14 still had a midrange fight and an in-close or visual option—inside 10 miles. It was here, in the visual arena, where the performance parameters were less defined and the performance delta against other fighters was more reliant on the skills of the individual fighter pilot.

The Tomcat rated well against all the competition in specific excess power, specific excess energy, wing loading, and elevator authority (pitch rate). But there were safeguards, computer algorithms, lifting-device limiters, and other systems designed to keep the jet well within its designed operating envelope. By no stretch of the imagination were the Tomcat's limiters as bad as those Hawk had wrestled with on his first and only flight in the Dutch air force's F-104 Starfighter. After that two-versus-two sortie, Hawk had commented that "never in my life have I experienced so many systems, safety backups, override controls, and warning tones so disconcerting and effective at keeping a pilot from flying his jet."[1]

In contrast to the F-104, a skilled Tomcat pilot learned to short-circuit or bypass some of these safeguards. When the crew had learned all the tricks and techniques of the mighty Tomcat, they held total mastery of the jet and were able to unleash the full brawn, power, and performance capability of the F-14.

The Black Lions most likely excelled at this beyond most other F-14 squadrons at NAS Miramar at this time. Although there were some variations in tactile skill levels and technical cleverness across the board, the Lions' crew became gifted in bringing into the air battle every pound of thrust, every foot of lifting area, every nuance of pitch authority, and every kinetic unit of power within the array of onboard weapons systems.

The most widely used aircraft in the adversary mission was the McDonnell Douglas A-4 Skyhawk, affectionately called the "Scooter." It began life on June 12, 1952, as a light-attack, carrier-based jet with a nuclear mission. It had a 27-foot wingspan and weighed in at 11,000 pounds empty.

The early Scooters had neither the top speed nor the energy addition rate of a MiG-21, nor did they have the low-speed turning performance of the MiG-17. However, if the MiG-21 and the MiG-17 mated, their offspring might look and act very much like the A-4. It represented an acceptable cross between the two real-world threat aircraft and was one of the few aircraft that could perform the dissimilar air combat training mission with aplomb.

During the late 1970s and into the early 1980s, the little bogies flown by TOPGUN and the adversary squadrons—the F-5E Tiger II and the A-4—seemed to have their way with the leviathan F-14 more often than they should. The Super Fox was persistently and particularly annoying to Tomcat drivers. There was no reason an aircraft designed in the early 1950s as an attack airplane should be in the same league as the Tomcat in the visual arena—but it was.

The performance deltas between these aircraft were not an original topic during happy hour, especially between the fighter and adversary pilots, but this time Cmdr. Jim "Tarzan" Nunn, CO of VF-126, one of the adversary pilots flying in the Fighter Derby, made this beer-laced acclamation: "Ain't nobody in an F-14 can beat me in a Super Fox!"

Tarzan was a former Phantom pilot and a highly respected adversary pilot, but this boast went well beyond the pale—*thems was fightin' words!* by Hawk's thinking.

Hawk waited a few seconds to see if anyone would counter the statement. Ordinarily, boasts of this sort were considered a breach into the *no-no land* of fighter pilot / adversary pilot protocol. This breach, on occasion, could put the *who* into the sauce and detract from the professionalism of the relationship. However, this level of balderdash screamed for a champion from the fighter community.

When it was clear there was no one willing to come to the rescue of the Tomcat community, Hawk, with typical statesmanlike diplomacy, politely retorted, "Now Tarzan, come on—that's complete bullshit and you know it!"

"That's no bullshit, Hawk. I've never lost a one-versus-one against a Tomcat, and I never will!"

"Tarzan, I know you been doing this awhile, and I know the Super Fox is a mighty impressive little airplane, but one-on-one I don't think you can beat any of my Black Lions."

Hawk wasn't sure that was a true statement, but he held such pride in all his aircrew he was honor-bound to say it. Surely, few F-14 pilots at Miramar were better trained, but Tarzan was a talented, adversary pilot, and the Super Fox was nothing to poke a stick at, as Hawk well knew.

"Yeah, well, there's lots of days left in the Fighter Derby. I guess we'll just have to see how your young kitty cats do against my Super Fox."

"Yeah, Tarzan, I reckon we will!"

Two days later, in one of those amusing little quirks of destiny, a Black Lion section was scheduled for a Fighter Derby event against a TOPGUN F-5 and a VF-126 Super Fox flown by none other than Tarzan. None of the Black Lions knew which adversaries they were scheduled against, but a few minutes after the end of a very successful two-versus-two engagement, word raced back to Hawk that Buck Jones scored a tracking-gun kill on a Super Fox, the pilot of which was the man who could not be beaten by an F-14.

Pipper's On!

"Davie 'Buck' Jones was a big guy," according to Hawk. "He stood well over 6 foot 3 and was built like a Brink's truck. And the boy could eat. He could whammo two supersize Big Macs and a huge stack of fries while you were still unwrapping your burger.

"Buck had been a plowback,[2] so he was a more senior lieutenant and came to us with a ton of hours. He had made the '79 deployment, but he wasn't that stellar around the boat, so that didn't make CAG Ready or the LSOs very happy. It was difficult for him to use the riflescope, but he had an incredible set of eyes and could pick the fly shit out of the pepper at 100 yards. The other thing he could do very well was get the Tomcat into an old-fashioned slugfest and win. He was dazzling!"

During the Fighter Derby event with Buck and Tarzan, there was nothing remarkable during the setup or the radar intercept. The Black Lion RIOs' radar work was typically superlative. Both VIDs were solid; there were two missiles in the air well prior to the merge. Shortly after the merge, similar to Hawk's fight, the engagement broke down into two one-versus-ones. This was something the Lion aircrew ordinarily tried to avoid, but for which they were prepared to execute if an advantage was to be gained. And this time, Buck saw an advantage. And this one went far better than Hawk's.

Just after merge plot, Tarzan, in the Super Fox, quickly glommed on to Buck—not really a surprise. The Super Fox was quick to commit and initially had a clear positional advantage on the F-14. There was an early gun attack attempt by Tarzan, and while he still retained a positional advantage, he sacrificed a good deal of energy in that attempt.

Buck played it smart. He worked on building energy and watched intently as he figured out the game plan of the Super Fox driver.

It didn't take long. Tarzan did what he did best and pushed Buck into a rolling scissors.[3] All in all, this was an acceptable if not perfect situation for a Super Fox driver. Tarzan was happily surprised that this idiot Tomcat pilot choose to engage a Super Fox in the fight the A-4 did best—a rolling scissors.

But then a funny thing happened. As the rolling scissors developed, the Tomcat didn't deplete its energy as it should have. Buck, now with considerably more airspeed, responded with several large rolling-scissor maneuvers around the Super Fox. Initially the match seemed even, but as it progressed, the Super Fox just couldn't compete with the big TF30 engines roaring like twin volcanoes, and the enormous wing—now full forward.

As the energy of both jets diminished, the vertical displacement began to collapse. As that happened, the fight naturally transitioned into a flat scissors.[4] This wasn't exactly what Tarzan had in mind. Usually by this point, Tarzan would have had several snapshots and one or two long, stable tracking gunshots, which would be followed by a very joyous "That's a kill—knock it off!" call.

A peek at the F-14 revealed several cues vital to a bogey pilot. The Tomcat was abeam the A-4, slightly higher, cospeed, with the wings extended—a dead giveaway indicating that the F-14 was running out of smack. But suddenly Tarzan in his "can't be beat" Super Fox had a new surprise. This fight was turning into something completely different.

Buck, per Black Lion tactical doctrine, thumbed the maneuvering flaps down. With clean, undisturbed air flowing over the horizontal stabilizers, the Tomcat's controllable airspeed dropped by nearly another 15 knots, and Buck coaxed the Tomcat's nose up into the vertical an additional 10 degrees higher than Tarzan dared point the nose of his scooter.

Tarzan marched slowly out in front of and below the Tomcat, while Buck skillfully balanced the 20-ton jet on two white-hot plumes. Tiny stick and rudder inputs by Buck ensured maximum lift over drag. Buck waited patiently and watched; he made a slight turn to keep the little Super Fox in sight as the vertical and lateral separation increased.

It was a cold blow to Tarzan. Never before had he seen a Tomcat literally stand on its tail and still have such remarkable pitch authority.

Tarzan wrestled with his jet and, with the last few knots of airspeed, tried desperately to take the vertical and positional advantage away from Buck.

It wasn't going to happen—not that day.

Buck rolled slightly, eyed the Super Fox (now well below him and slightly in front), and noted that the flaps were down and the slats were fully extended. It was quite obvious that whoever was flying the little jet knew his business, but it was moot at this point. Buck was about to rack up big points for the Black Lion team.

When Buck was sure he had sufficient lateral and vertical separation to converge on the Scooter without overshooting, he pulled a bit of power, dipped his wing into the A-4, and started down, all the while positioning the bobbing gun pipper in front of the A-4 for a shot.

Buck ignored the Fox-two (AIM-9 Sidewinder shot) opportunity and closed for guns. At 1,800 feet he pulled the trigger activating the gun camera and announced, "Pipper's on!"

For the next four seconds Buck closed on the hapless Scooter and refined the placement of the gunsight.

There was no disputing the shot, and no possibility of a Monte Carlo miss. TACTs telemetry equipment recorded the pipper tracking on the centerline of the airplane, from the nose, through the canopy, and down the tail.

It was a precision gunshot against the man who couldn't be beaten by a Tomcat.

The engagement was hardly over when one of the Lion JOs rushed into Hawk's office and made an unofficial announcement: "Skipper . . ." Huff. Huff. "Buck gunned Tarz!" Before he got the third word fully formed, Hawk was in a dead run for the TACTS trailer to review the engagement replay.

Hawk replayed the video several times and studied it carefully. It was stupendous footage and captured some extraordinary maneuvering.

Hawk loathed gloaters, and he tried very hard to remain stoic, but his excitement was nearly off the chart. One of his young Lions had reigned supreme against one of the best adversary pilots in the business, flying one of the toughest bogey aircraft in the Navy. Hawk reveled in the moment and realized that the unwavering insistence on tactics, training, airmanship, discipline, and fighter doctrine innovation that was now part of the Black Lion genetic coding had paid off.

Here there are Lions!

On the Podium

Buck's fight proved to be rallying point of the Black Lions' performance in the Fighter Derby. The Lions were never short on innovative techniques or spirit, or grit, but on that day, that victory became the moment of truth that allowed everything to coalesce.

When all the scores were tallied and the results were reviewed and finally released by the ComFit staff to the Miramar fighter community, the Black Lions had taken first place.[5] So skillful was their airmanship, so sound was their combat section discipline, and so determined was their esprit de corps that their score was nearly as high as the sum of the scores of the second- and third-place fighter squadrons combined.

To Hawk, at least as important as their accomplishments was the fact that his boys had risen to the occasion. Nearly every Lion, from the greenest airman to the most salt-encrusted chief to the most combat-hardened officer, shared the load. They pulled together, embraced every challenge, overcame every obstacle, and, as a team, had broken the chains of the status quo. Hawk knew they would remember and cherish their part of this triumph for the rest of their days.

CHAPTER 10

Here There Are Lions

I wish to have no connection with any ship that does not sail fast, for I intend to go in harm's way.

—Capt. John Paul Jones, in a letter to le Ray de Chaumont, November 16, 1778

Ascent to Mount Olympus

Everything following the Fighter Derby seemed somewhat anticlimactic. There were several turnaround events to complete before the sail date of USS *America*. Many were major, and all required the command's full attention, but after the Fighter Derby, the Black Lions were riding the groundswell of success, and nothing was too hard. The mechanical precision of the squadron, the brotherhood, and the leadership, as well as a willingness to accept new challenges, allowed everything to magically fall into place.

By the fall of 1980, Hawk's version of *Mr. Toad's Wild Ride* was drawing to a close. And though it was the end of Hawk's last squadron tour—his last hurrah in the fighters that had become part of his very being—it was also his proudest hour.

The Fighter Derby cleared the decks for all that followed. It hailed a victorious conclusion to a long, sometimes torturous climb from chaos and impossibility to recognized supremacy in the fighter mission. A year of struggle, training, and tactical innovation had thrust the command to a new apogee. The road seemed always uphill and fraught with obstructions and frustration, but in the end, in those final moments, Hawk had achieved his dream—*the consummate fighter squadron.*

"These guys were something special. They were all fine men and plenty smart to start with, and certainly they all had their fair share of fight in their blood. All I did was fire 'em up, challenge them, empower them, and turn 'em loose. But it was a team effort; they took the job seriously, accepted responsibility, and, under their own power, rose to the occasion. They completed every task and every mission we set out to accomplish."

From November until the Black Lions departed for cruise in February 1981, it was—as always before each deployment—a very busy time. This time, however, it was doable. They now had trained personnel, groomed aircraft, proper funding, and the right *go-for-it spirit* to make things happen, with a minimum of surprises, setbacks, and "ah, shits." This time the Lion leaders were leading, taking charge, and making it work.

Ever so humble, to hear Hawk speak of his squadron, one might get the impression that his team was manned with tacticians, innovators, and leaders when he arrived. One might conclude that all he did was inherit the Black Lions as up-rounds and combat ready—just add water, a ship, and end speed—but Capt. Jack Ready had a much-different story to tell.

Capt. Ready detached as commander of Air Wing 11 on July 2, 1980. He scripted the final fitness reports on all his commanding officers, as required. In Cmdr. John M. Smith's fitness report[1] for the period March 1, 1980, to July 2, 1980, Capt. Ready so eloquently wrote, "Cmdr. Smith has clearly outpaced seven other skippers through unsurpassed imaginative and effective leadership. VF-213 is now the best fighter squadron in the Navy, and Cmdr. Smith has been the driving force behind this accomplishment. Cmdr. Smith's aggressive approach to mission readiness objectives, coupled with a sincere, effective approach to people, allowed his squadron to achieve: a sixty-percent increase in flying sortie rate, highest full-mission capable rate within the VF community, eighty-three-percent reduction in NJP [nonjudicial punishment], and the best retention and advancement statistics within the air wing and functional wing. Cmdr. Smith has literally led his squadron from average to an unsurpassed state of readiness while faced with the usual supply and personnel shortages.

"Cmdr. Smith is a topnotch F-14A fighter pilot, tactician, and strike leader. He led by example. He is a first choice to lead in combat. He is my number one choice for command of an air wing and accelerated promotion to captain."

And to avoid the mistake of assuming that this extraordinary fitness report may have been a fluke, after six months of observation, the new commander of Air Wing 11, Capt. R. E. Smith, wrote the following in Hawk's departing fitness report:[2] "Cmdr. John Monroe Smith is the number one ranked commanding officer in CARRIER AIR WING 11. He provided the brilliant leadership that produced the most effective and combat-ready fighter squadron in the Navy today. His enthusiasm and exuberance lifted spirits and improved attitudes throughout the air wing. He works for his people, and they respond superbly in support of objectives. From top to bottom, his command knows who they are, where they are going, and why."

These were fitting and well-deserved accolades to Hawk's tour as commanding officer of the Black Lions.

Change of Command

Cmdr. Jim Haley took command of VF-213 on Saturday, December 13, 1980. RAdm. Gillcrist, Miramar ComFit commander, was the guest speaker. His words were most complimentary both to Hawk and his Black Lions. He addressed some of the more lofty achievements and noted that the Lions were the submission by COMFITAEWWINGPAC (Commander, Fighter Airborne Early Warning Wing, US Pacific Fleet) for the Arleigh Burke Fleet Trophy.[3] There was no higher achievement for a fighter command.

When it was Hawk's turn to speak, he kept it focused and short. "You men of the Black Lions have brought this squadron to a new level of professionalism, set new benchmarks for tactical achievement and leadership, and coined a new meaning for the word 'teamwork.' You petty officers, and chiefs, and junior officers—Black Lions all—consistently completed the mission, all too often in the face of persistent obstacles—lacking funding, people, equipment, parts, and, always, it seemed, fighting against the clock. To borrow a quote from Miss Jenny: 'You did stuff because you didn't know you couldn't!'

"My pride in you runs far deeper than I can describe. I know I can take great comfort in knowing that under the leadership and vision of Cmdr. Jim Haley, you will persevere in completing the tough missions in the future, and you will endeavor to make good things happen simply because you have no appetite for second place.

"I could stand up here and rehash the record, but I don't need to. We don't have to talk about what everybody already knows. We are simply the best. The best only because you—each one of you—pitched in to work as a team and made us the best."

And that was a true statement. One look at the faces of his men and it was obvious that they knew they were Black Lions, the finest fighter squadron in the Navy.

Hawk cut to his closing lines and kept his points centered on the most important message. "Just stay true to our mission. Stay true to your shipmates. Stay true to our squadron. Stay true to our Navy.

"That is all!"

And with that, Hawk invited RAdm. Gillcrist and Cmdr. Haley, the new skipper of the Black Lions, to the podium and announced, "I will now read my orders."

CHAPTER 11

Blue Skies, White Water

Old men forget: yet all shall be forgot,
But he'll remember with advantages
What feats he did that day.

—Shakespeare, *Henry V*

Last Romp in the Big Blue

On December 13, 1980, Hawk left his cherished Black Lions and his last fleet flying assignment. That assignment, and each that followed, was packed with their own set of challenges, frustrations, and rewards. Hawk enjoyed them all, but nothing brought the satisfaction or the endorphin spike of the ride down the catapult track strapped in a fire-breathing dragon in the guise of an F-14.

Follow-On Orders

There is probably no experience worse for a TACAIR pilot than to be close enough to touch the jets, hear the thunder of their engines, and smell the JP-5 but not actually be in one. That was Hawk's personal conundrum on his next assignment. He reported to USS *Ranger* (CV-61) as her air operations officer and operations department head, a postcommand position of high prominence on a carrier. Hawk spent thirty months assigned to *Ranger* and then received orders for a two-month, postcommand course at Naval War College in Newport, Rhode Island.

In an ironic twist of fate, Hawk was then ordered to Commander, Fighter and Airborne Early Warning Wing, Pacific, at NAS Miramar as staff operations officer on August 1, 1983, under RAdm. George "Skip" Furlong. Hawk considered him a fabulously talented officer and devoted leader as commander of Air Wing 14 and as commander of ComFit; it was obvious that he brought that same sense of devotion to his people and exuberance for the mission to Miramar.

The admiral had put a heavy shoulder into overhauling ComFit and improving both morale and operational readiness—worthy objectives, but something that many predecessors believed to be a paradox. Hawk, though, seasoned with the experience of once being on the other side of the ComFit fence and knowing both can be accomplished, quickly poured his considerable energies and imagination into the admiral's objectives.

Before Adm. Furlong departed for his next set of orders, NAS Miramar became a beehive of operational efficiency and—surprising to many senior officers—a tour of duty for which many enlisted personnel aggressively campaigned.

It wasn't until July 1985 that Hawk finally fulfilled the promise he made to Miss Jenny some fifteen years earlier. They were headed back to the East Coast. By this time, however, much of the calling to return to her roots had lost urgency. Her transformation to the California lifestyle, except for her pervasive honey-coated southern accent, had been complete. She considered California her home.

Hawk's new orders were somewhat troubling. He had been, up to that point, successful in straight-arming one of the least desirable assignments in the armed forces. But he was a captain at this time, having been promoted in January 1984, and his services were demanded at the Navy's largest headquarters—the pulse point of Navy policy, doctrine, programs, and funding. As much as Hawk dreaded it, he had finally been swept into the tempest of the *five-sided wind tunnel*—the Pentagon.

For two years, Hawk navigated the corridors of the Pentagon, rubbed elbows with the movers and the shakers, and worked with key decision makers in the highest circles. It was interesting work and enlightening in the ways of politics and policymaking, but, by his account, "It was too far removed from the heart of the Navy—the people." He couldn't wait for his next set of orders.

In May 1987, Hawk got his wish. He was ordered out of the Pentagon, far away from the wind tunnel and back into an environment where he was more at home. Hawk had been selected for major shore command, and a large overseas base at that: commanding officer, Naval Station Rota, Spain. This assignment also double-hatted Hawk as the commander of US Naval Activities Command in Spain.

These were high-visibility and highly sensitive positions. He was responsible not only for the Navy base but for thirty-one component activities as well. It required solid organizational abilities and leadership competencies, but also statesmanship skills. As the senior naval officer in Spain, Hawk represented the United States and reported directly to the US ambassador to Spain in the nation's capital, Madrid.

Miss Jenny, as wife of the commanding officer, took on the role of hostess, tour guide, and social director for foreign dignitaries, high-ranking visiting foreign service members, and senior military officers. It was a job for which she was perfectly suited and enjoyed immensely.

For nearly two and a half years, Hawk commanded one of the Navy's largest overseas bases. He studied the culture, learned the language, and treated the members of the command—the sailors, officers, and civil service personnel as well as the Spanish nationals employed at the base—as if they were part of a squadron and therefore like a family. They responded well to Hawk's and Miss Jenny's refreshing approach to leadership and genuine southern hospitality.

Hawk and Miss Jenny departed Rota in September 1989 and returned to Norfolk. On October 1, 1989, he reported to Commander, Naval Air Forces, US Atlantic (COMNAVAIRLANT). The commander of AIRLANT was none other than his pilot in his first fleet squadron (VF-102), his associate on the Tomcat Project, and his commander in CVW-11, VAdm. John "Stinger" Ready.

Hawk's initial assignment under VAdm. Ready was assistant chief of staff for shore activities. This placed him in the conduit between the admiral and the commanding officers of thirteen naval air stations and naval stations, from Keflavik, Iceland, to the Panama Canal.

Hawk took the position just in time for Hurricane Hugo to take a swipe at Naval Station Roosevelt Roads, Puerto Rico; wander down to Guantánamo Bay, Cuba; and then tumble over NAS Key West, causing serious damage to all three AIRLANT component commands.[1]

His previous assignment as commander of US Naval Activities, Spain, gave him precisely the requisite experience and background needed to coordinate immediate material shipping, repair teams, and other needed supplies to those affected facilities. And for the long term, Hawk placed a strong and steady hand in resolving numerous readiness, manpower, funding, and deteriorating base infrastructure problems that had beset all the CNAL commands in previous years.

After considerable success in researching, planning, and executing tailored restoration projects for each command, VAdm. Ready asked Hawk if he'd consider coming up to the front desk as his chief of staff. At this time, the current chief of staff, Capt. Ron Stoops, was slated for retirement, and Hawk, the admiral hoped, would fill the position upon Capt. Stoops's departure. Hawk jumped at the opportunity and began the turnover in early 1991, just as Operation Desert Storm was kicking off.

During peacetime, the position of chief of staff is an exceptionally complicated and demanding job that can utterly deplete one's energy and sense of humor, but the exigency during the Gulf War increased the workload, the urgency, and the complexity dramatically. Even then, Hawk embraced each day of his assignment. He was in his element. His penchant for creative thinking under fire, desire to make good things happen, and concern for training, morale, and combat readiness became widely known throughout the NAVAIRLANT commands.

Given the opportunity, Hawk would have remained in the Navy indefinitely, but all good things come to pass. On Friday, September 5, 1993, at the Norfolk Naval Base Theater, in front of a large gathering of friends, relatives, associates, and squadron mates, Capt. John Monroe "Hawk" Smith read his retirement orders and, hand in hand with Miss Jenny, was ceremoniously piped over the side.

Full Circle

In a way, Hawk had come full circle. A short thirty years and four months earlier, he had signed a contract with the Navy at that very base—Naval Air Station Norfolk. The adventure and the odyssey, however, were set in motion much earlier, when Hawk, as a young boy, had first stared in wide-eyed wonder into the blue abyss over Columbia, South Carolina, straining for a glimpse of the source of the deep-throated thunder in the sky—a jet airplane. If there was a defining moment in Hawk's life, it was at that instant. The sight, the thrill, and the experience ignited a passion in Hawk that would burn for years. But even then, Hawk was a pragmatist. He believed that flying military jets was reserved for a group of highly skilled and exceptionally talented people—special people.

Hawk was partially right. All the service branches are propelled by a special group of people: men and women of high energy, exceptional leadership qualities, enthusiasm, vision, and commitment, and with a quiet sense of duty to country. Hawk shared these values . . . and much more. He had an insatiable drive for the objective, a spirit of adventure, a proclivity to circumvent arcane practices, and a willingness to accept the risk that goes with accomplishing anything of consequence.

On the inside cover of Hawk's personal copy of *TOMCAT! The Grumman F-14 Story*, the author, RAdm. Paul T. "Gator" Gillcrist, penned this short note:

To: Hawk (28 August 1995)

There were twenty-eight fighter squadron commanding officers in 1980 (I counted them up in a spare moment). Of all of them, you were the most inspired, most gifted in leadership qualities, most competent as a Naval officer and Naval Aviator, most candid, most unpretentious, and most dedicated to the "least common denominator" of leadership to the preservation of human dignity of all the people under your cognizance.

It was an honor and a privilege to have served with you. I am enriched by the experience.

"Speed is life."

"Gator"

Paul T. Gillcrist. RAdm., USN (Ret.)

Fly Navy!

Hawk took the oath of enlistment on August 23, 1963. On that day, he became part of the fellowship of carrier aviation. He joined the ranks of thousands who went before him, hundreds he worked and flew with, and the countless warriors who will carry the naval mission and the tradition forward into the future. They were and will be cast from the same steel. They were and will be much like Hawk—adventurers, pathfinders, and pioneers—naval aviators all. Aviators who over the course of decades of trial and error perfected the art of carrier operations, adapted technologies to bring carrier aviation to its full potential, designed tactics to meet the evolving threat, and accepted the frightening personal challenges of flying from the decks of ships day and night, in good weather and in poor, in peace and in war.

Collectively, these are an exceptional people. They are also normal everyday Americans who have an abnormal drive for adventure and achievement. They are common people filled with an uncommon sense of duty to country and devotion to their team. They are ordinary people who, by extraordinary strength of character, brave the hazards of nature and the weapons of man to project power to the shores of America's enemies. And . . . for as long as these ordinary men and women are annealed in the foundry of naval aviation, the world's despots and America's enemies will hold in reverie the extraordinary power of naval aviation and tremble at its colossal fury.

Hawk was part of this lineage of naval aviation, and he counted himself fortunate, beyond measure, to have served.

Capt. John Monroe "Hawk" Smith retired from the Navy on October 1, 1993. For both him and Miss Jenny, it was a long run and an exhilarating odyssey of trial, sacrifice, and achievement. It was far more than a young boy from South Carolina could ever have imagined, and the adventure of a lifetime for one who had dared to dream that he could one day *Fly Navy!*

Epilogue

The day comes in every aviator's life when he will walk to their airplane either knowing or not knowing it will be their last. Regardless the outcome, it will be a horrific and gut-wrenching end.

—Donald E. Auten

The shooter recognized Hawk by his helmet. He smiled and nodded. With a slight tip of his helmet, Hawk returned the gesture.

As two final checkers made a last inspection of doors, panels, and external stores and checked for fluid leaks, the shooter noted the weight scribbled in chalk on the nose gear door and scanned the configuration of the Tomcat. He then raised his right hand and gave a two-finger *turn-up* signal, to which Hawk responded by moving both throttles forward to the military power detent. The nose of the beast crouched low, like a tiger ready for the attack.

The shooter's two-finger turn signal changed into a clenched fist, followed by an open hand, and then he repeated the gesture a second time. Hawk brought both throttles around the detent position into zone 2 afterburner. The Tomcat bucked and quaked and shook side to side. A tremendous howling, a chest-rattling roar that would have deafened anyone on the flight deck without earplugs and sound suppressors, erupted from the twin TF30 infernos.

Hawk made his final scan of the engine instruments, gauges, and indicators—those last-chance telltales of the wellness of the jet. He cycled the flight controls through all four corner stops and checked the center mirror to ensure the seat pin was out.

Satisfied their Tomcat was good to go, Hawk yelled above the rumble, "You ready, Chief?"

"Up and up, Hawk.

"And Hawk," almost as an afterthought, Chief declared, "It's been a pleasure to serve with you, Skipper!"

"Thanks, Chief. Truly, the pleasure's been mine, but it ain't over yet!"

Hawk flipped a final thumbs-up and saluted the shooter for the last time. In response, the shooter saluted, rotated slightly to get a clear view of the entire length of the catapult, bent down on one knee, tapped the flight deck, and then pointed forward.

In anticipation, Hawk had eased his helmet back into the headrest, locked his left arm forward, and rested his right arm across his right thigh, his hand carefully caressing the stick grip.

Almost instantly, Hawk was rewarded with an exhilarating rush as 60,000 pounds of airplane rocketed from zero to 155 knots in less than three and a half seconds. In the length of a football field, the Tomcat, with afterburners scorching the flight deck, was airborne and skimming the cerulean sea. He and Chief were squashed like bugs against the seats, with three times the force of gravity. Hawk, at 170 pounds of muscle and hard sinew, weighed the equivalent of a small horse. It was a spike of excitement Hawk anticipated and craved.

Hawk made a crisp clearing turn, steadied out on heading, deftly snapped the gear handle up, and came out of blower. Wing sweep and flaps came next as he accelerated to 300 knots and stabilized at 500 feet.

"Black Lion One's airborne, switching departure," Chief announced on the radio.

"Roger, Black Lion One. Cleared to switch."

But before Chief could switch to the new frequency, there was another transmission: "Hawk, Boss!" This was a nonstandard transmission, a breach of radio protocol ordinarily sternly addressed by the "boss" or one of his assistants, but since this transmission obviously came from the "boss," no one objected.

Hawk keyed the mike: "Go, Boss!"

"We're gonna miss you around the chicken coop, Hawk. Fair winds, lad!"

Well, that about did it. Hawk was in close combat with his own demons and struggling with a day in his destiny he always knew would come. He fought to maintain the strict emotional control and radio discipline he was known for. "Roger, Boss. Fair winds, shipmate! Switching."

Fair winds, shipmate. I guess that says it all.

For a sailor, no three words uttered in a single phrase had more meaning. No syntax conveyed a clearer wish for the well-being of a brother, and no sentiment better acknowledged the bond of comradeship, trust, and deference that is the Navy family.

Chief had switched frequencies to departure control: "Departure, Black Lion One, 5 miles," Chief reported on the UHF.

The transmission was lost on Hawk.

There's no gettin' around it. I'm going to miss this. I'm going to miss the ship's crew, my squadron, the air wing guys . . . I'm going to miss 'em all!

Hawk felt his chest tighten a bit. *And still I miss all my friends, my squadron mates, those who didn't make it. Too many good men lost before their time. Too many husbands and fathers and sons and patriots who, for any number of reasons, crashed into the sea, crashed into other airplanes, or blew up in the air. No! I miss the people, but I won't miss the agony of losing my friends. I know it comes with the territory, but . . .*

Once again he engaged the question he'd been thrashing with all morning—all week, really . . . *Was it all worth it?*

"Black Lion One, departure. Roger! Squawk four-one-two-zero, come right to zero-two-zero to avoid Cuban airspace, switch to Miami Center on three-eight-one point four, and avoid penetrating flight level one-eight-zero until contact with Miami. Have a safe trip, Black Lion One!"

"Four-one-two-zero, right to zero-two-zero, switching to Miami on three-eight-one point four. Chief dialed in the assigned IFF codes and frequency and checked in with Miami. "Miami Center, Black Lion One is with you squawking four-one-two-zero, coming right to zero-two-zero."

"Good morning, Navy Black Lion One. Got your squawk. You're cleared to climb to flight level four-one-zero."

"Black Lion One climbing to four-one-zero."

Chief noticed they were 6 miles from the ship. To avoid conflict with overhead traffic, departing airplanes were supposed to stay at 500 feet until 5 miles from the ship. Ordinarily, Hawk, at precisely 5.0 miles, would start his climb. *Hawk,* Chief thought, *must be thinking about something else.*

"Hawk, we're coming up on 7 miles. Were you planning on a low-level route to Oceana? If you were, it's okay with me, but I better refile the flight plan and look for a tanker because we're going to need a ton more gas."

"Yeah, Chief. I was just thinking. Okay, we're heading up to 41,000. Hold onto your helmet, boy!"

Hawk moved the throttles forward, around the detent position into afterburner. After nine years flying the F-14, he was still mystified by the results. In mere seconds, 300 knots turned into 400 knots, and that into 500.

And I'm sure as hell not going to miss all the time I've spent away from home either, away from Miss Jenny and Jack. I've missed my son's first steps, his first words. Hell, he didn't even recognize me when I came home from my second cruise. He was two then, and I'd been gone seven months. I've missed birthdays, Christmases, and anniversaries. These are days I'll never make up. I'll never get 'em back. I've got a lot of making up to do.

"Gee, Hawk, I didn't think these jet thingies could go so fast," Chief chided.

Hawk's eyes quickly snapped to the airspeed indicator. The needle was quickly moving through 650 knots and just a hairsbreadth from Mach 1.

"We're you planning to climb sometime today, or were you trying to give all the sea life in the area earaches?"

"Yeah, Chief, I was just thinking about climbing! You know how I love 600 knots and accelerating."

And with that, Hawk made a gentle but firm pull on the stick. The nose of the F-14 began a sweeping arc into the vertical. When the nose was pointed almost straight up, when the gyro indicated a nearly perfect vertical climb, Hawk eased the stick forward to hold attitude. The airspeed indicator began to slowly unwind. The altimeter looked more like a child's top than a precision aircraft instrument, and the needle of the vertical-speed indicator, the instrument that registered climb and descent rates, was pegged "up."

Seconds later, Chief whispered, "Two-nine-nine-two on the altimeter, Hawk," reminding him to reset the barometric altimeter to the standard setting when operating above flight level one-eight-zero—18,000 feet.

"Got it, Chief!'

Hawk continued with his thoughts: *I've given so much. I've given of things that weren't even mine to give. This career has been long and hard and sometimes just too damned painful. Had it not been for the thrill and the experience, those small victories, the camaraderie, the accomplishments, and the chance to serve my Navy and my country, I'm just not sure it would have been all worth it. But would I do it all over again . . . if I could . . .*

The Miami Center flight controllers at first thought they had an equipment malfunction. Black Lion One had picked up a tremendous amount of speed, but the target remained at low altitude for some time. Then the next sweep of the radar indicated there was literally no horizontal progress, but the climb rate was astronomical. In fact, it looked more like a shuttle launch than the climb-out of a military jet.

The Tomcat was climbing through 30,000 feet when Hawk smoothly rolled 180 degrees and began to pull the nose from nearly pure vertical back to the horizon. Still inverted, Hawk eased the stick back to bring the nose to the horizon. He then inputted lateral stick to roll the aircraft upright and pulled the throttles back to 88 percent. When the Tomcat finally settled out, it was steady at flight level four-one-zero, cruising precisely at 0.78 Mach, and exactly on heading zero-two-zero degrees.

"Miami Center, Black Lion One at flight level four-one-zero," Chief proudly announced.

"Black Lion One," Miami Center came back, "yes . . . duly noted!"

Black Lion One had climbed nearly 7 miles straight up in under two minutes. The horizontal travel was less than 5 miles. Confusing, *What-in-the-hell-is-that?* looks were shared by the several controllers huddled around the radar.

With his mighty Tomcat on altitude, heading, and airspeed, Hawk thought back on an age-old aviation adage. *The day comes in every aviator's life when they will walk to their airplane either knowing or not knowing it will be their last flight. Regardless the outcome, it will be a horrific and gut-wrenching end.*

It seemed an appropriate axiom for the situation, but not for this glorious day. Hawk refused to succumb to the depression that tried to envelop him. Instead he divorced himself from his conundrum and, for a moment, reveled in the panorama.

He could see 200 miles in any direction. Clearly visible was the entire island of Cuba. He could make out Key West, a good emergency divert if needed, and the toe of the Florida coast. It was absolutely beautiful and breathtaking, and for a moment in time Hawk was sitting on top of the world.

But if I could . . . would I do it all over again?

Well . . . hell yeah, I would! I wouldn't miss it for the world!

Endnotes

Prologue

1. At this time, USS *America* was designated CVA-66. The "CV" designation did not come about until 1975, when *Kitty Hawk* and *Saratoga* completed cruises with S-2 Trackers on board to test the viability of having ASW fixed-wing assets on board the larger carriers. Attack carriers went to the CVA designation, and ASW carriers became CVS in October 1952, having previously been CV or, in the case of Midway-class ships, CVB. After 1975, the conventional carriers were CV, and the nuclear-powered ships were CVN [*Enterprise* had been CVA (N)-65 before this]. Cmdr. Jan Jacobs, USN (ret.).

2. 5-MC: the public-address loudspeaker for the flight deck.

Chapter 1

1. Many of the following sections relied heavily on passages from Donald E. Auten, *Roger Ball!* (New York: iUniverse Star, 2008), in order to provide comprehensive subject background and maintain fidelity.

2. Naval flight officer (NFO): Naval officers qualified and designated to fly as crewmen in naval aircraft, including navigators, bombardier-navigators (BNs), radar intercept officers (RIOs), and tactical air control officers (TACOs). But the NFO designation and double-anchor wings did not come about until 1968. Before that, non–naval aviator crew members were called naval aviation observers (NAOs) and were awarded a set of gold wings with a circle and an anchor in the middle, centered between the gold wings.

3. From official USS *America* (CVN-66) Command History Submission.

4. CONUS: continental US.

5. VX-4; the "Evaluator's" call sign was "Vandy."

6. CVW: Carrier Air Wing. Prior to 1962, Carrier Air Group (CAG) was the official term, but old habits die hard, and in many circles, CAG and CVW are now used interchangeably.

7. Waving: providing the aircrew landing guidance to come aboard a carrier.

8. In 1977, two developments added a certain urgency to TOPGUN's mission. The TOPGUN staff was beginning to gather AIMVAL/ACEVAL results and intelligence information that proved the Soviets had built their own third-generation fighters. AIMVAL/ACEVAL was the biggest and most complex air combat tactics and weapons evaluation in history, and a watershed event for USAF, Navy, and Marine Corps tactical squadrons. In the twelve months of AIMVAL/ACEVAL testing, over three thousand sorties were logged and over nine hundred engagements recorded. Although analysis, findings, and lessons learned would be digested and debated for months following the conclusion of the evaluation, AIMVAL/ACEVAL stands today as a triumphant turning point in the catharsis of twenty-first-century fighter doctrine. It forced a revolutionary overhaul of fighter combat philosophy and sketched a blueprint for the design of new tactics, aircraft, and weapons systems for future battlefields.

9. TACAIR: tactical aviation—those carrier-based aircraft with kinetic kill capability. Also called "shooters."

10. "Fenner" was a pseudonym used so as to avoid embarrassment for the actual character in *Roger Ball!* The admiral's actual name was Fellows. At this time Fellows was the commander of both the Fighter Wing and the Airborne Early Warning Wing.

11. Lt. Mike "Smiles" Bucchi had a distinguished career as a TOPGUN instructor. Before retiring as vice admiral, his assignments included CO of VF-33, commander of CVW-3, commander of Carrier Group 6, chief of Naval Air Training, and commander of US 3rd Fleet. He was kind enough to provide the foreword for this work.

12. This event is believed to be following a Navy Reserve fighter conference at NAS Miramar in mid-1977, where the two Dallas-based F-4 squadrons (VF-201 and VF-202) came out to fly against the West Coast Reserve F-4 squadrons (VF-301 and VF-302). Adversary support was supplied by VC-13, flying TA-4J Skyhawks. There were several former TOPGUN instructors in the squadron. At the end of the exercise there was a formal dining out, and Fellows was invited. According to the a Dallas RIO who had just accepted a post with the US Diplomatic Service and was leaving the Reserves (and therefore had nothing to lose) made this toast: "To Admiral Fellows, the man who contributed more than anyone for Navy Reserve recruiting!"

13. First-generation fighter, 1950s: Korean-era fighter with low-loaded wing whose primary air-to-air weapon is a rapid-firing cannon. Second-generation fighter, 1960–early 1970s: fighter design with emphasis on short-range to medium-range air-to-air missiles; poor turn capability, but good thrust-to-weight rating. Third-generation fighter: supersonic capability with high thrust-to-weight rating and high turn rates.

14. Black Program: a highly classified, sensitive project with national security implications; usually associated with TOP SECRET and Special Access Project (SAP) security levels.

15. NATOPS: Naval Aviation Training and Operating Procedures—the aircraft-operating manual.

16. Radome: conical, structural, weatherproof enclosure that protects a radar antenna.

17. Turkey feathers: variable-exhaust nozzles.

18. At this time, the missile was designated AAM-N-6a Sparrow III. It became the AIM-7 after 1963.

Chapter 2

1. *SteelJawScribe*, "Flightdeck Friday! Douglas F4D-1 Skyray (Part 1)," *Naval History Blog*, US Naval Institute, 2010, https://www.Navalhistory.org/2010/04/16/ flightdeck-friday-douglas-f4d skyray-part-1.

2. At this time, the missile was designated AAM-N-6a Sparrow III. It became the AIM-7 after 1963.

3. In 1963, the proper designation would have been McDonnell F-4B Phantom II. The merger between McDonnell and Douglas didn't take place until 1967.

4. "VFA-213." Wikipedia, https://en.wikipedia.org/wiki/VFA-213.

5. Division: four aircraft within a group. Two aircraft in formation make a section; two sections (4 a/c) complete a division.

6. PERSMAR: Personnel Manning Report.

7. BUPERS: Bureau of Naval Personnel.

8. FRAMP: Fleet Readiness Aviation Maintenance Program.

9. LPA: life preserver; LPA-1 was the first Navy life preserver with inflatable neck lobes.

10. Shroud cutters were part of the survival gear at this time and, indeed, mandatory as a primary piece of survival equipment.

11. "Carrier Air Wing ELEVEN," Wikipedia, https://en.wikipedia.org/wiki/Carrier_Air_ Wing_Eleven.

12. The Air Corps became a subordinate element of the Army Air Forces on June 20, 1941, and was abolished as an administrative organization on March 9, 1942. It continued to exist as a branch of the Army (similar to the infantry, quartermaster, or artillery) until reorganization provisions of the National Security Act of 1947 (61 Stat. 495), July 26, 1947. "History of the United States Air Force," Wikipedia, https://en.wikipedia.org/wiki/History_of_the_United_States_Air_Force.

13. "Carrier Air Wing Eleven," Wikipedia, https://en.wikipedia.org/wiki/Carrier_Air_Wing_Eleven.

14. "Carrier Air Wing Eleven [CVW 11]," Global Security, https://www.globalsecurity.org/military/agency/navy/cvw11.htm.

15. Japan formally surrendered during a ceremony in Tokyo Bay aboard USS *Missouri* on September 2, 1945. At the time, President Truman declared September 2, 1945, as VJ-day.

16. "Carrier Air Wing Eleven," Wikipedia, https://en.wikipedia.org/wiki/Carrier_Air_Wing_Eleven.

17. "Fatherland Liberation War," June 25, 1950–July 27, 1953, Wikipedia, https://en.wikipedia.org/wiki/Korean_War.

18. "Inchon Landing," History.com editors, 2010, https://www.history.com/topics/inchon.

19. "Carrier Air Wing ELEVEN [CVW 11]," Global Security, https://www.globalsecurity.org/military/agency/navy/cvw11.htm.

20 Allan R. Millett, "Battle of the Chosin Reservoir," *Encyclopedia Britannica*, https://www.britannica.com/event/Battle-of-the-Chosin-Reservoir.

21. "Carrier Air Wing Eleven," Wikipedia, https://en.wikipedia.org/wiki/Carrier_Air_Wing_Eleven.

22. VAW-122 was an East Coast (NAS Norfolk) E-2C Hawkeye unit from 1967 to 1996. The E-2C was just coming online and was based only on the East Coast initially. To spread the new capabilities evenly, some East Coast Hummers made cruises with West Coast air wings, and some West Coast E-2B squadrons went east and made Med cruises in the late 1970s and early 1980s.

23. US-3As were stripped-out versions of the antisubmarine S-3A aircraft.

24. VQ-1 was based at NAS Agana at this time and rarely ever made it to CONUS. The shipboard EA-3B aircraft assigned usually sent a det of one or two aircraft and met the deployed air wings at NAS Cubi Point, Philippines. VQ-2, out of NAS Rota, Spain, would do the same for Med cruising air wings.

25. "Welcome to NAS Fallon," CNIC, https://www.cnic.navy.mil/regions/cnrsw/installations/nas_fallon.html.

26. "Naval Strike and Air Warfare Center," Wikipedia, https://en.wikipedia.org/wiki/Naval_Strike_and_Air_Warfare_Center.

27. "Naval Air Station Fallon," Wikipedia, https://en.wikipedia.org/wiki/Naval_Air_Station_Fallon.

28. First-generation fighters: Subsonic jet aircraft, highly maneuverable with rear-quadrant air-to-air weapons. Examples include F-86 Saber, F9-F Panther, MiG-15 Fagot, and MiG-17 Fresco.

29. Second-generation threats: Supersonic jet aircraft with heavier-loaded wings and reduced maneuverability, but with improved air-to-air radar and weapons.

30. October 3, 1979: F-15A, 77-0072, of the 9th TFS, 49th TFW, USAF, crashed near NAS Fallon, Nevada, after colliding with F-15A, 77-0061, which landed safely.

31. This incident was witnessed by the author, who at the time was the wingman of the A-4 that was being prosecuted by the F-15s. The F-15 wingman missed the A-4 wingman by several hundred feet but, unfortunately, did not avoid the lead F-15.

32. Guard frequency: a frequency assigned to general and military aviation and reserved for in-flight emergencies and priority announcements; 121.5 MHz for VHF and 243.0 MHz for UHF.

33. Operational Readiness Evaluation (ORE) is the final assessment of the ship's readiness for deployment. Consequences are usually brutal for commanding officers of ships that fail to pass the ORE.

34. CARGRU: carrier group.

Chapter 3

1. While the Soviets had taken the keenest interest while running intelligence, surveillance, and reconnaissance (ISR) missions against US Navy forces, many other unfriendly nations conducted similar flights, including Libya.
2. Although gathering intel on American CVGBs was high priority, but Russia and other nations routinely ran intercepts on surface battle groups also.
3. BEAREX: live exercise against a friendly aircraft simulating a Russian reconnaissance aircraft.
4. Combat Information Center (CIC) is now called Combat Direction Center (CDC); provides information and control to airborne fighter and attack aircraft.
5. Judy: notifying the controller that the crew of the prosecuting aircraft has a radar contact and to cease all additional calls until assistance is requested.
6. Midnight: running with no external lights at night.
7. Commander, 6th Fleet (C6F): The 6th Fleet is the US Navy's operational fleet and staff of United States Naval Forces Europe and is headquartered at Naval Support Activity Naples, Italy. C6F conducts the full range of Maritime Operations and Theater Security Cooperation missions, in concert with coalition, joint, interagency, and other parties, in order to advance security and stability in Europe and Africa. "United States Sixth Fleet," Wikipedia, https://en.wikipedia.org/wiki/United_States_Sixth_Fleet.
8. Hawk had liberty in Naples on his first cruise. It had not been a pleasurable experience. Details provided in Auten, *Roger Ball!*, 118.
9. ACEVAL/AIMVAL: Joint Navy and USAF back-to-back Joint Test & Evaluations chartered by the US Department of Defense, which ran from 1974 to 1978 at Nellis Air Force Base in Nevada. US Air Force and Navy participated, contributing a team of F-15 Eagle and F-14 Tomcat fighter aircraft and using TOPGUN F-5E Aggressor aircraft as the Red Force. The fundamental question that needed to be answered was one of "quantity vs. quality." Mock engagements showed that in greater numbers, cheaper, lower-technology fighters armed with all-aspect missiles were able to destroy the more advanced and more expensive F-15s and F-14s. Results of the AIMVAL/ACEVAL testing led to the Air Force decision to structure its fighter forces with a balance of cheaper F-16s, along with the more expensive F-15s. The Navy took a similar strategy in procuring cheaper F-18s to complement the more expensive F-14s. "ACEVAL/AIMVAL," Wikipedia, https://en.wikipedia.org/wiki/ACEVAL/AIMVAL (accessed in October 2017).
10. "Chops": nickname for supply personnel, as in "pork chops."
11. Aircraft handler: Also called the "mangler." Responsible for movement, positioning, and security of aircraft on the flight and hangar decks.
12. Deck multiple: number of aircraft on the flight deck.
13. 3M: maintenance, material, management.
14. Brow: ladder or gangway between the dock and ship when secured to the quay.

Chapter 4

1. Upon completion of a command assignment, the officer may continue to wear the command pin on the left side, below the pocket of a uniform shirt or uniform jacket.
2. Despite the interchangeability of the terms "CVW" and "CAG" when referring to the carrier organization of air wings / air groups, most commonly at this time the commander of the air wing / air group was referred to as "CAG."
3. "Sweet": military aviator jargon to indicate that the tanker package is operating properly and passing gas.

Chapter 5

1. Decarrierize: process to reduce the air pressure to improve performance, increase coefficient of friction for field operations, and reduce the possibility of a tire blowout.
2. Bravo Sierra: Falcon/phonetic code for "bullshit."
3. VFR: visual flight rules—indicating that the weather conditions are generally clear enough to allow the pilot to remain clear of clouds.

Chapter 6

1. TARPS: Tactical Airborne Reconnaissance Pod System.
2. Flexi Flyer: Popular in the mid-1900s, the Flexi Flyer was a wooden and steel cart with four wheels, made steerable by a cross-member connected to the front wheels. The wheels were generally painted bright red or blue.
3. Twelve aircraft were assigned to VF-213 at that time; however, three of those were at NAS North Island undergoing depot-level maintenance.
4. SPINTAC: an aircraft that is not available for operational flights for thirty days and is considered a Special Interest Aircraft.
5. "A" status: full-mission-capable (FMC) aircraft.
6. NORS: aircraft not operational; available for supply (parts).
7. James Perry Stevenson, *Grumman F-14 Tomcat* (Blue Ridge Summit, PA: Aero, 1986).

Chapter 7

1. Chord: The imaginary straight line joining the leading and trailing edges of an airfoil. The chord length is the distance between the trailing edge and the leading edge.
2. Camber: The convexity of the curve of an *aerofoil* from the leading edge to the trailing edge. Also explained as the asymmetry between the top and the bottom surfaces of an aerofoil. An airfoil that is not cambered is called a symmetrical airfoil. "Camber (aerodynamics)," Wikipedia, https://en.wikipedia.org/wiki/Camber_(aerodynamics), accessed June 2017.
3. Section takeoffs: a simultaneous takeoff with two aircraft.
4. The F-14 Tomcats were equipped with the 10× power Television Sight Unit (TVSU), but it needed improvement. The follow-on was the Television Camera Set (TCS), but it was not delivered to the fleet until 1982.
5. With riflescope in hand, Hawk went straight to the Black Lions' airframe shop to talk with Petty Officer Vergara. Now the challenge was to fabricate a stable mount that would not interfere with the HUD or standby compass, yet be safe, adjustable, and effective. Within two days, Vergara had handcrafted a stainless-steel prototype mount that attached the scope to the right-side frame of the windscreen. The following day, Hawk was scheduled for a CAP and SSSC mission with a wingman. He briefed 25-mile intercepts with maneuvers that would facilitate early visual acquisition using the riflescope. When they returned to the ready room, Hawk exclaimed that "this thing is TITS!" Skipper Applegate (at the time) said, "Well, why don't you name it that!" In less than a minute, the acronym was announced: "the Tomcat Integrated Telescope System." TITS on a Tomcat! Over the remainder of the deployment aboard USS *America*, Hawk evaluated the riflescope's application to various missions and segments. By September 1979, when the Black Lions returned to NAS Miramar, Hawk had created a better mounting bracket out of aluminum that could be easily attached to the VDIG by using existing screw holes with ¼-inch-longer screws. He wanted

supply to open-purchase at least six Weaver six-power riflescopes for all F-14 squadrons, beginning with the Black Lions and the Aardvarks.

6. Much of the discussion on Capt. Ault's report was extracted from *Roger Ball!* in order to provide comprehensive subject background and maintain fidelity.

7. Ron "Mugs" McKeown had a distinguished war record in Vietnam, including a MiG kill. Jack "Fingers" Ensch and Mugs were in VF-161 "Chargers." Together they shot down *Midway's* sixth and seventh MiGs: two MiG-17s with AIM-9 Sidewinders on the same day, May 23, 1972.

8. Capt. Foster S. "Tooter" Teague was a well-known and highly respected officer in the fighter community. He had six fighter squadron assignments, his last as executive officer and commanding officer of VF-51. On June 11, 1972, while flying an F-4 as commanding officer VF-51 aboard USS *Coral Sea* (CVA-43), Tooter was given credit for downing a MiG-21. Additionally, he was assigned to the highly classified joint Have Drill project and flew several Soviet-built fighter aircraft. Capt. Teague was commander of Carrier Air Wing 11 on board USS *Kitty Hawk* during his WestPac deployments and flew over 450 combat missions.

9. Break turn: the hardest turn available on the basis of airspeed, altitude, and aircraft weight.

10. Interview with Capt. Ronald "Mugs" McKeown on October 7, 2004.

11. Constant Peg: a joint program managed by the USAF, designed to expose tactical US air forces to the flight characteristics of fighter aircraft used by the Soviet Union during the Cold War. "4477th Test and Evaluation Squadron," Wikipedia, https://en.wikipedia.org/wiki/4477th_Test_and_Evaluation_Squadron (accessed May 2016).

12. Constant Peg was declassified in 2006. "Constant Peg," *Air Force Magazine*, April 2007, http://www.airforce-magazine.com/MagazineArchive/Pages/2007/April%202007/0407peg.aspx (accessed April 2016).

13. Red Eagle: The 4477th Test and Evaluation Squadron (4477 TES) of the US Air Force under the claimancy of the USAF Tactical Air Command (TAC). The unit was created to expose the tactical air forces to the flight characteristics of fighter aircraft used by the Soviet Union. The declassified history of the squadron shows that it operated MiG-17s, MiG-21s, and MiG-23s between 1977 and 1988, but it was not formally disbanded until July 1990. "4477th Test and Evaluation Squadron," Wikipedia, https://en.wikipedia.org/wiki/4477th_Test_and_Evaluation_Squadron (accessed May 2016).

14. "The pros from Dover" is an American slang term for outside consultants who are brought into a project to troubleshoot and solve problems.

15. The 64th and 65th Aggressor Squadrons at Nellis AFB simulate real-world threat platforms. They perform missions similar to TOPGUN, including basic fighter maneuvers, advanced air combat maneuvering, tactics, and weapons system training.

16. Gunner: normally a senior aviation ordnanceman, who is responsible for weapons, ammo, ordinance, and associated aircraft systems.

17. Hawk remembers the return to NAS Miramar: "We had a total of eight F-14s on deck at Nellis on our last day of deployment. I wanted to return to Miramar in two diamond formations and called Cmdr. Lee Tillotson, the COMFIT operations officer, to seek approval. Lee made it happen. So we performed section takeoffs. Joined in two diamonds for a flyover salute to Nellis and returned to Miramar and entered the break with eight Tomcats in two diamonds. Esprit was sky high that day!"

18. TAD: temporary additional duty; orders directing an individual or group to perform a mission out of the geographic region of his permanent duty station.

19. Gene Tye worked for General Electric and designed the merged, multireference gunsight.

20. *Fighter Squadron Two One Three (VF-213)*, Command History Submission of January 29, 1980.

21. Century banner: a target banner containing at least 100 bullet holes.
22. Gene Tye opined that it was statistically improbable to break that record, given the firing time, the gun's spin-up time, and the number of rounds expended.
23. In favor of day and night field carrier-landing practice.

Chapter 8

1. TACTs: This range provides real-time electronic readout of all dynamic flight data and aircraft presentations within the confines of the range for all the aircraft equipped with a telemetry pod.
2. VIDs: visual identification process.
3. Phantom squadrons were not allowed to simulate gunshots, since the Navy F-4 did not carry an internally mounted cannon.
4. AIM-9D: A dated version of the Sidewinder heat-seeking, air-to-air missile. Heart of the envelope was described as a rear-quadrant missile with ranges from 3,000 to 9,000 feet, but it was susceptible to decoy flares to confuse the heat-seeking head. The Soviet-built AA-2 Atoll missile was very similar in almost every way to the AIM-9D.
5. Midnight: Bill Dollard, a retired Marine aviator, ran the TACTs range.
6. Talley: I have the bogey in sight. Visual: I have you in sight.
7. YOYO: "Fighterese" for "You're on your own!"
8. Pipper: the aiming point on a gunsight, designating where the projectiles were calculated to intercept the target.
9. Hawk thought he was out of the area and clear of any further engagement.
10. Super Fox A-4: 1950s-vintage light-attack aircraft built by McDonnell Douglas. Low-loaded wing with several variations of engines. The last and best-performing A-4 was the Super Fox, weighing in at about 10,000 pounds; a Pratt & Whitney J52-P-408 developing 11,700 pounds of thrust (uninstalled) made the Super Fox quite a terror in the visual-dogfight arena.

Chapter 9

1. Auten, *Roger Ball!*, 388.
2. Plowback: a pilot or NFO whose first assignment was in the training command, not the fleet.
3. The rolling scissors is described as two aircraft flying along the sides of a gigantic striped barber pole. One aircraft traverses the white-striped helix, and the other the red helix. The lift vectors of the aircraft are pointed toward one another. Both aircraft fly this helix-type flight path in an attempt to maneuver to the rear hemisphere of the opponent's aircraft, or their opponent's six o'clock. When both aircraft have high energy, the axis of the rolling scissors might be elevated far above the horizon. As the energy of the aircraft is depleted, the axis of the flight arcs toward the horizon, and if the energy continues to diminish, the rolling-scissors maneuver may descend below the horizon. The rolling scissors requires that the pilot maneuver the aircraft in all three dimensions, using the elevator for pitch and nose control, aileron for roll, and rudder to assist in roll and nose position. It is an exceptionally complex maneuver requiring continuous adjustment of all three control surfaces as the dynamics of the engagement change. Auten, *Roger Ball!*, 155.
4. Flat scissors: As with the rolling scissors, the objective of the flat or horizontal scissors is to maneuver to the opponent's six o'clock position and into a firing solution. Toward that end, this maneuver often develops when two opposing aircraft are flying at nearly the same altitude, heading, and airspeed, and each pilot attempts to flush his opponent to the front of his aircraft in order to arrive

at that firing solution. Commonly, this engagement results in slow-speed maneuvering with a very high angle of attack and requires good energy management techniques, an exceptional feel for the aircraft, and judicious use of trim, flaps, speed brakes, and other lift devices.

5. *Fighter Squadron Two One Three (VF-213)*, Command History Submission for 1980 (VF-213/PAO: jr, 5700, dated November 23, 1980).

Chapter 10

1. Report on the Fitness of Officers, Smith, John Monroe, Commander, Period of Report: 80Mar01 to 80Jul02, Reporting Senior: Ready, J. K., 80Jul02.

2. Report on the Fitness of Officers, Smith, John Monroe, Commander, Period of Report: 80Jul03 to 80Dec13, Reporting Senior: Smith, R. E., 80Dec15.

3. The Arleigh Burke Fleet Trophy is awarded annually to the most improved combat unit (ship, submarine, or squadron), Ref, OPNAVINST 3590.11F.

Chapter 11

1. Hurricane Hugo took the roof off the gym at NAS Key West and caused other serious damage.

Bibliography

"1975 Eagle Pull, Frequent Wind, the End of an Era." Scarface-USMC. Accessed April 04, 2004. www.scarface-usmc.org.

"4477th Test and Evaluation Squadron." US Department of the Air Force. Wikipedia. Accessed May 2016. https://en.wikipedia. org/wiki/4477th_Test_and_Evaluation.

"ACEVAL/AIMVAL," Wikipedia. Accessed October 2017. https://en.wikipedia.org/wiki/ACEVAL/AIMVAL

Ault, Frank W., Capt. USN (Ret.). *Report of the Air-to-Air Missile System Capability Review (U), Naval Air Systems Command, November, 1968.*

"A TOPGUN For Air-Ground Ops." *US Naval Institute Proceedings*, Annapolis, Maryland, 2002.

Auten, Donald E. Capt., USN (Ret.). *Roger Ball! Odyssey of a Navy Fighter Pilot.* New York: iUniverse Star, 2008.

"AV-8B Harrier History." Accessed September 9, 2004. www.globalsecurity.org/.../av-8-.history.htm.

Bucchi, Michael, VAdm., USN (Ret.) interviewed by the author in San Diego, California, 30 June 2004.

"Camber." Wikipedia. Accessed June 2017. https://en.wikipedia.org/wiki/Camber_(aerodynamics)

"Carrier Air Wing ELEVEN." Wikipedia. Accessed April 11, 2018. https://en.wikipedia.org/wiki/Carrier_Air_Wing_Eleven

"Carrier Air Wing ELEVEN [CAG ELEVEN]." Global Security.org, p. 1. Wikipedia. Accessed January 12, 2017. https://www.globalsecurity.org/military/agency/navy/cvw11.htm

"Constant Peg." *Air Force Magazine*, April 2007. Accessed April 2016. http://www.airforce-magazine.com/MagazineArchive/Pages/2007/April%20 2007/0407peg.aspx

"Carrier Air Wing ELEVEN." Wikipedia. Accessed April 29, 2017. https://en.wikipedia.org/wiki/Carrier_Air_Wing_Eleven

"Carrier Air Wing ELEVEN (CVW-11)." Global Security. Accessed June 8, 2017. https://www.globalsecurity.org/military/agency/navy/cvw11.htm.

Cunningham, Randy and Ethell, Jeff. *Fox Two.* Mesa, Arizona: Champlin Fighter Museum, 1984.

"Fatherland Liberation War, June 25, 1950–July 27, 1953". Accessed June 20, 2018. https://en.wikipedia.org/wiki/Korean_War

"Flightdeck Friday! Douglas F4D-1 Skyray (Part 1)." US Naval Institute, Naval History Blog, 2010. Accessed March 24, 2017. https://www.Navalhistory.org/2010/04/16/flightdeck-friday-douglas-f4d-skyray-part-1.

"The Flight Jacket, A. O. C. Classes 1-50 1972". Naval Aviation Schools Command 1972,

Gillcrist, Paul T., RAdm., USN (Ret.). *Feet Wet.* California: Presidio Press, 1990.

Gillcrist, Paul, T., RAdm., USN (Ret.). *Tomcat! The Grumman F-14 Story.* Pennsylvania: Schiffer Publishing Ltd, 1994.

Gunston, Bill. *The Encyclopedia of World Airpower*. London, England: Aerospace Publishing Limited, 1981.

Gunston, Bill. *Illustrated History of Fighters*. New York: Exeter Books, 1981.

Heatley, C. J., Capt., USN (Ret.). *The Cutting Edge*. Japan: Dai Nippon Printing Co. Ltd., 1986.

"History of Vietnam, Vietnam War Statistics and Facts 5." 25th Aviation Battalion. Accessed 15 November 2004. http://25thaviation .org/id795.htm,

"History of the United States Air Force." National Security Act of 1947 (61 *Stat*. 495), July 26, 1947. Wikipedia. Accessed January 12, 2017. https://en.wikipedia.org/wiki/ History_of_the_United_States_Air_Force.

Howard, Michael and Paret, Peter. *Carl von Clausewitz on War*. New Jersey: Princeton University Press, 1976.

Hurt, H. H. *Aerodynamics for Naval Aviators*. Issued by the Office of the Chief of Naval Operations Aviation training Division, NAVAIR 00-80T-80, 1965.

"Inchon Landing." History.com Editors, 2010. Accessed October 27, 2018. https://www.history. com/topics/inchon

Jones, Lloyd S., *US Fighters*. Fallbrook, California: Aero Publishers, Inc., 1975.

Kao, James C. "VF-103 Squadron History." Accessed 1 July 2004. http://www.topedge.com/ alley/squadron/lant/vf103his.htm

Karnow, Stanley. "*Vietnam, A History.*" New York: Viking Press, 1983.

Lehman, John F. *Command of the Seas*. New York: Charles Scribner's Sons Macmillan Publishing Company, 1988.

McKeown, Ronald "Mugs" Capt., USN (Ret.), interviewed with the author in San Diego, California, 7 October 2004.

Millett, Allan R. "Battle of the Chosin Reservoir." *Encyclopedia Britannica*. Accessed May 31, 2018. https://www.britannica.com/event/Battle-of-the-Chosin-Reservoir.

"Naval Strike and Air Warfare Center." Wikipedia. Accessed March 22, 2018. https://en.wiki-pedia.org/ wiki/Naval_Strike_and_Air_Warfare_Center

"Naval Air Station Fallon." Wikipedia. Accessed March 22, 2018. https://en.wikipedia.org/ wiki/ Naval_Air_Station_Fallon

Naval Air Station Pensacola. Accessed August 17, 2003. www.globalsecurity.org/military/ facility/pensacola.htm,

"Operation Frequent Wind." Global Security. Accessed April 13, 2004. www.globalsecurity. org/military/ops/frequent_wind.htm.

Pawloski, Dick and Ball, H. Glenn. *Fighter Performance*. Fort Worth, Texas: General Dynamics, 1986.

Pawloski, Dick. *Changes in Soviet Air Combat Doctrine and Force Structure*. Fort Worth, Texas: General Dynamics, 1987.

Petry, W. A., Cmdr., USN (Ret.). *F-8 Cockpit Crossfeed*. "Report of November 1968".

"The Royal Maces, History and Information." Accessed June 25, 2005. www.usscoralsea.net/27/ pages/history.html.

Redditt, Richard, Cmdr., USN (Ret.) interviewed with the author in San Diego, California, 4 June 2004.

Sherwood, John Darrell. *Fast Movers*. New York: The Free Press, 1999.

Sherwood, John Darrell. "*Afterburner.*" New York: New York University Press, 2004.

Smith, Clint, Capt., USN (Ret.), phone interview with author in San Diego, California on 19 August 2003.

Smith, Leighton W., Adm. USN (Ret.) interviewed with the author by phone on 17 September 2005.

Smith, Virginia Hudgins, a.k.a. *Miss Jenny.* Interviewed with the author in San Diego, California, 4 July, 2005.

Stevenson, Jim. *Grumman F-14 Tomcat.* Aero Series, 1986.

Toliver, Raymond F. and Constable, Trevor J., *The Blond Knight of Germany.* Pennsylvania: TAB/Aero, Division of McGraw-Hill, Inc, 1970.

Turbak. Gary. "Korea: The Carrier War." *VFW Magazine:* Issue: December 2002.

"United States Sixth Fleet." Wikipedia. Accessed June 26, 2019. https://en.wikipedia.org/wiki/United_States_Sixth_Fleet.

US Department of the Navy. *USS America (CVN-66)* Command History Submission for 1966. CVA66/3800, Code 32, Ser: 2791, 15 November 1967.

US Department of the Navy. *Command History Submission for Fighter Squadron One Hundred Three*, Submission 1968.

US Department of the Navy. *Fighter Squadron One Hundred Three (VF-103)*, Command History for 1969, VF-103, dated 1970.

US Department of the Navy. *Air Test and Evaluation Squadron Four (VX-4), Activity Report for the Week Ending 7 May 1971*, FF12/VX4/JSD:dr, 3930. Ser 035, dtd 10 May 1971.

US Department of the Navy. *Air Test and Evaluation Squadron Four (VX-4), Command History Submission for 1970*, FF12/VX-4/DRM:pbs, 5000, Ser 060, dtd 20 Aug 1971.

US Department of the Navy. *Air Test and Evaluation Squadron Four (VX-4), Activity Report for the Week Ending 10 December 1971*, FF12/VX4/MSW:dr, 3930. Ser 081, dtd 13 December 1971.

US Department of the Navy. *Air Test and Evaluation Squadron Four (VX-4), Activity Report for the Week Ending 4 February 1972*, FF12/VX4/MSW:dr, 3930. Ser 013, dtd 8 February 1972.

US Department of the Navy. *Air Test and Evaluation Squadron Four (VX-4), Activity Report for the Week Ending 9 June 1972*, FF12/VX4/MSW:sc, 3930. Ser 039, dtd 13 June 1972.

US Department of the Navy. *Air Test and Evaluation Squadron Four (VX-4), Activity Report for the Week Ending 8 December 1972*, FF12/VX4/DKH:jlj, 3930. Ser 077, dtd 12 December 1972.

US Department of the Navy. *Enemy Aircraft Shot Down by Naval Aviators in Southeast Asia, 1965–1973, Appendix E.* Naval Historical Center, Washington Navy Yard.

US Department of the Navy. *USS Enterprise (CVAN-65), 1974* Command History, CVAN65/.bn, 5750, Ser C13, dtd 28 February 1975.

US Department of the Navy. *Attack Carrier Air Wing Fourteen*, Command History for 1974, 10:PAR:sa, 5700, Ser C9, dtd 4 April 1975.

US Department of the Navy. *Carrier Air Wing Fourteen*, Command History for 1975, 13/GEB:sa, 5750, Ser 41, dtd 19 March 1976.

US Department of the Navy. *USS Enterprise 1975 (CVAN-65)*, Command History Submission, CVN65/32:bn, 5750, Ser., C59, dated 26 April 1976.

US Department of the Navy, Commander, Naval Air Systems Command. *A-7C, A-7E Tactical Manual (C).* NAVAIR 01-45AAE-IT, 1977.

US Department of the Navy. *US Marine Corps Participation in the Emergency Evacuations of Phnom Penh and Saigon: Operations Eagle Pull and Frequent Wind (U).* Arlington Virginia, Center of Naval Analysis, June 1977.

US Department of the Navy, Chief of Naval Operations. *NATOPS General Flight and Operating Instructions Manual*, OPNAV Instruction 3710.7G, 1973.

US Department of the Navy. *Air Test and Evaluation Squadron Four (VX-4)*, Command History Submission for 1973, FF12/VX-4/JRW:dh, 5750, Ser 197, dtd 2 April 1974.

US Department of the Navy. *USS Enterprise (CVAN-65)*, Command History for 1974, CVAN65/.bn, 5750, Ser 013, dtd 28Feb1975.

US Department of the Navy. *A-7C, A-7E Tactical Manual, (C)*. Commander, Naval Air Systems Command, NAVAIR 01-45AAE-IT, 1977.

US Department of the Navy. *Fighter Squadron Two One Three (VF-213)*, Command History Submission of January 29, 1980.

US Department of the Navy. *Report on the Fitness of Officers, Smith, John Monroe, Commander*, Period of Report: 80Mar01 to 80Jul02, Reporting Senior: Ready, J. K., 80Jul02.

US Department of the Navy. *Fighter Squadron Two One Three (VF-213)*, Command History Submission for 1980. VF-213/PAO: jr, 5700, dated November 23, 1980.

US Department of the Navy. *Report on the Fitness of Officers, Smith, John Monroe, Commander*, Period of Report: 80Jul03 to 80Dec03, Reporting Senior: Smith R. E., 80Dec03.

US Department of the Navy. *The Arleigh Burke Fleet Trophy. OPNAVINST 3590.11F.*

US Department of the Navy. *United States Naval Aviation 1910–1980*. Deputy Chief of Naval Operations (Air Warfare) and the Commander, Naval Air Systems Command. 1981.

US Department of the Navy. "Operation "Frequent Wind", Evacuation of Saigon, South Vietnam, from USS Hancock (CVA-19)" Accessed November 15, 2004. http://ships.bouwman.com, 13 Apr 2004

"USS *Saratoga*, (CVA-60), Command History for 1969, CVA60/5750, Ser 623, dtd 1 April 1970." USS *Saratoga* Association. Accessed February 21, 2004. www.uss-saratoga.com,

"VFA-213." Wikipedia. Accessed March 14, 2018. https://en.wikipedia.org/wiki/VFA-213

Watts, Barry D. *Doctrine, Technology, and War*. Air & Space Doctrinal Symposium, Montgomery, Alabama: Maxwell AFB, 1996.

"Welcome to NAS Fallon," CNIC. Accessed August, 17, 2018. https://www.cnic.navy.mil/regions/cnrsw/installations/nas_fallon.html

Wilson, George C. *Flying the Edge*. Annapolis, Maryland: Naval Institute Press, 1992.

Zahalka, Joe, Cmdr. USN (Ret.), interviewed with the author in San Diego California, on 6 July, 2005.

Glossary

first-generation fighter: Jet-propulsion fighter aircraft exhibiting low wing loading, high turn rates, and low thrust to weight; primarily gun/cannon equipped

second-generation fighters: Supersonic, jet-propulsion, pulse-radar fighter aircraft exhibiting high thrust to weight, high wing loading, and, consequently, lower turn rates; equipped with guns and air-to-air missiles

third-generation fighter: Fighter aircraft with the combination of low wing loading (allowing exceptional maneuvering) and high thrust to weight (allowing high acceleration rates and supersonic flight). The F-14 was considered the world's first third-generation fighter.

fourth-generation fighter: Supercruise, high agility; sensor fusion, active electronically scanned arrays; reduced signatures or active stealth technology

fifth-generation fighter: Supercruise, all-aspect stealth with internal weapons bays, extreme agility, full-sensor fusion, integrated avionics

20 millimeter: High-rate-of-fire cannon caliber used by most US fighters and attack aircraft. Also called 20 "mike-mike."

AAA: antiaircraft artillery

ACM: Air combat maneuvering. Engaged maneuvering between two or more aircraft.

active mode: In relation to an air-to-air missile, specifies that the missile uses an onboard radar to locate a target and is actively seeking or tracking its intended target.

ADIZ: Air Defense Identification Zone

AIM-7 Sparrow: Medium-range, radar-guided, air-to-air missile for US fighter-interceptors

AIM-9 Sidewinder: Heat-seeking dogfight missile for US fighter-interceptors

air breather: Aircraft requiring ambient oxygen for engine combustion

air boss: Senior commander or captain in charge of all flight deck activity and flight operations

Aldus lamp: A powerful, handheld spotlight

all-aspect missile: Air-to-air missile with the capability to guide and attack a target aircraft, within range of the weapon, from any aspect angle

Alpha strike: Co-coordinated, multiaircraft attack using complementary packages of selected aircraft to overcome defenses and inflict damage. An Alpha strike package might include twenty-five or more aircraft to defeat enemy air defense systems, attack several target sets, perform poststrike bomb damage assessment, and provide combat search-and-rescue missions and counter air assets.

alternate ejection handle: A yellow-and-black-striped handle on the forward side of the seat pan, between the crewman's legs. Also termed the "secondary" ejection handle.

ball: Meatball. Primary glide-slope reference source on the flight deck of carriers. A powerful direction-sensitive light emitted by the Freznel lens.

barricade: Large nylon net erected in the landing area to trap crippled aircraft coming aboard a carrier

BDHI: Bearing-distance-heading indicator—a compass card with integrated needles that indicate magnetic direction to selected navigation aids or radio transmission sources

Bear alert: Alert posture of the ship when in an area of possible Russian aircraft overflights

below the radar horizon: The area in which radar does not have coverage due to the curvature of the earth

BFM: Basic fighter maneuvering. Elementary maneuvers between two or more aircraft.

bingo fuel: Fuel state at which an aircrew terminates mission and returns to base **"black" classification:** Highly classified information. Access to "black" material ordinarily requires a Top Secret clearance, an "in-brief," and a "need-to-know."

blackout curtain: Cloth cover that snapped over the RIO's head and cockpit area to reduce sunlight and improve the radar picture

blower: Afterburner

blow through: Continue through the merge; terminating or attempting to "reset" the engagement

blue bomb: Practice bomb

blue-on-blue: Engagement with a friendly aircraft

BN: Bombardier/navigator. Naval flight officer trained to operate navigation, communication, EW systems, and weapons systems in attack aircraft.

BNAO: Basic naval aviation observer

bogey: Hostile or enemy aircraft

bolter: A carrier pass resulting when the arresting hook misses or skips over all arresting cables

Book of Naval Aviation Wisdom: Does not exist—but should.

BOQ: Bachelor officers' quarters

bouncing: Field carrier landing practice in preparation for actual carrier qualification landings

brace: Assume the position of attention.

Bravo Zulu: "Well done" adulation

break turn: Hardest turn available on the basis of airspeed, altitude, and aircraft weight

bring-aboard characteristics: Related to handling and aerodynamic performance in the landing configuration during carrier operations

buffet: Term associated with airframe/wing vibration during high-angle-of-attack maneuvering. Usually an indication of a stalled wing or a wing approaching a stalled condition.

bug out: To exit a fight after engaging

bulkhead: Wall

BUPERS: Navy Bureau of Personnel

CAG: Commander and an air group or carrier air group. Often referred to as the "airwing."

call sign: Nickname

calling the ball: First voice report to the LSO, seconds from landing on the flight deck, requesting pilot's interpretation of the position of the meatball

campaign cover: Stiff-brimmed hat. Distinguishing uniform article worn by a Marine Corps drill instructor.

Case I approach: Circular racetrack pattern used during fair weather in daylight hours to recover aircraft

Case II approach: Straight-in, carrier-controlled, nonprecision approach used during night, poor weather, or both, or when aircrew are experiencing difficulties

Case III approach: Straight-in, carrier-controlled, precision approach used during night, poor weather, or both, or when aircrew are experiencing difficulties

catapult: Steam driven mechanism that assists in accelerating aircraft to takeoff speed

catapult officer: Officer responsible for safe, efficient catapult launch of aircraft from the flight deck of a carrier

CB: Cumulus buildups; often termed "bumpers"

CCA: Carrier-controlled approach

Charlie time: Time identified for commencing carrier landings

Chief: Chief petty officer; senior enlisted personnel in pay grades E-7 (chief petty officer), E-8 (senior chief petty officer), and E-9 (master chief petty officer)

CIC: Combat Information Center. Later termed Combat Direction Center (CDC). Provides information and control to TACAIR aircraft.

Clara: Report from the pilot to the LSO that the "ball"—the glide-slope reference light—is not visible

clearing turn: Turn performed following a cat shot to avoid being run over by the ship in the event the airplane fails to complete a successful climb-out

clinch control: Navy controllers responsible for coordinating aircraft in the Virginia Capes area

Combat Air Patrol (CAP): Primarily a fighter mission in which the primary objective is to detect and engage hostile aircraft

combat spread: A tactical formation in which the wingman maintains a position approximately 6,000 feet abeam the lead aircraft

combat weight: Aircraft weight calculation used to compare fighter performance. Usually considered as the basic weight of the aircraft, plus half internal fuel, plus the weight of a normal combat load-out.

Courage: Tactical call sign of USS *America*

CQ: Carrier qualification or CARQUAL

crew concept: Practice of distributing cockpit tasks among the crew members under the coordination of the mission commander, or the pilot in command IAW NATOPS

cubi dog: Local hot dog at NAS Cubi, Philippines

cut lights: A row of green horizontal lights at the top of the Freznel lens, which, when illuminated, direct a jet pilot to add power and a prop pilot to pull power and land

dead-reckoning: Form of navigation by using a previously determined position, or fix, and advancing that position on the basis of known or estimated speeds over elapsed time and course to arrive at desired destination

Delta stack: Holding pattern near the ship where returning aircraft assemble in preparation for landing

det: Detachment. "DET" identifies a component of aircraft and personnel that is part of a larger squadron temporarily assigned to a carrier. HC-2, DET 66, for example, identifies a detachment of helicopters from HC-2 temporarily assigned to USS *America* (CV-66).

division: Four aircraft flying as a unit compose a division.

down: A grade on a particular learning objective indicating unsatisfactory performance. Usually a "down" required the student to refly the sortie.

drown-proof: A procedure to conserve energy in a water survival situation

dry suits: Anti-exposure suits enhance the survivability of aircrew in cold-water or cold-weather conditions in the event of an ejection/bailout.

Dutch roll: Ship phenomenon in which wave action produces a roll coupled with yaw and pitch. These three oscillations cause the stern of the ship to scribe a pattern similar to a figure eight on its side.

EMCON: Electronic emission control status

empennage: Tail section of an aircraft

face shot: Forward-quadrant missile shot

FAM 1: First familiarization hop

firewall: Throttle position full forward

flex deck: An open deck allowing simultaneous launches and recoveries, unrestricted by hard schedules

flight level: Altitude of aircraft operating in the jet route structure. Flight level four one zero is 41,000 feet.

Fox one: Term used to announce the firing of a radar-guided missile during mock combat. Transmitting the calls over the UHF allows those involved in the engagement an opportunity to see and evaluate the parameters at the time of the shot.

Fox two: Term used to announce the firing of a heat-seeking missile during mock combat. Transmitting the calls over the UHF allows those involved in the engagement an opportunity to see and evaluate the parameters at the time of the shot.

Freznel lens: The Freznel lens is part of the optical landing system that provides glide-slope information to pilots on approach to the ship. It consists of a series of green horizontal "datum" lights affixed perpendicular to and on either side of five vertically stacked light cells that project glide-slope information to the pilot. The top four glide-slope cell lights are amber; the bottom cell is red. Light emitted from any cell can be seen only within a narrow field of view or illumination beam—similar to viewing direction-sensitive traffic lights.

GCA: Ground-controlled approach; an approach to a runway monitored and controlled by radar operators

guard frequency: 243.0 megahertz, standard UHF emergency frequency. All military aircraft are required to monitor this frequency for emergency or MAYDAY transmissions.

gyro: The artificial horizon displays angle of climb, descent, and bank information.

hangar queen: Aircraft requiring extensive repair work

hard deck: A rule-of-engagement altitude limitation below which no maneuvering is permitted

hard wing: The original Phantom design without leading-edge or maneuvering slats/flaps

high Yo-Yo: Basic fighter maneuver used to convert energy/velocity into the vertical in order to avoid a horizontal overshoot

holdback fitting: A 5-inch metal bar that holds the aircraft in position on the catapult until the catapult actually fires. At that point the holdback breaks and allows the aircraft to accelerate the length of the catapult track.

huffer: Small jet engine mounted on a cart, used to start aircraft jet engines

ICS: Internal communications system. The system that aircrew use to communicate with one another.

IFF: Identification friend or foe. An electrical identification system that controllers use to identify and track aircraft.

IFR: Instrument flight rules that govern the operation of aircraft in poor weather

IR missile: Infrared or heat-seeking missiles

JAG: Judge advocate general; a military lawyer

jammed radar environment: Condition in which a radar transmitter floods an area with radar energy in an attempt to confuse or "jam" the enemy radar

JBD: Jet blast deflector. Large hinged section of flight deck set behind each catapult, which is raised behind aircraft on the catapult to direct prop wash and jet exhaust up and over personnel and equipment on the flight deck.

JOs: Junior officers: lieutenant (Lt.), lieutenant junior grade (Lt. j.g.), and ensign (Ens.)

JP-4: Standard, high-grade kerosene mixed with gasoline, primarily used by the US Air Force and Army for jet engines

JP-5: Standard high-grade kerosene for use in jet engines; considered to be the naval equivalent of JP-4

Judy: Declaration that the fighter aircrew have a radar contact and a request to radar controllers to terminate all additional calls until assistance is required

KIO: Knock it off. Safety of flight transmission requiring immediate cessation of all maneuvering.

laminar flow: The smooth, uninterrupted molecular flow of air over the aircraft surface areas

L/D max: Lift over drag—maximum. A quotient of the lift of a surface area divided by the drag of the surface area. L/D max identifies the optimum angle of attack both for an approach and an energy-sustaining turn.

lens: Freznel optical landing device, also called simply the "ball" or "meatball"

lens roll angle: Roll angle of the Freznel lens. Each aircraft has a different roll angle both for normal landings and barricade approaches. The roll angle is set by the air boss.

Lemooron: Light-attack and strike-fighter crews and support people based at NAS Lemoore, California

lift vector: Directional component of lift generated by a wing producing lift

look-down, shoot-down: Firing aircraft shoots at targets below the horizon. This aspect can cause the radar to confuse ground clutter with enemy aircraft, and complicates the radar picture.

low Yo-Yo: Basic fighter maneuver used to convert altitude into velocity to reduce nose-to-tail separation

LSO: Landing signal officer. Carrier pilots designated to control the safe and expeditious recovery of aircraft returning to the ship. LSOs stand on the port side of the landing area and provide information and commands to the aircrew during the terminal portion of an approach to the ship.

LSO comments: LSOs grade each carrier approach. Both the pilot's technique and the wire caught are considered in assigning a grade. A perfect approach is an "OK," no comment, three-wire pass. In descending order, other grades are "OK" with comment; "Fair," expressed as "(OK)"; "No Grade," expressed as "NG"; and finally "Cut." A "Cut" pass usually violates a safety procedure. Each squadron aboard a carrier maintains a "Greenie" board, which lists the assigned pilots and records the grades of each of their passes.

LSO pickle: Handheld switch used by the primary and backup LSOs to activate the "cut" signal lights, which advise pilots to add power, and the "wave off" signal lights, which command an immediate wave-off.

Mach doughnut: Compression vapor, often generated by an airplane in supersonic or transonic flight. It may appear to be a small cloud formed around the leading-edge surfaces of the aircraft. Also referred to as a Mach cloud.

Marshal: Radio call sign of flight controllers aboard ships who are responsible for providing separation between aircraft and issuing holding instructions, traffic advisories, and weather reports

max trap: Maximum allowable weight with which an aircraft can safely come aboard

midnight: Operating without external lights at night

military doctrine: Refers to the maxims of organizing, equipping, training, and sustaining forces. While VX-4 at the time did not have a hand in all four elements of doctrine, they had, nonetheless, a major influence on fighter doctrine.

mis-light: A condition in which selection of afterburner does not result in afterburner

MODLOC: Modified location. A geographical area that a ship is scheduled to transit to or operate in.

Mustang: Enlisted person who receives a commission on the basis of superior performance

NATOPS Manual: Naval Aviation Training and Operations Manual. A NATOPS Manual exists for each naval aircraft. It delineates limitations, restrictions, operating procedures, and emergency procedures for that aircraft.

needles: Aircraft navigation instrument that provides course and glide-slope information for instrument approaches. The information is superimposed over the artificial horizon in the form of a vertical needle (course information) and horizontal needle (glide slope). Following these "fly-to" commands will assist the pilot in arriving on glide slope and on centerline.

NFO: Naval flight officer; a commissioned naval officer designated to act as a crewman in naval aircraft, other than as a pilot. The designation was changed from naval aviation observer (NAO) to naval flight officer (NFO) in the early 1970s.

ninety, the: The position of an aircraft in a circling approach in which it has 90 degrees remaining to roll onto centerline

O3 level: Third level above the hangar deck

"on and on": "On" glide slope and "On" centerline

one-circle turn: Two engaged aircraft turning in the same horizontal direction scribe a single circle over the ground.

ops boss: Operations officer; responsible for the conduct of safe flight operations on an aircraft carrier

optimum AOA: Optimum or best angle of attack; provides the best lift-over-drag angle of attack for a sustained turn and approach for landing

ordies: Ordnance personnel

"P" CAG: The "prospective" commander of the air group / air wing

pad eyes: Recessed tie-down points on the flight deck and hangar deck

padlock: To maintain visual contact on a target aircraft

paint: Establish a radar return on a target

paraloft: Work center for parachute riggers. Aircrew gear and survival equipment are generally stored in the paraloft.

passageway: Hall, corridor

piped over the side: A longtime naval tradition in which the retiree marches through a column of saluting side boys. Once through the column, the retiree cuts his salute and is, at that point, considered to be released from the Navy.

pitch rate: Performance characteristic of tactical aircraft addressing the ability of the aircraft to develop "pitch"

Plan of the Day (POD): A command document, printed daily, that delineates all events and watch assignments for a twenty-four-hour period

plat: Television monitors located in each ready room and crew assembly area. The plat normally shows ships' latitude/longitude position, time, course, speed, and environmental data. The plat is turned off when the ship exceeds its classified speed.

pointability: Fighter aircraft performance attribute addressing the ability to direct the nose at a desired direction by using all available flight controls: elevator, rudder, and ailerons

poopie: Term derived from the poopie suit, drab-green overalls issued to new candidates upon arrival at Aviation Officer Candidate School. Candidates wore these for the ten days of "indoctrination." In the humidity and heat of Pensacola, the overalls quickly began to emit the very personal odor of their wearer, and due to that odor, wearers were called poopies.

push time: Time scheduled to commence a penetration from holding

QF-9 drone: F-9 Cougar configured for remote control

quarterdeck: Main entrance, lobby

radar missile: Radar-guided missile

rails pass: LSO term indicating a perfect pass, as if on "rails"; "OK," no comment, three-wire pass

ready room: The nerve center of the squadron and sovereign territory of the squadron duty officer (SDO)

riggers: Parachute riggers; technicians whose main job is to inspect, maintain, and repair air crew gear and survival equipment

RIO: Radar intercept officers; NFOs trained to operate navigation and weapons systems in fighter aircraft

Rutkowski paths: Minimum time to climb to altitude performance calculations/ schedules

roaring 20s: Wind sprints with the added difficulty of carrying one's mattress up and down the staircase. Amusing collisions were the norm when more than one poopie was involved.

round-down: Aft end of the flight deck and the edge of the landing area that is rounded and slopes toward the water

rules of engagement (ROE): Authoritative guidelines for combat intervention and activities. In peacetime scenarios, ROEs articulate engagement safety rules.

Russian AGIs: Intelligence-gathering ships that commonly shadow Navy units

SAM: Surface-to-air missile

sea course: A 1.6-mile fitness trail on grass, dirt, and soft sand at NAS Pensacola

section: Two aircraft flying as a unit make up a section. Two sections compose a division.

ship's complement: Souls on board. A carrier's total complement is approximately five thousand: twenty-five hundred assigned to the air wing and twenty-five hundred assigned to the ship.

shit-hot: Tailored flight suit designed with the colors and logo of the wearer's squadron

shooter: Term for "catapult officer"

Sidewinder (AIM-9): Primary heat-seeking dogfight missile for US fighter-interceptors. Also termed "heater."

SLUF: Slow little ugly fellow

soft deck: A rule of engagement altitude limitation below which aggressive maneuvering is restricted

Sparrow (AIM-7): Primary medium-range, radar-guided, air-to-air missile for US fighter-interceptors

squadron duty officer (SDO): The SDO is the designated representative of the commanding officer. He handles all routine matters, keeps the flight schedule current, and keeps the skipper and XO abreast of all developments throughout a twenty-four-hour period.

TACAIR: Tactical aviation assets/mission. Primarily associated with kinetic power projection: air-to-air, air-to-surface, and electronic-warfare missions. Also termed "shooters."

TACAN: Tactical Air Navigation. Primary en route and terminal navigation aid used by the military.

tally: Visual sighting of a bogey or hostile aircraft

tanker orbit: Airborne tanker's location in reference to the ship

thrust to weight: Ratio of an aircraft's thrust to its weight. High thrust-to-weight aircraft exhibited better vertical performance, climb, and acceleration characteristics.

tilly: A large, self-propelled crane used primarily to hoist and move aircraft on the flight deck

tower burble: Turbulent air produced by winds over and around the tower or island on the flight deck of a carrier

turkey feathers: Titanium strips assembled around the aft end of the tailpipe to allow variable constriction of exhaust gases, in order to produce maximum thrust for a selected power setting

turnaround cycle: Training period between deployments

two-circle turn: Two aircraft turning in opposite directions scribe a horizontal figure eight over the ground—two separate circles.

up and up: Term used to indicate that an airplane is "up" and all systems are working properly

VA: Navy designation for fixed-wing (V) attack (A) squadron. The number following the designation identifies the specific squadron; thus VA-27 is Attack Squadron 27.

vectored thrust: A system in which thrust is discharged through fore and aft nozzles and can pivot more than 90 degrees down, allowing thrust to lift the aircraft off the deck vertically. When in flight, the nozzles pivot rearward to accelerate the aircraft in order to allow the wings to generate lift.

vertical nose position authority: Ability of a tactical aircraft to develop and sustain a nose-up position. Associated with "pointability" and nose position authority.

VF: Navy abbreviation for fixed-wing (V) fighter (F) squadron

VFR: Visual flight rules; associated with fair-weather flying conditions

VFR navigation: Visual flight rule navigation—use of ground reference points and terrain to navigate from point to point

visual: Sighting of a friendly aircraft

"V" max: Maximum structural velocity limit. Also termed "Q" limit.

VP: Navy abbreviation for fixed-wing (V) patrol (P) squadron

VS: Navy abbreviation for fixed-wing (V) antisubmarine warfare (S) squadron

VT: Navy abbreviation for fixed-wing (V) training (T) squadron

VTAS: Visual Target Acquisition System

VX-4: Air Test and Evaluation Squadron 4, responsible for aircraft performance evaluations and weapons compatibility testing for fighter aircraft

wands: Flashlights fit with colored plastic cones to improve soft illumination

wave-off lights: A set of red lights on both sides of the Freznel lens, which signal the pilot to add full power and terminate his approach

waving: Term passed down from the early days of naval aviation, when LSOs, wearing brightly colored overalls, stood near the stern of the ship and "waved" two flags to guide the pilots aboard the carrier

"white" classification: Unclassified information

winder growl: The audio cue of a Sidewinder missile indicating that the seeker head is trained on a heat source

wing loading: Ratio of wing surface area to aircraft weight. Low wing loading allows aircraft to produce a better sustained turn rate than high-wing-loaded aircraft.

workups: Training associated with preparation for deployment

writing book (verb): Scripting the LSO's abbreviated comments in the LSO book in order to record the passes and later debrief the pilots

zoom bag: Flight suit; also called "bag"

Zuni rocket pods: Rocket pack containing four 5-inch Zuni rockets

Index

#

1973 Yom Kippur War, 63

1st Marine Division, 46–47

64th and 65th Aggressor Squadrons, 110

A

A-4 Skyhawk/Scooter, 48–49, 116–117, 120, 123, 125, 141

A-4E Mongoose, 114

A-4F Super Fox, 114, 121, 123–126

A-5 Vigilante, 47

A-6 Intruder, 13, 47,49, 72, 77

A-7 Corsair II, 13, 29, 49, 54, 61–62, 82–84

ABC's *20/20* documentary team, 97–100

ACEVAL/AIMVAL, 23, 58, 104, 111

ACM, 12, 43, 48, 102, 112–113, 120–121

ADMAT Inspection, 89–90

Adriatic Sea, 61

AGIs, 71–72

AIM-7 Sparrow, 54, 77, 114, 121

AIM-9 Sidewinder, 29, 54, 77, 111, 114, 118, 121, 126

AIM-54 Phoenix, 29, 77–78

air boss, 12, 14, 58, 76, 136

air combat maneuvering (ACM), 20, 48, 102, 114

Air Test and Evaluation Squadron Four (VX-4), 21–22, 28, 36, 106–107, 110

Alexandria, Egypt, 62–63, 66

Allen, Ed "Bulldog," RAdm. USN, 63, 71–73

Anderson Dan "Chief," Lt., 13, 70, 82–85, 114–116, 118–121, 135–138

Angle-of-attack (AOA), 43

Applegate, Terry "Gator," Cmdr. USN (Ret.), 35, 37, 39, 52, 69

Augusta Bay, 75–76

Ault Report, 106, 109

Ault, Frank W, Capt. USN, 106

Auten, Donald, "Duck," Capt. USN (Ret.), copyright page, epigraph, foreword, 135

B

Balearic Islands, 68

Barcelona, Spain, 70–71

Barricade, 22

basic fighter maneuvers (BFM), 48

Battle of Midway, June 6, 1942, dedication, 10, 45

Bear alert, 54–55, 81

Benedict, "Eggs," Lt. Cmdr. USN, 114

Blower, 72, 117, 119–120, 136

blow-through, 115

Bogey, 49, 104, 114, 116, 120, 125, 126

Bucchi, Michael, RAdm. USN (Ret.), foreword, 11, 27

Buccho, Lennie "Toado," Capt. USMC (Ret.), 114–115, 117–119

bug-out, 120

BUPERS, 38

C

CAG (COMANDER AIR GROUP), 69, 77, 89, 91

Cannon AFB, 82–85

carrier qualifications, 28, 39, 42, 113

Catania, Sicily, 62

catapult officer, 43

Chief of Naval Operations (CNO), 106

Chosin Reservoir Battle, 46–47

Coleman, Frederick D., AMHC USN, 57

Command at Sea pin, "Texaco Star," 68–69

Commander, Naval Air Forces, US Atlantic (COMNAVAIRLANT), 132

Constant Peg, 109–110

Crowley, Blake, Ordnance Chief Petty Officer, 111

CVW-11, 32–33, 36, 38, 45, 47, 50, 54, 66, 77, 79, 94, 113, 132

CVW-14, 21, 36, 97
CVW-9, 31

D

Davis, Tommy, JR (Junior), Lt. USN, 114
DeGruy, Charlie, Lt. Cmdr. USN (Ret.), 38, 102
Digiovani, Mr., "Mr. Dee," 40
Disher, John S., RAdm USN, 96
division, 34, 40, 42, 46, 60, 102, 111
Douglas F4D-1 Skyray, 32
Dunn, Robert, RAdm. USN (Ret.), 51

E

EA6-B Prowler, 47
Egypt, 62

F

F/A-18 Hornet, 29, 46
F-104 Starfighter, 123
F-11 Tiger, 15, 49, 115–121
F-111 Aardvark, 33–34, 47, 63, 82, 89, 99
F-14 Tomcat, 11–16, 21–22, 27–30, 33–34, 36–38, 43, 50, 63, 69, 72–75, 77–79
F-15 Eagle, 29, 49, 104, 110–111
F-16 Viper, 29
F-2H Banshee, 32
F3H-2 Demon, 32
F-4 Phantom, 11, 20, 32–33, 54–56, 74, 75, 94, 105–106, 108, 115, 124
F-8 Crusader, 47, 94
F-9 Cougar, 20
Fairgame IV, 19
Feist, Bob "Ranger," Lt. USN, 77
Fellowes, G. Frederick Jr., RAdm., 24–27, 74
Fenner, RAdm. USN, 24–27, 74
Fighter Derby, 113–115, 121–122, 124–126, 128
Fighter Town USA, 16, 24, 32–33, 88, 93, 113
flat scissors, 125
Fleet Replacement Group (FRS), 15, 21
flight level, 115, 136–138
Forchet, Mike "Weasel," Lt. USN, 71, 76
Fox One, 116

Fredrickson, A. W., Cmdr. USN (Ret.), 51, 58, 70
Furlong, George "Skip," RAdm. USN (Ret.), 131

G

Genoa, Italy, 75
Gerard, Greg "Mullet," Lt., 113
Gillcrist, Paul T. "Gator," RAdm. USN, 75, 86, 88–89, 91, 95–100, 104, 129–130, 133–134
Gilleece, Pete, Lt. Cmdr. USN, 107, 109
Grumman Aircraft Corporation, 13, 21, 28, 36–37, 58, 94, 100, 102, 133
Guard frequency, 49, 56, 64
Gulf of Sidra, 71

H

Haley, Jim "Comet," Cmdr. USN (Ret.), 87, 89, 129–130
Have Doughnut, 28, 106, 109
Have Drill, 28, 105, 106–107, 109
Head's-up Display (HUD), 104
Heatley, Charles "Heater," Capt. USN (Ret.), 24, 26
Heatley, Kay, 24
Henninger, Steve, 11
Honor, Craig "Tweety," Lt. (USN), 63
HS-12 "Wyverns," 47, 77
Huiseman, Capt. USN (Ret.), 85–86, 88, 95

I

Independence Day, 66
Inshas airbase, Egypt, 63, 66
Israeli Air Force, 63–64, 66

J

Jacanon, Jake, Cmdr. USN (Ret.), 35, 39
Jacobs, Jan, Cmdr. USN (Ret.), 11, 139
JAG (Judge Advocate General), 25–26, 74
Japanese attack on Pearl Harbor, 45
jet blast deflector (JBD), 14, 43
Jim Stevenson, 97–99
Johnson, Duke, Lt. Cmdr. USN, 107

Jones, Dave "Buck," Lt. USN (Ret.), 124–126
JP-5, 12, 37, 77, 120, 131
Judge Advocate General (JAG), 25–26, 74
Judy, 55

K

Korean air war, 105
Korean War, 32, 46
Korean War, 32, 46

L

Landing Signal Officer (LSO), 12, 21, 97, 66, 77, 84, 125
Latendresse, Tom, Capt. USN (Ret.), 83–84
Lawson, Robert "Photo Bob," Senior Chief Petty Officer Photomate, cover
Leeds, Rene "Sam" W., Capt. USN (Ret.), 75–76

M

M-4 Bison, 54
Marash, Dave, 97–99
MCAS Yuma, 114–115
McDonnell Douglas, 32, 49, 123
McDonnell F2H Banshee, 32
McKeown, Ronald "Mugs," Capt. USN, 106–109
Meyer, Capt. USN (Ret.), 51, 53, 57, 75–76
midnight, 55, 115–116, 118
MiG-15 "Fagot," 48
MiG-17 "Fresco," 105
MiG-21 "Fishbed," 49, 63, 105
MiG-23 "Flogger," 49, 63, 105
MiG-29 "Fulcrum," 29
Mk. 45 parachute flares, 62, 66, 77
More, Tom "Rookie," Lt. Cdr. USN, 20
Morris, Max, Cmdr. USN (Ret.), 20
Mostoller, Bernie "Mo," Senior Chief USN, 58
Muammar Gaddafi, 71
mustang, 40

N

Naples, Italy, 57, 61
NAS Key West, Florida, 20, 132, 138
NAS Miramar, California, 13, 16, 20, 22–23, 32–34, 47, 50, 52, 75, 82, 85, 87–89, 95 97, 100, 105, 110, 113–115, 122–124, 126, 129
NAS Moffett Field, California, 31
NAS Norfolk, Virginia, 17, 47, 50–52, 57, 132–133
NAS Oceana, Virginia,19, 21, 50, 52
NAS Pensacola, Florida, 20
NAS Pt. Mugu, California, 21
National Week XXVII Exercises, 71, 74–76
NATOPS, 28, 96, 101, 104
Naval Air Systems Command, 21
Naval Aviator, 20, 109, 134
Naval Flight Officer (NFO), 19
Naval Investigative Service (NIS), 61
Naval Station Rota, Spain, 132
Navy Fighter Weapons School, 16, 22, 27, 48
Nellis AFB, 63, 107–108, 110–112
Nesby, Chuck "Sneakers," Lt. USN, 63
Nise, Jim "Nice Guy," Lt. USN, 114–116
Norfolk, Virginia, 17, 47, 50–52, 57, 132–133
North Vietnam, 33, 47, 109
Nunn, Jim "Tarzan," Cmdr. USN (Ret.), 124

O

Operation Frequent Wind, 22
Operational Evaluation (OPEVAL), 28, 111
Operational Readiness Evaluation (ORE), 51, 131
Ore, Bud "Budman," Capt. USN (Ret.), 84
Ostertag, Mark "Tag," Lt. USN, 32

P

P-3 Orion, 54
Pacific campaign, 45
padlock, 118
Palma de Mallorca, 68, 70
Palma, 61, 68, 69–70

Parrot, Ralph, Cmdr. USN (Ret.), 76
Pentagon, 132
Philippines, 46
Phoenix, AIM-54, 29, 77–78
Pieper, Bruce "Peeps," Lt. USN, 28
pitch-rate, 119
Pollensa Bay, Spain, 66
Power Projection, 47–48, 56
preflight, 13–14, 30

R

RA-5C Vigilante, 47
Radar Intercept Officer (RIO), 11, 13, 19–20, 30, 34, 77
Ramenskoye Soviet jets, 29
Ready, Jack "Stinger," VAdm. USN (Ret.), 61, 69, 77, 89, 125, 128, 129, 132–133
Reddit, Richard "Turtle," Capt. USN (Ret.), 24, 26
Report of the Air-to-Air Missile System Capability Review (Ault Report), 106
RF-8G photoreconnaissance aircraft, 47, 94
riflescopes, 13, 58, 104–105
Rogers, "Buck," Lt. USN, 54
rolling scissors, 125
Rota, Spain, 77, 132
Rules of Engagement (ROE), 19, 105, 114
Ruliffson, "Cobra," Cmdr. USN, 23
Russian AGIs, 71

S

Scharff, "Hard" Richard, Cmdr. USN (Ret.), 88, 91, 97, 104
Ship's Habitability Improvement Team, "SHIT Team," 60–61
Sidewinder (AIM 9), 29, 54, 77–78, 105, 111, 114, 118, 121, 126
Small, W. N., VAdm. USN (Ret.), 79
Smith, Jack, 14, 20, 53, 57, 85–86, 137
Smith, John Monroe "Hawk," Cmdr. USN, 9, 11–12, 16, 20, 23, 68, 75, 87, 128–129, 133–134
Smith, Miss Jenny, 14, 16, 18–21, 53, 57, 61–70, 85–86, 92–93, 96, 129, 132–134, 137

Smith, Warren "Snuffy," VAdm. USN (Ret.), 25–27
Southeast Asia, 32, 106
Soviet Union, 105
Sparrow (AIM-7), 29, 32, 54, 77, 114, 121
Split, Yugoslavia, 61
Strait of Messina, 75
Su-27 "Flanker," 29
Sullivan, Mike "Lancer," Col. USMC (Ret.), 115

T

TACAIR, 23–25, 27, 54, 63, 71, 105, 109–110, 130
Tactical Airborne Reconnaissance Pod System (TARPS), 93–94, 100
Tactical All Aircrew Meetings (T-ACM), 102, 112
Talcott, Michael, Lt. USN, 61–62
Teague, Tooter, Cmdr. USN, 107–108
thrust-to-weight, 29
Tillotson, Lee "Tilly," Cmdr. USN, 99
Tinker AFB, Oklahoma City, 50
TOPGUN Christmas Card, 24–27, 74–75, 91
TOPGUN, 9–11, 14, 16, 22–28, 30–31, 48, 58, 63, 74, 75, 91, 96–97, 101, 106, 109–110, 112, 114–115, 124
Trieste, Italy, 61–62
Tu-16 "Badger," 54–56
Tu-20/Tu-95 "Bear," 54–56, 79, 81
turkey feathers, 28
two-circle turn, 119

U

US Air Force, 17, 33, 39, 49 58, 61, 63, 65, 83, 104–106, 110–111, 123, 132
US Army, 39, 45, 48
US Marine Corps, 117
US Navy, 9–13, 17, 18–19, 21–23, 26–28, 32–33, 36, 38, 40–41, 45–49, 52–53, 58–60, 63–66, 68–70, 74–76, 79–80, 82–83, 88, 90–92, 94–99, 103–106, 108–111, 122, 123, 126, 129–130, 132–134, 136–137

Uniform Code of Military Justice (UCMJ), 41, 74

US X Corps, 46

USS *America*, 12, 14, 19, 38, 50, 60, 84, 104, 113, 128

USS *Arthur W. Radford* (DD-963), 54, 66, 71, 73

USS *Barry* (DD-993), 54

USS *Bon Homme Richard* (CVA-31), 32

USS *Coral Sea* (CV-43), 45

USS *Enterprise* (CV-6), 10, 45

USS *Enterprise* (CVN-65), 11, 21

USS *Hornet* (CV-8), 10, 46

USS *Joseph Hewes* (FF-1078), 54

USS *King* (DDG-41), 54

USS Kitty Hawk (CV-63), 31–32, 47, 113

USS *Lawrence* (DDG-4), 54

USS *Lexington* (CVA-16), 32, 45

USS *Midway* (CVA-41, 74–75

USS *Nimitz* (CVN-68), 79–80

USS *R. K. Turner* (CG-20), 54

USS *Ranger* (CV-61), 131

USS *Sampson* (DDG-10), 54

USS *Saratoga* (CV-60), 20–21 45, 54–57, 84

USS *Yorktown* (CV-5), 10, 45

V

VA-147 "Argonauts," 84

VA-192 "Golden Dragons," 47, 82–84

VA-195 "Dambusters," 47, 61–62

Valencia, Italy, 76–77

Vance, Moon, Cmdr. USN (Ret.), 95–96

VAQ-131 "Lancers," 47

VAW-122 "Steel Jaws, 47

VF-1 "Bullets," 21

VF-1 "Wolfpack," 21

VF-2 "Bounty Hunters," 21

VF-101 "Grim Reapers," 95, 19–21

VF-102 Diamondbacks, 19–20, 40

VF-103 "Sluggers," 20–21, 54

VF-114 "Aardvarks," 13, 47, 59

VF-124 "Gunfighters," 16, 28–29, 37, 43

VF-126 "Bandits," 114, 124

VF-213 "Black Lions," 10, 12–13, 23, 25, 30–36, 38, 45, 47, 50, 52, 59–60, 69, 72, 78, 82, 85, 87–89, 91, 94, 98–99, 101–105 109–113, 115, 123–126, 128–131

VFP-63 (Det 4), 47

VFR, 85

Vietnam War, 9, 22, 32–33, 47–48, 62, 105

Vietnam, 20, 45, 47–48 105, 109

Visual Identification (VID), 104–105

VQ-1 "World Watchers," 48

VS-33 "Screwbirds," 47

VT-8 Torpedo Squadron, 8

VX-4 "Evaluators," 21–22, 28, 36, 106–107, 110

W

Waldron, John C., Lt. Cmdr., 3

Washington, DC, 58

waving, 22, 53

wing loading, 123

workups, 51

World War II, 32, 45–46, 48

Y

Yeager, Chuck, Gen. USAF, 53

Yuma Tactical Air Combat Training (TACTs), 114–115

Z

Zahalka Joe, "Crash," Cmdr. USN (Ret.), 87, 104

Zonk, Mike "Zonk," Lt. USN (Ret.), 114, 117, 120